PSYCHOPATHOLOGY

A CASE BOOK

PSYCHOPATHOLOGY

A CASE BOOK

Robert L. Spitzer, M.D.
Andrew E. Skodol, M.D.
Miriam Gibbon, M.S.W.
Janet B. W. Williams, D.S.W.
Columbia University
New York State Psychiatric Institute

McGRAW-HILL BOOK COMPANY

New York   St. Louis   San Francisco   Auckland   Bogotá
Hamburg   Johannesburg   London   Madrid   Mexico   Montreal   New Delhi
Panama   Paris   São Paulo   Singapore   Sydney   Tokyo   Toronto

This book was set in Times Roman and Helvetica by J. M. Post Graphics, Corp.
The editors were Patricia S. Nave, Stephen Wagley, and Jo Satloff;
the production supervisor was Leroy A. Young.
The cover was designed by Infield, D'Astolfo Associates.
R. R. Donnelley & Sons Company was printer and binder.

PSYCHOPATHOLOGY

A Case Book

5 6 7 8 9 0   DOCDOC   8 9 8 7 6

ISBN 0-07-060350-2

Library of Congress Cataloging in Publication Data
Main entry under title:

Psychopathology, a case book.

   Bibliography: p.
   Includes index.
   1. Psychology, Pathological—Classification—Case
studies.   2. Psychology, Pathological—Diagnosis—Case
studies.   3. Diagnostic and statistical manual of
mental disorders.   3rd ed.   I. Spitzer, Robert L.
RC455.2.C4P79   1983   616.89   82-17193
ISBN 0-07-060350-2

CONTENTS

FOREWORD

It was with particular pleasure that I accepted the invitation from the authors to write an introduction to this volume of case studies because of my own involvement in the conception of the idea for this casebook. It began when Robert Spitzer and I found ourselves seated together at lunch during a conference on *Risk Factor Research in the Major Mental Disorders,* which was held at the National Institute of Mental Health. We had much to talk about. I was aware of the central role Spitzer had played in directing a massive third revision of the *Diagnostic and Statistical Manual of Mental Disorders* (DSM-III) of the American Psychiatric Association. He was aware of a critical article I had published challenging the use of the term "mental disorder" as applied to the specific developmental disorders of childhood that were a component of axis II of that revision. Although my article had been critical with respect to this area, I had also praised the advances that he and his associates had made in providing specific descriptions of the symptom criteria for the major mental disorders of adults.

Our conversation turned to a casebook he was preparing for practitioner-users of DSM-III, which would highlight issues of differential diagnosis (Why this disorder and not that one?). I was intrigued with his case descriptions, and in my role as McGraw-Hill's advisory editor, I asked Spitzer whether he had ever considered writing a casebook for students enrolled in courses in psychopathology. My interest was directed toward the undergraduate student taking an abnormal psychology course and to the beginning graduate student in clinical psychology. Spitzer indicated that he had thought about such a possibility and hoped that such a casebook might prove valuable as well to students in related disciplines who were training in psychiatric nursing, social work, counseling, and so on.

That conversation took place on April 3, 1980, and here is the final product in printed form. More than two years has gone into its preparation, and it is a casebook unlike any other hitherto published. It contains a larger and more representative set of cases than has previously been available to the student reader, and the cases are designed to reflect a newly revised American psychiatric classification system that is markedly similar to patterns of case categorization used throughout the Western world. This is important to instructors because the framework of DSM-III is evident in the organization of contents of almost every abnormal psychology text now in use. Although the order of chapters in a given text may be different, the instructor and the student can readily locate those cases grouped together in the casebook that are related to specific chapters in the adopted text.

This volume contains 50 cases that not only capture the range of contemporary psychopathology, but have come from distinguished clinicians in the various mental health disciplines. The casebook is representative of the state of the art in many ways: it portrays the multiform nature of behavior disorders, it describes the various modes of treatments now in use, and it reflects the clinical talents of the wide band of professions that have responsibility for those who have known the anguish of mental disorder.

To take as one example, here are some of the various interventions discussed in this volume—drug therapy and other somatic forms of treatment, behavior modification and behavior therapy, skills training, social support, and community placements. While some instructors may find discomfort with one form of treatment and others with another, none will be able to deny that here is the range of interventions as practiced today, whatever their virtues or shortcomings. Nor will one dispute that the authors have succeeded in assembling an ecumenical group of talented clinicians to portray the status of therapy as currently practiced.

The emphasis in these 50 case studies is on both diagnosis and attendant modes of treatment. It is not on case dynamics, although each case presents background information that will enable you and the students to discuss factors that may have played a central role in the development of the disorder. All the cases are written in a clear and interesting style. The authors' titling of the cases reflects their goal of not only investing this casebook with a rigorous attention to case details, but also capturing the inherent interest that the study of psychopathological behavior generates in students.

In reading and rereading these cases I have been fascinated with their diversity. One is simply drawn into a case by the clarity and style with which the authors have presented the background of the patient, the significant life events that took place, the potentiating factors, the course of the disorder, the treatment and its outcome, the description of the alternative diagnoses posed by a case, and the final diagnostic decision.

There are other casebooks in print. How is this volume different from the others?

1. It introduces the student reader to the key element in any effort to create a science of psychopathology—the act of classification of the phenomena of the field; in this instance it is the critical act of diagnostic specification.

2. It provides in-depth representation of a grouping of disorders and thus portrays for the student a vision of the complexity and breadth of psychopathology. Thus, instead of a single case of schizophrenia, five are described. Rather than one or two cases of affective disorders, six are offered. By fine tuning the patterns of differences between *and* within categories of disorder, the authors have invited the student to see the complexity of psychopathology. A single case standing alone can foster a false sense of understanding; five or six aggregated begin to provide a grasp of central themes reflected within a category of mental disorder, but with important variations kept intact.

3. As I have noted, the structure of DSM-III matches the organization of many texts. It should be simple for the student to match up text and casebook simply by referring to the table of contents in each.

4. The cases are relatively brief, and as a result students are unlikely to get caught in a thicket of case dynamics.

5. The authors have provided relevant readings for the various disorders, which can serve as supplementary reading assignments.

6. The authors present four historically significant case studies by three of the great figures of the past: Kraepelin, Breuer, and Freud. Using these famed cases, the authors have linked past and present by writing a diagnostic reappraisal of each case.

7. The quality of clinical talents tapped is exemplary. Turning to my own discipline, I note with pleasure the contributions of such clinical psychology leaders as Ellis, Kazdin, Lazarus, Lewinsohn, Strupp, and others.

What broad purposes are served by a casebook? Beyond the advantages listed above is the powerful evocative quality of a case study. Anyone who has taught a course in abnormal psychology knows the motivational power of a case recital. Begin a case history and the most restive class quiets, and all focus their attention on the lecturer.

What is behind this fascination that we all have with individual cases of psychopathology? Is it a form of psychological voyeurism—the welcome peek (for a change) at someone else's psyche? Is it one's search to understand the mysterious world of "madness?" Is it that we find in the troubled state of another a welcome relief from our own anxieties? Or that it exacerbates concern about our own adaptations? (Thus the authors' comment in their introduction that, given the similarity to be found between the normal and the abnormal, students should not worry if some of the case histories resemble aspects of their own lives as well.)

Whatever the reasons, the reality exists. We are all captured by the vicissitudes of life, and those are most powerfully realized in children and adults who have begun to exhibit marked signs of deviant behavior. (Would we be captured as strongly by a casebook of achievements? I rather doubt it.)

But if this were the only reason for case studies, they would enjoy only a fleeting moment in the sun. Case histories—significant ones—have a basic importance that account for their long-lived status. In the attempt to construct a science of human behavior—whether normal or abnormal—the study of the single case provides the fundamental base for the scientific agenda. Our understanding of the phenomena of a discipline begins with observation. In the case of psychopathology these observations focus on individuals, their history, their behavior, and the biological and psychological processes that may underlie such behavior. The case study is the beginning point of understanding.

The next important step in enhancing that understanding is the act of aggregating those cases that seem to share certain behavioral or background factors in common. Thus begins the act of classification that is the foundation stone of every science. Psychopathology is no exception to that scientific enterprise, but its satisfactory resolution is always an arduous task, and in psychopathology that goal has not yet been achieved. The structure of this casebook is DSM-III. But that system is not the last word in the classification effort. There will, in future years, be a DSM-IV followed by a DSM-V, and so on. We still have a long way to go, as the authors point out in their introduction to the volume. Diagnosis should be accompanied by a knowledge of etiology, course, treatment, and outcome. This lies beyond our current achievements. But categorization is the first step, and hence the importance of a casebook that does not deny the importance of the classification task. In psychopathology that task takes the form of diagnoses based upon symptomatology. The venture is a boot-strapping operation in which we hope to arrive at finer differentiations as we learn more about symptoms and their underlying processes. One can criticize the status of a classification system, but not the scientific goal of devising one whose correlates will help us to organize domains of behavior that we must understand to get at the roots of the behavior disorders. That is the position taken by the authors of this casebook. It illustrates the status of the psychopathologies as defined by the DSM-III. It is a small but important step toward ultimately helping us to achieve a greater understanding of aberrant behavior. And that is the task that instructors in courses of abnormal psychology hope to communicate to students.

Some writers (e.g., Shontz, Kazdin) have described the many uses of individual case studies. One that I have mentioned is its utility in aggregating individuals who share behaviors in common as in the efforts to classify different types of behavior disorders. But an equally important virtue lies in the power of a superb case study to provide a source of the origins of a discipline. Great historical cases have performed this vital role, and several are offered toward the end of this volume. Another value of a case study is to describe unusual phenomena, and this volume is replete with descriptive accounts of cases that capture the interest of the reader. The individual case can also test the efficacy of unique therapeutic techniques to demonstrate their success or failure in easing anxiety or modifying deviance. Again, this volume illustrates the differential power of different forms of intervention for different types of cases.

And then there is the function of a case study in suggesting possible areas for future research. To instructors who will use this volume I commend the tough task of separating out within the cases those unanswered questions from others that seem to suggest at least partial answers and to communicate to your students the role of research in freeing us from ignorance. Many of your students will be future witnesses to the solutions of the mysteries of the etiology of the most severe mental disorders. Yours is the significant task of motivating them to think seriously about a range of disorders that poses one of the greatest public health problems of our time.

Psychopathology is an adventure. Reading these histories is a beginning point for that adventure. I hope that you and your students find them as stimulating and as provocative as did the authors and clinicians who framed this volume for you, the teacher, and for those who study with you.

Norman Garmezy
Professor of Psychology
University of Minnesota

TO THE STUDENT

PURPOSE

The purpose of this book is to provide students of abnormal psychology with a broad range of clinical cases drawn from the experiences of mental health professionals across the country. This book grew out of the realization that abnormal psychology is taught in classrooms where frequently there is little opportunity for firsthand observation of individuals who actually seek help for psychological disorders, symptoms, and behavioral complaints. (Throughout the book we will refer to individuals who enter the mental health system as "patients," although we recognize that many prefer to use the more neutral, nonmedical term "client.") Although attending actual case conferences is probably the ideal way to learn about psychopathology, we feel that a case book is the next best thing. In fact, it has several advantages. The cases presented here represent an extremely varied collection of different types of patients and problems. In addition, the professionals who have provided these cases represent many different viewpoints regarding the causes and treatment of psychological problems. Such diversity of patients and professional points of view is not to be seen in any single clinical setting.

THE CASES

Each case is presented in two parts: the clinical material, followed by a discussion. The clinical material was provided by the clinicians who evaluated the patients. In most cases this takes the form of a case summary written by the clinician and edited by us. In a few instances patients allowed us to use their own accounts of their problems. In all but one case the identities of the patients were disguised by altering names, ages, occupations, etc.

The case summaries reflect the evaluation process. In most cases the summary begins with a statement of the problems that caused the patient to come into contact with the mental health system. These may be the patients' complaints about their own problems or complaints about their behavior made by others, such as family members or agencies within the community. Usually there then follows a description of the context in which these problems developed, how they evolved over time, and the extent to which they have interfered with other areas of the individual's life. There is usually a discussion of past personal history which often provides clues about factors that may have influenced the development of the disturbance.

In some of the cases, special evaluation procedures such as psychological or biological tests are described. These tests were used to help the clinician make a differential diagnosis; that is, to determine the most likely diagnosis from among those that could account for the disturbance.

In most cases there is also a description of the treatment the patient received and the results of that treatment. In some instances there is also a long-term follow-up that describes how the patient has functioned in the years following treatment.

The discussions that follow each case have been prepared by us. We begin by noting the most salient features of the patient's psychopathology and then discuss the most likely diagnosis. For many of the cases, theories of the causes (etiology) of the particular disorders and alternative approaches to treatment are noted. Frequently we also include a discussion of the prognosis, by which we mean the expected course and outcome.

WHAT YOU WILL LEARN

In reading these cases you will become familiar with the full range of psychopathology that is seen in clinical practice and with the technical terms used to describe signs and symptoms of psychological disturbance. You will learn how clinicians conduct an evaluation and then summarize the clinical information into a diagnosis and treatment plan.

Over 250 "brands" of psychological treatment have been described in the literature. Although we have obviously not included all of these, you will read about cases that involve the following major forms of psychotherapy: psychoanalysis, psychodynamic psychotherapy, behavior therapy, cognitive behavior therapy, in vivo systematic desensitization, social skills therapy, brief psychotherapy, group therapy, family therapy, milieu therapy, sex therapy, supportive psychotherapy, rational emotive therapy, hypnosis, special education, Alcoholics Anonymous, and rape counseling. In addition, we have described the major biological approaches to treatment, including several forms of drug therapy and electroconvulsive treatment.

The treatment described for each case is the one that was actually given. We do not mean to imply that it was necessarily the only appropriate treatment, or even the most effective. The cases illustrate the range of possible outcomes from total recovery to chronic incapacitation. Although we believe that many of the favorable outcomes that are described do commonly occur, there probably was a tendency for clinicians to select their successfully treated cases.

THE IMPORTANCE OF DIAGNOSIS

Mental health professionals need a common language with which to communicate about the types of psychological problems for which they assume professional responsibility. A diagnosis is simply a way of summarizing a large amount of clinical information into a shorthand term. A diagnosis is valid to the extent that it identifies a group of individuals who share common clinical characteristics, such as presenting symptoms, course, outcome, and response to treatment. Ideally, a diagnosis also suggests the etiology, but for most of the mental disorders the etiology is still unknown. We believe that effective treatment planning begins with an accurate diagnosis. However, we recognize that diagnosis of mental disorders has been criticized on several counts: first, that the diagnosis of mental disorders is unreliable (clinicians often not agreeing on the diagnosis they assign to patients); second, that the diagnoses lack validity in that they offer little information useful in planning treatment. Finally, it is said that the application of diagnostic labels to people with psychological problems focuses only on psychopathology and ignores strengths and is inherently stigmatizing.

The diagnostic system used in this book is that of DSM-III, the third edition of the American Psychiatric Association's *Diagnostic and Statistical Manual of Mental Disorders*. We believe that the innovations in this system render these criticisms less valid than they were in the past.

For each of the diagnostic categories in DSM-III there are diagnostic criteria: explicit descriptions of the clinical features that must be present before the diagnosis can be made. Studies have shown that when clinicians use these criteria, diagnostic reliability is considerably improved over previous systems that provided only very general descriptions of the categories. A wealth of recent research indicates that for many of the diagnostic categories there are very clear treatment implications. Therefore, modern diagnosis is increasingly relevant to effective treatment planning.

It is true that diagnostic labels can be misused, with very unfortunate results for the individuals so labeled. However, in DSM-III it is emphasized that what is being classified is not the *individuals* themselves, but the *mental disorders* that they may or may not have. Thus it is a mistake to refer to "a schizophrenic," but rather one should speak of "an individual with schizophrenia." Finally, DSM-III includes a multiaxial system for evaluation. In this system, each individual is evaluated on five separate axes. The first two axes describe the mental disorders (psychological functioning). The third axis is for noting physical disorders that are important in treatment or management (biological functioning). Axis IV is for noting the severity of psychosocial stressors that have contributed to the development or exacerbation of the mental disorder. Finally, the fifth axis is for noting the highest level of adaptive functioning during the past year. (Axes IV and V describe aspects related to social functioning.) Therefore, the DSM-III multiaxial system provides a systematic and comprehensive bio-psycho-social evaluation that does include positive aspects of functioning (axis V) as well as psychopathology (axes I and II).

Because of our own special interest and expertise in the area of diagnosis, a major focus of our discussions has been in this area. We realize that some readers will be less interested in diagnosis than we are and will want to use the cases to focus on other areas, such as treatment or different theories of etiology.

The modern concept of mental disorder is very different from the old idea of "insanity" and includes many mild conditions which cannot be sharply differentiated from normality. Therefore, students should not be unduly alarmed to find similarities between their own problems and those experienced by some of the individuals described in this book.

ORGANIZATION OF THE BOOK

The volume includes 50 contemporary cases and four historical cases. The contemporary cases are grouped together according to the major diagnostic classes of DSM-III. However, the order of the groups does not follow the DSM-III classification. Instead, it follows the order generally found in most textbooks of abnormal psychology. The DSM-III approach to classification is descriptive and generally not based on theories of etiology. For that reason there is no diagnostic class of neuroses, a term that implies the psychoanalytic conception that unconscious conflicts cause these disorders and the use of particular defense mechanisms characterizes them. Instead, "neurotic" disorders are classified with other disorders according to their predominant clinical features. For example, "phobic neurosis" is called phobic disorder and is classified with the anxiety disorders; "depressive neurosis" is called dysthymic disorder and is classified as an affective disorder.

The historical cases described in the volume were treated by famous clinicians of the 19th century. The vivid and complete descriptions of these patients enable us to compare and contrast their notions of psychopathology, diagnosis, and treatment with those of the present day.

The book concludes with a list of references that includes articles and books on the diagnostic categories, as well as on the treatments that were employed in the cases.

We have alluded to the clinicians' possible bias in selecting successfully treated cases. We must acknowledge that we also had a bias, in that we selected cases that were interesting and often dramatic. We hope, therefore, that the book will prove to be not only instructive but also enjoyable for you—the student.

Robert L. Spitzer

Andrew E. Skodol

Miriam Gibbon

Janet B. W. Williams

About the Authors

Robert L. Spitzer, M.D., Chair (1974-80), APA Task Force on Nomenclature and Statistics during the development of DSM-III; Professor of Psychiatry, Columbia University; Chief, Biometrics Research, New York State Psychiatric Institute.

Andrew E. Skodol, M.D., Assistant Professor of Clinical Psychiatry, Columbia University; Research Psychiatrist, Biometrics Research, New York State Psychiatric Institute; Private Practice.

Miriam Gibbon, M.S.W., Assistant Clinical Professor of Psychiatric Social Work (in Psychiatry), Columbia University; Research Scientist, Biometrics Research and Director of Training, Research Assessment and Training Unit, New York State Psychiatric Institute.

Janet B. W. Williams, M.S.W., A.C.S.W., DMS-III Text Editor and Field Trial Coordinator; Assistant Professor of Clinical Psychiatric Social Work (in Psychiatry), Columbia University; Research Scientist, Biometrics Research and Assistant Director (for Research Training) of the Social Service Department, New York State Psychiatric Institute.

ACKNOWLEDGMENTS

We gratefully acknowledge the contributions of our colleagues listed below. Without their cases, this book would not have been possible. In order to ensure the anonymity of the patients, contributors are listed in alphabetical order rather than in association with the cases that they have provided.

HAGOP S. AKISKAL, M.D.
Affective Disorders Program
University of Tennessee College
   of Medicine
Memphis, Tennessee

ROBERT L. ARNSTEIN, M.D.
Yale University Health Services
Yale University
New Haven, Connecticut

PATRICIA BARTONE, M.S.N.
Western Psychiatric Institute and Clinic
University of Pittsburgh School
   of Medicine
Pittsburgh, Pennsylvania

AARON T. BECK, M.D.
Department of Psychiatry
University of Pennsylvania
Philadelphia, Pennsylvania

JUDITH V. BECKER, Ph.D.
Department of Psychiatry
Columbia University College of
   Physicians and Surgeons
New York, New York

DAVID BEHAR, M.D.
Unit on Childhood Mental Illness
National Institute of Mental Health
Bethesda, Maryland

MALCOLM B. BOWERS, Jr., M.D.
Department of Psychiatry
Yale University School of Medicine
New Haven, Connecticut

ROSEMARY CATHER, B.S.N.
Western Psychiatric Institute and Clinic
University of Pittsburgh School
   of Medicine
Pittsburgh, Pennsylvania

CARLO C. DICLEMENTE, Ph.D.
Texas Research Institute of
   Mental Sciences
Houston, Texas

ANN LOUISE DONEY, B.S.N.
Western Psychiatric Institute and Clinic
University of Pittsburgh School
   of Medicine
Pittsburgh, Pennsylvania

ALBERT ELLIS, Ph.D.
Institute for Rational-Emotive Therapy
New York, New York

M. JEROME FIALKOV, M.B. Ch.B.,
D.P.M.(U.C.T.), F.F.Psych.(S.A.)
Western Psychiatric Institute and Clinic
University of Pittsburgh School
   of Medicine
Pittsburgh, Pennsylvania

LESLIE M. FORMAN, M.D.
Department of Psychiatry
New York University School of Medicine
New York, New York

ALLEN J. FRANCES, M.D.
Department of Psychiatry
Cornell University Medical College
New York, New York

NANCY H. FRENCH, R.N., M.S.
Western Psychiatric Institute and Clinic
University of Pittsburgh School
   of Medicine
Pittsburgh, Pennsylvania

RICHARD C. FRIEDMAN, M.D.
Department of Psychiatry
Cornell University Medical College
White Plains, New York

ABBY J. FYER, M.D.
Department of Psychiatry
Columbia University College of
   Physicians and Surgeons
New York, New York

LAURENCE L. GREENHILL, M.D.
Department of Psychiatry
Columbia University College of
   Physicians and Surgeons
New York, New York

DEBORAH GREENWALD, Ph.D.
Western Psychiatric Institute and Clinic
University of Pittsburgh School of
   Medicine
Pittsburgh, Pennsylvania

RAYMOND P. HARRISON, Ph.D.
Department of Psychiatry
University of Pennsylvania School
   of Medicine
Philadelphia, Pennsylvania

GERARD E. HOGARTY, M.S.W.
Western Psychiatric Institute and Clinic
University of Pittsburgh School
   of Medicine
Pittsburgh, Pennsylvania

ROBERT J. HOWELL, Ph.D.
Department of Psychology
Brigham Young University
Provo, Utah

HELEN S. KAPLAN, M.D., Ph.D.
Department of Psychiatry
Cornell University Medical School
New York, New York

ALAN E. KAZDIN, Ph.D.
Western Psychiatric Institute and Clinic
University of Pittsburgh School
   of Medicine
Pittsburgh, Pennsylvania

DONALD F. KLEIN, M.D.
Department of Psychiatry
Columbia University College of
   Physicians and Surgeons
New York, New York

ARNOLD A. LAZARUS, Ph.D.
Graduate School of Applied and
   Professional Psychology
Rutgers, The State University of
   New Jersey
Piscataway, New Jersey

PETER M. LEWINSOHN, Ph.D.
Department of Psychology
University of Oregon
Eugene, Oregon

JOHN R. LION, M.D.
Department of Psychiatry
University of Maryland School
   of Medicine
Baltimore, Maryland

RUSSELL R. MONROE, M.D.
Department of Psychiatry
University of Maryland School
   of Medicine
Baltimore, Maryland

J. LAWRENCE MOODIE, M.D.
Department of Psychiatry
Cornell University Medical School
New York, New York

PETER F. NATHAN, Ph.D.
Graduate School of Applied and
   Professional Psychology
Rutgers, The State University of
   New Jersey
Piscataway, New Jersey

JUDITH L. RAPOPORT, M.D.
Unit on Childhood Mental Illness
National Institute of Mental Health
Bethesda, Maryland

CONWAY REDDING, Ph.D.
Southeast Community Mental
   Health Clinic
San Diego County Department of
   Health Services
San Diego, California

DOUGLAS REISS, Ph.D.
Western Psychiatric Institute and Clinic
University of Pittsburgh School
   of Medicine
Pittsburgh, Pennsylvania

RICHARD B. RESNICK, M.D.
Department of Psychiatry
New York Medical College
New York, New York

GRAENUM R. SCHIFF, M.D.
Chippenham Hospital
Richmond, Virginia

BENJAMIN SELTZER, M.D.
Department of Neurology
Boston University School of Medicine
Boston, Massachusetts

ARTHUR K. SHAPIRO, M.D.
Department of Psychiatry
Mount Sinai Medical Center
New York, New York

ELAINE SHAPIRO, Ph.D.
Department of Psychiatry
Mount Sinai Medical Center
New York, New York

DAVID A. SOSKIS, M.D.
Department of Psychiatry
Temple University School of Medicine
Philadelphia, Pennsylvania

HANS H. STRUPP, Ph.D.
Department of Psychology
Vanderbilt University
Nashville, Tennessee

LINDA TERI, Ph.D.
Department of Psychology
University of Oregon
Eugene, Oregon

B. TIMOTHY WALSH, M.D.
Department of Psychiatry
Columbia University College of
   Physicians and Surgeons
New York, New York

DAVID A. WASSERMAN, M.A.
Department of Psychology
University of Oregon
Eugene, Oregon

KATHERINE WHIPPLE, Ph.D.
Department of Psychiatry and the
  Behavioral Sciences
University of Southern California
  School of Medicine
Los Angeles, California

LORNA WING, M.D.
Medical Research Council
Social Psychiatry Unit
London, United Kingdom

STUART C. YUDOFSKY, M.D.
Department of Psychiatry
Columbia University College of
  Physicians and Surgeons
New York, New York

PSYCHOPATHOLOGY

A CASE BOOK

ANXIETY DISORDERS

COOKIES AND PEANUTS

Ms. B. is a 48-year-old housewife who was referred for behavior therapy after a two-year trial of psychodynamically oriented psychotherapy proved to be unsuccessful in alleviating her symptoms.

In the first session, she related that for the past fifteen years she has had a fear of choking to death on food. The fear is so severe that she has not been able to eat normally for this entire period, and during this time has eaten only soft foods, such as ice cream, yogurt, mashed potatoes, baby foods, and liquids. Her greatest fear is that a piece of food, such as meat, will lodge in her throat, obstructing her airway and causing her to choke to death. She therefore eats extremely slowly, often taking up to 2 hours to finish a very simple meal. When she tries to overcome her fear and eat solid food, she finds she cannot swallow and experiences a "lump in her throat."

At the initial interview Ms. B. related well to the therapist, but appeared very anxious—fidgeting in her seat, speaking in short, staccato sentences. Her affect was markedly constricted, and her mood was anxious and slightly depressed. She expressed feelings of hopelessness because of the duration of her problem and her unsuccessful prior therapy. Although she recognized that her fear was irrational, she continued to think that choking to death was a strong probability in *her* case. Her judgment was intact in other areas of her life.

Ms. B. cried as she recalled that her problem began fifteen years ago, shortly after an episode during which her 5-year-old son choked for a few seconds on some food during a meal at home. Ms. B. subsequently became extremely concerned about a recurrence of this event; she started chopping up food for her children and worried when her children ate at school. Although she feels she has been a "nervous person" all her life, she experienced an increase in her usual level of anxiety at this time, which has persisted to the present. Over the course of one year from the episode with her son, Ms. B. gradually began to fear that she herself could choke to death on food that became lodged in her throat. She gradually decreased her solid food intake, ate more and more slowly and carefully, worried up to several hours after a meal that, unbeknownst to her, some food *may* have lodged in her throat and could cause her to choke hours after eating. Because of her unusual eating habits she gradually stopped eating meals with her family. She states, "I feel like an outsider in my own family." Her husband eventually became quite exasperated with her. She was no longer eating with the family, nor was she dining out on social occasions, and their marital relationship suffered for it. Ms. B. became increasingly intolerant of herself, demoralized, and eventually depressed. Tranquilizers prescribed by her family physician alleviated some of the anxiety symptoms, but her fears persisted. Over the years she consulted numerous doctors to determine whether there was a physical basis for her inability to swallow, but physical examinations and numerous sophisticated tests were all negative.

Finally, feeling increasingly hopeless, withdrawing from contact with others, losing interest in her usual activities, Ms. B. decided with great trepidation to seek psychiatric treatment. She feared that a psychiatrist would diagnose her as "crazy." For two years she was in psychodynamically oriented psychotherapy without any positive effect. At one point she was on a low dose of antidepressant medication, also without any beneficial results. She ultimately left treatment and called another psychiatrist, who referred her for behavior therapy.

In order to determine the severity of her problem, the therapist suggested that the patient try to eat a cookie which he happened to have. Ms. B. agreed to try, held the cookie, and began to shake all over. She finally took a miniscule bite and then chewed for several minutes, appearing very fearful and continuing to shake the entire time. Finally she asked for some water to drink. The first session ended after Ms. B. and the therapist agreed to meet in one week, and Ms. B. would bring peanuts to the office.

The second session began with an explanation of the treatment. The therapist explained that children who are afraid of the water can gradually overcome this fear by first wading in up to their ankles, then their knees, and eventually their entire body. Their fear disappears as they realize that with gradual exposure to the feared situation, nothing bad happens. Therefore the therapy would consist of the patient gradually exposing herself to eating different kinds of solid food, beginning with very small amounts, in the presence of the therapist.

Then Ms. B. was gently encouraged to eat one peanut—she split it in half and with much shaking and fear gradually nibbled half of it. This was repeated several times, and she was instructed to practice this at home frequently. It appeared that her anxiety eased somewhat as the session progressed. The third session was similar to the second, with carrots and apples introduced. Ms. B.'s face lit up with joy as she bit into an apple for the first time in fifteen years. Once again, she was to practice at home what had been done in the session.

By the fourth visit the therapist began to realize that Ms. B. had a strange conception of the anatomy and physiology involved in eating. She believed that it was possible to choke on food several hours after it had been eaten. The therapist therefore began the fourth session by drawing a diagram of the esophagus and its relation to other bodily organs. He then described the swallowing process and the natural safeguards against choking to death. Ms. B. expressed great relief at obtaining this information. During the second part of the session she ate some bread, taking very small bites and chewing very slowly and carefully, but with less anxiety. As he had throughout the treatment, the therapist gently and with good humor encouraged Ms. B., reassured her, at times joked with her, and modeled the desired behavior as they ate together. The atmosphere was as relaxed as possible, and the decision of which food to try next was made by agreement of Ms. B. and the therapist, with the idea of gradually increasing the difficulty to Ms. B. as she became comfortable at each step. There was always homework after each session.

On the fifth visit the therapist attempted to teach Ms. B. a relaxation exercise that she could use in order to reduce her anxiety when eating. She was told to close her eyes and imagine a line down the center of her thoughts. On the left side she should put all her worries, and on the right side imagine the most pleasant scene possible. She was then to concentrate on gradually moving the line over to the left so that eventually she would only have pleasant thoughts. Ms. B. felt this was not helpful, since when she tried to relax, intrusive thoughts of choking would increase her anxiety level. In the same session Ms. B. began to eat a sandwich. On the sixth visit she was able to finish very slowly half a tunafish sandwich.

The remaining four therapy sessions consisted of continued progress in eating foods Ms. B. considered difficult, with steadily decreasing levels of anxiety. Ms. B. was instructed to use a small kitchen timer to help her eat at a normal rate, and reduce the time she spent chewing her food. With continued practice, she eventually was able to eat solid foods without difficulty, at a slow-normal rate, by the time therapy was terminated after the tenth session.

The therapist called Ms. B. three years later to find out how she was doing. She reported that she was no longer fearful of eating solid food, but she occasionally would find herself starting to worry about the possibility of choking. She also mentioned that about a year after stopping therapy she had a relapse but decided that rather than reentering therapy, she would first try to treat herself. She therefore began the gradual exposure process, beginning with peanuts and a timer. In a few weeks she was able to eat as well as she had at the end of therapy. She told the therapist that what she remembered most vividly about the therapy were the times that they laughed together as they ate the cookies and peanuts.

DISCUSSION

Psychopathology and Diagnosis   Ms. B. had a fear of an activity (eating solid foods) that was grossly out of proportion to any actual danger inherent in that activity (choking to death). Her fear was so overwhelming that she avoided the activity, with the result that her avoidance interfered with important life activities (eating meals with her family) and caused her great distress. Despite her preoccupation with her fear, she recognized that it was irrational. A persistent and irrational fear of an activity or situation that results in avoidance of the activity, causing the individual significant distress, but recognized by the individual as irrational or excessive, is a phobia.

Phobias may occasionally occur as associated symptoms of other illnesses such as major depression and schizophrenia and are then not diagnosed as a separate disorder. However, when the phobia is not part of another mental disorder, as in Ms. B.'s case, it is diagnosed as a phobic disorder, within the broader rubric of anxiety disorders.

Anxiety disorders are disorders in which either anxiety is the predominant disturbance, as in panic disorder (see Case 2, "Anxious Anne") and generalized anxiety disorder (see Case 3, "Fathers and Sons"), or anxiety is experienced if the individual attempts to master the symptoms, as in confronting the dreaded object or situation in a phobic disorder or resisting the obsessions or compulsions in obsessive compulsive disorder (see Case 4, "Keeping Things Straight"). Phobic disorders, the most common type of anxiety disorder, are divided into three types. The most incapacitating type is agoraphobia (see Case 2, "Anxious Anne"), in which there is a marked fear of being alone or being in public places. Important activities, like going out of the house alone, are increasingly avoided, and the person's life may eventually become so constricted that the person is totally house-bound. In social phobias there is fear and avoidance of activities in which the individual could be embarrassed or humiliated. Common examples include fear and avoidance of public speaking, using public lavatories, and eating or writing in public.

Finally, all other phobias, such as Ms. B.'s, are called *simple phobias.* (In Ms. B's case, since her fear of eating was due to a fear of choking to death rather than embarrassment or humiliation from choking in public, it was a simple phobia.) The most common simple phobias involve irrational or excessive fear of animals, such as dogs, snakes, insects, and rodents.

Many people feel somewhat uncomfortable in certain situations that pose little or no real danger. For example, many people feel mildly anxious when exposed to insects or high places or when they have to speak in front of a group of people. It is only when such fears are persistent, involve a compelling desire to avoid the dreaded activity or situation, and cause significant distress that they would be termed phobias.

Treatment The most effective treatment of simple phobias, such as Ms. B.'s fear of eating solid food, involves a form of behavior therapy, called desensitization. In this therapy the individual is gradually exposed to the feared stimulus. It was previously thought that such gradual exposure could be accomplished as well by having the patient vividly imagine getting closer to the feared stimulus (systematic desensitization using imagery). Now it is recognized that it is far more effective if the treatment is carried out actually using the feared stimulus (desensitization in vivo).

Ms. B.'s therapist applied this behavioral therapy with skill and ingenuity. His use of humor, gentle coaxing, assignment of homework, and education (he corrected her anatomic misconceptions about eating) all contributed to the success of the therapy.

Prognosis As is often the case, there was a relapse after having stopped therapy, but the patient was able to make use, on her own, of the techniques that she had learned to overcome her problem. Therefore, her long-term prognosis is very good.

ANXIOUS ANNE

Anne Watson, a 45-year-old married woman, was self-referred for evaluation at an outpatient psychiatric clinic. Over the past two years she had been troubled by increasingly frequent "anxiety attacks" and constant nervousness. In the past several months she had begun to dread common activities that took her away from home, such as shopping and driving. Though her fears seemed unreasonable to her, she found herself unable to overcome them. Her family and friends began to notice changes in her behavior, but she was ashamed to disclose her condition to them. While visiting a friend she read an article describing a treatment program for people suffering symptoms similar to hers. The next day she called the clinic for an appointment.

Ms. Watson reported that until the onset of her current problems two years ago, she had led a normal and happy life. At that time an uncle to whom she had been extremely close in her childhood died following a sudden unexpected heart attack. Though she had not seen her uncle frequently in recent years, Anne was considerably upset by his death. Nevertheless, after two or three months her mood returned to normal. Six months after his death she was returning home from work one evening when suddenly she felt that she couldn't catch her breath. Her heart began to pound, and she broke out into a cold sweat. Things began to seem unreal; her legs felt leaden, and she became sure she would die or faint before she reached home. She asked a passerby to help her get a taxi and went to a nearby hospital emergency room. The doctors there found her physical examination, blood count and chemistries, and electrocardiogram all completely normal. They did note that when she first arrived her heart rate was somewhat elevated, but this subsided within 20 minutes. By the time the examination was finished Anne had recovered completely and was able to leave the hospital and return home on her own. The incident had no effect on her daily life.

Four weeks later Ms. Watson had a second similar attack while preparing dinner at home. She made an appointment to see her family doctor, but again, all examinations were normal. She decided to put the episodes out of her mind and continue with her normal activities. Within the next several weeks, however, she had four attacks and noticed that she began to worry about when the next one would occur. She tried to find explanations for their occurrence, but each time she felt certain she had figured it out, an episode would take her by surprise. She returned to her family doctor, who diagnosed her problem as "nervous strain" and prescribed a minor tranquilizer to be taken three times a day. Ms. Watson reported that the medication made her calmer, but had no effect on her anxiety attacks. She found that alcohol was extremely helpful in alleviating her constant tension, and gradually, over the next several months, she developed the habit of having two cocktails at lunch and several drinks both before and with dinner.

She then found herself constantly thinking about her anxieties as attacks continued; she began to dread leaving the house alone for fear she would be stranded, helpless and alone, by an attack. She began to avoid going to movies, parties, and dinners with friends for fear she would have an attack and be embarrassed by her need to leave. When household chores necessitated driving, she waited until it was possible to take her children or a friend along for the ride. She also began walking the twenty blocks to her office to avoid the possibility of being trapped in a subway car between stops when an attack occurred.

A year before her clinic visit she started seeing a psychiatrist twice a week at the advice of her family doctor. She described the psychotherapy as helpful in increasing her understanding of her relationship with her husband and in dealing with certain decisions that had to be made about her career. However, there was no effect on her anxiety attacks or increasing fears. Anne reported that her husband had become aware of and extremely concerned about her increased drinking, and that this had motivated her to follow up on the article she had seen in the newspaper about the clinic's program.

Ms. Watson is one of three children who grew up in a small southern city. Her father was a middle-level executive for a national corporation; her mother was a housewife. She describes her home as hectic, but her childhood as generally content. She came to New York City to attend college, and met her husband while in her sophomore year. They married soon after her graduation. Her husband was at that time a first-year law student. After graduation, Ms. Watson worked as a copywriter until the birth of her first child, three years later. She did not return to work after the child's birth. She and her husband decided to have a second child, who was born eighteen months later. Anne describes this as a happy time in her life. She and her husband were extremely active in local politics, and the house was usually full of people, since both enjoyed entertaining.

When her children reached adolescence, Ms. Watson decided to return to work and took a job with a company concerned with the development of special educational programs. She has since received several promotions and is currently in charge of a department. She has found the work interesting and satisfying, but refused her most recent offer of promotion because of her fear that her anxiety would make her unable to handle the responsibility.

Ms. Watson is a thin, well-dressed, and attractive middle-aged woman. During the interview she sat rather rigidly and fidgeted continually with her gloves. Her speech was rapid, her voice soft. Her conversation was completely coherent and relevant. Though while discussing her difficulties she at times became tearful, she was also able to respond to humor appropriately. She described her recent mood as desperate, terrified, and unhappy, but also noted that if her husband were with her or activities did not require her to be alone or leave the house, she enjoyed things fully and was in fact her normal self. She denied any recent change in eating or sleeping habits.

Ms. Watson was started on an antidepressant medication at bedtime, to be increased until a certain nightly dose was reached. She was to remain at this dose until her return visit, the following week. She was told to continue her use of the tranquilizer. At her second visit, the panic attacks were unchanged. She was instructed to increase the antidepressant every three days until a maximum dose was reached. Six days later, Ms. Watson telephoned to say that she "couldn't stand up." When she did she got dizzy, lightheaded, and almost passed out. In order to minimize this common side effect, a drop in blood pressure when suddenly standing up, medication was reduced, and then increased at a slower rate to a lower maximum dosage. The patient tolerated this well. At her third visit she stated that her panic attacks still occurred daily, but lasted only about half as long as before and seemed not as bad. An increase of medication was continued at the same rate, to a somewhat higher dose. At her next visit two weeks later Ms. Watson reported only one or two mild panic attacks. Medication was again increased slightly. At this dose she reported that she sometimes felt she was about to have an attack—but the attack never occurred. Over the next few weeks the medication was maintained at that dose, and it soon became clear that she was no longer having panic attacks. She reported she was again able to enjoy doing things like going out to dinner or a concert—"things I didn't realize I was avoiding." At the end of the second month of treatment she and her husband began to discuss summer vacation plans. She was reluctant to plan a long trip, but felt she did want a chance to see if she could do it. She also stated that she had stopped her evening routine of several drinks as she "no longer needed it."

Eight months after starting treatment Ms. Watson returned from her summer vacation reporting that she had had a wonderful time and felt like her "old self." She was able to play tennis, swim, and travel comfortably. Visits to theaters and restaurants had become a pleasure rather than a trial. She was also considering accepting the job promotion which she had refused during her illness. She had decreased her tranquilizer intake to a very small dose on her own.

Plans to gradually discontinue her antidepressant were discussed since she had had six months of treatment, the usual point at which medication can be stopped without a serious risk of the reappearance of the panic attacks. She expressed much hesitation about this, fearing a relapse. It was decided to postpone the decrease until after her job change was accomplished.

DISCUSSION

Psychopathology and Diagnosis   Ms. Watson's chief complaint was anxiety that took the form of discrete episodes of intense fear that were not precipitated by a life-threatening situation (such as being attacked) or by a specific stimulus (such as heights or public speaking). Such episodes of panic are generally accompanied by various physical symptoms of autonomic arousal. Ms. Watson experienced difficulty breathing, faintness, palpitations, accelerated heart rate, and sweating. There were also characteristic psychological symptoms: She had derealization (felt that things were unreal) and feared that she would die.

Recurrent panic attacks of this kind indicate panic disorder. Often the illness begins following a psychosocial stressor, such as the death of a loved one or the termination of an important relationship. Because Ms. Watson's uncle had died six months before her first panic attack, it is unclear whether this played a role in precipitating her illness. Many patients with panic disorder begin to restrict their activities as the anxiety generalizes to other situations, as did Ms. Watson, for fear that they will have an attack in a place or situation from which escape might be difficult or where help might not be available in case of sudden incapacitation. This complication is called *agoraphobia with panic attacks*. (Agoraphobia means "fear of the market place," actually a misnomer since what is actually feared is the occurrence of a panic attack rather than the place itself.) Agoraphobia can be extremely incapacitating. In some cases, individuals with the disorder restrict their lives so much for fear of having panic attacks that they eventually become captives in their own homes.

Treatment   Surprisingly, antianxiety agents (minor tranquilizers) are generally ineffective in preventing the occurrence of panic attacks, although they may be helpful in alleviating the anticipatory anxiety that an attack will occur. A most effective treatment, for reasons that are unclear, are certain antidepressant drugs, such as the one that Ms. Watson received. When these drugs are effective (in 70 to 90 percent of the cases), they block the occurrence of the panic attacks; however, the individual with agoraphobia must learn to overcome the anticipatory anxiety that remains, and to enter situations that had been avoided. In time, as the individual enters these situations and does not have an attack, the anticipatory anxiety gradually disappears.

Many behaviorally oriented clinicians would be strongly opposed to the use of medication as a first choice of treatment for such a case. In their view, there is a large research literature attesting to the efficacy of in vivo desensitization for this disorder (see Case 1, "Cookies and Peanuts"), often in a group with other patients with agoraphobia.

FATHERS AND SONS

Bob Donaldson was a 22-year-old carpenter referred to the psychiatric outpatient department of a community hospital in the northwest by his mother's boss, a doctor on the staff of the same hospital. Three months earlier, the patient's father had died after a protracted illness. The day of his father's funeral, Bob experienced an episode of dizziness, sweating, and an unusual feeling that things around him did not look quite real. This feeling waxed and waned for an hour or so and then disappeared. Over the ensuing month similar episodes became longer and more frequent, until about one month prior to his evaluation, when he admitted that he was never without some set of uncomfortable physical sensations that he was aware of.

During the initial interview Bob was visibly distressed. He appeared tense, worried, and frightened. He sat on the edge of his chair, tapping his foot and fidgeting with a pencil on the psychiatrist's desk. He sighed frequently, took deep breaths between sentences, and periodically exhaled audibly and changed his position as he attempted to relate his story:

Bob: It's been an awful month. I can't seem to do anything. I don't know whether I'm coming or going. I'm afraid I'm going crazy or something.

Doctor: What makes you think that?

Bob: I can't concentrate. My boss tells me to do something and I start to do it, but before I've taken five steps I don't know what I started out to do. I get dizzy and I can feel my heart beating and everything looks like it's shimmering or far away from me or something—it's unbelievable.

Doctor: What thoughts come to mind when you're feeling like this?

Bob: I just think, "Oh, Christ, my heart is really beating, my head is swimming, my ears are ringing—I'm either going to die or go crazy."

Doctor: What happens then?

Bob: Well, it doesn't last more than a few seconds, I mean that intense feeling. I come back down to earth, but then I'm worrying what's the matter with me all the time, or checking my pulse to see how fast it's going, or feeling my palms to see if they're sweating.

Doctor: Can others see what you're going through?

Bob: You know, I doubt it. I hide it. I haven't been seeing my friends. You know, they say "Let's stop for a beer" or something after work and I give them some excuse— you know, like I have to do something around the house or with my car. I'm not with them when I'm with them anyway—I'm just sitting there worrying. My friend Pat said I was frowning all the time. So, anyway, I just go home and turn on the TV or pick up the sports page, but I can't really get into that either.

Bob went on to say that he had stopped playing softball because of fatigability and trouble concentrating. On several occasions during the past two weeks he was unable to go to work because he was "too nervous." Recently he felt especially easily distracted by roadside stimuli while driving and described a frightening sensation that the passing trees were falling over onto his car.

Bob became tearful while describing his father's death. He clearly related the onset of his current difficulties to the funeral, but was unable to understand why he was having so much trouble. He was an only child and described his relationship to his father as follows:

Bob: My father and I were very close. I really admired the guy. He was strong and everybody liked him. He was a foreman for the same company I work for. He started out, you know, as an electrician's apprentice and worked his way up. Whenever we would be around the same job, we'd have lunch and everybody would come over and say "hi" and shoot the breeze for a while. He seemed so comfortable with everybody. I know, since I can remember, I wished I was like him.

Bob's only difficulty was that he sometimes felt intimidated by his father's gregariousness and apparent success in most of what he did. There were times, before his father's illness, that Bob had wanted to express certain feelings, particularly about sensitive issues, such as doubts he had about himself that led him to feel uncomfortable with girls, but he felt too embarrassed to bring them up. During his father's illness Bob felt uncertain about whether he should share his worries about his father with him or maintain the same "front" that "things were not all that bad," which several other members of his family had adopted. When his father finally died, Bob had many feelings of regret about how he had handled their relationship over the past several years.

Bob acknowledged that he actually had not cried a great deal after the death. He became preoccupied with his anxiety symptoms and with the support of his mother, who took her husband's death very hard and became rather dependent on her son for very basic details of living, such as paying the bills. At first Bob managed, but as his symptoms worsened, he was unable to take care of these chores, either. He stated that he found his mother's needs to be burdensome and that she was frequently demanding and intrusive:

Bob: She doesn't do what she used to do or go where she used to go. She just hangs around the house moping or complaining or talking to me about everything that goes on in her head—that must have been what she did with my father. She's always asking me questions, too, "when are you coming home, when are you going to take out the garbage, what are you going to do about this or that?" I don't even tell her what I'm thinking about or my worries— she's got enough problems of her own.

Doctor: It must be hard, going through what you're going through, and having to be supportive of your mother, too.

Bob: Yeah, but she can't help it. She really depended on him and now he's gone— she's got no one else to turn to except me.

Doctor: Do you ever get angry when she's complaining or pestering you when you're not up to it?

Bob: No, not really. I understand what she's going through.

Treatment for Bob involved relief from anxiety symptoms with small doses of the antianxiety agent Valium and supportive psychotherapy. Although reluctant at first to take medication, believing that it would further his feelings of loss of control, Bob ultimately got symptomatic relief and was able to work and see friends. In psychotherapy he was encouraged to mourn the loss of his father, including expressing some of the ambivalent feelings that he had had arising from unspoken demands he felt had been placed on him by his father's successes. He also expressed anger at his mother, who assumed that the loss was all hers and that he needed no support. Following a three-month period of therapy he felt considerably better. It emerged that he had become rather self-conscious and insecure during adolescence, and he decided to continue therapy to see if he could develop a better feeling about himself.

DISCUSSION

Psychopathology and Diagnosis The death of a close family member almost always produces a strong emotional reaction, usually symptoms of depression. This expected reaction is called bereavement, and is not regarded as psychopathology unless it is particularly severe, incapacitating, or prolonged. Bob's case is clearly not uncomplicated bereavement because the symptoms are primarily those of anxiety rather than depression.

At the time he was referred for a psychiatric evaluation he was experiencing motor tension (appeared tense, sat on the edge of his chair, tapped his foot, and fidgeted with a pencil), autonomic hyperactivity (dizziness, sweating, palpitations), apprehensive expectation (worried and frightened), hypervigilance (easily distracted by roadside stimuli while driving), and unusual perceptions (things did not look real, the sensation of passing trees falling).

Sometimes anxiety is focused on a particular object, situation, or activity that is then avoided (phobias—see Case 54, "Little Hans"). In other cases, anxiety is controlled by various ritualized behaviors or thoughts (obsessions or compulsions—see Case 4, "Keeping Things Straight"). When anxiety is primarily experienced as short, discrete episodes of terror accompanied by various physical symptoms, these episodes are called panic attacks (see Case 2, "Anxious Anne"). In Bob's case, the anxiety does not take any of these specific or focused forms, but rather is continuous and diffuse. For this reason, the name of this disorder is *generalized anxiety disorder*.

Course and Treatment   Generalized anxiety disorder may be precipitated by a specific stressor, as it was for Bob. In such cases, the disorder is generally short-lived. More typically, it is a chronic condition without any clear precipitants.

Bob received an antianxiety medication to temporarily suppress the symptoms that were frightening and disabling. Because such drugs have a potential for becoming addictive, they generally should not be prescribed for long periods of time. When Bob became less symptomatic, he was able to discuss his ambivalent feelings toward his father with the therapist and to express grief over his death, which he had been unable to do previously. This is an example of the way in which somatic therapy can sometimes make it easier for a patient to make use of a psychological therapy, since the combination of drugs and psychotherapy seems to have contributed to Bob's recovery.

KEEPING THINGS STRAIGHT

Ted is a 13-year-old referred to a midwestern inpatient psychiatric research ward because of "senseless rituals and attention to minutiae." He can spend 3 hours "centering" the toilet paper roll on its holder or rearranging his bed and other objects in his room. When placing objects down, such as books or shoelaces after tying them, he picks them up and replaces them several times until they seem "straight." Although usually placid, he becomes abusive with family members who try to enter his room for fear they will move or break his objects. When he is at school, he worries that people may disturb his room. He sometimes has to be forced to interrupt his routine to attend meals. Last year he hid pieces of his clothing around the house because they wouldn't lie straight in his drawers. Moreover, he often repeats to himself, "This is perfect; you are perfect." He makes a gesture of head bowing, hand saluting, and sniffing. When outside, as in a movie house, he points his gestures in the direction of the house. To him, the gesture is a form of tribute to the "perfection" of his room. It's "like letting me know the room is straight."

There is little other thought activity during his compulsive behavior. His attitude and resistance fluctuate; he knows it takes time from his other interest—film making and projecting. He can get through his rituals quickly if he wants to do something else. Otherwise he is quite slow about them. He has little interest in school or socializing, and doesn't appear overly concerned about his condition. Because he spends the whole day in compulsive arranging and gesturing, he has not been able to attend school and is being tutored at home by his father.

Until he started kindergarten, his parents saw him as an average child who was cheerful and outgoing. His early development had been normal except for head banging as a toddler. Upon entering school, however, his teachers saw him as "withdrawn."

He could not tolerate contact sports or anyone touching him. He was also quite apathetic, just "sitting there."

He always had a fear of water, in spite of the fact that no untoward incident had ever occurred. He could not go any further than ankle deep without panicking and protesting strongly, and could only dangle his feet over the edge of a pool.

At 10 he also began fearing contamination with germs. He needed to know who had prepared his food before eating. He picked up his food with paper if his hands were not washed and placed the last piece of food back, fearing it was "drugged." At 11 he began to wear two layers of clothing, even in sweltering heat, so he would avoid "catching pneumonia." The teacher was disturbed because he spent too much time washing his lips and mouth with his own smuggled-in mouthwash and soap. Again, he feared germs were entering his mouth. On reflection, he always acknowledged that these habits and thoughts were unreasonable. Paradoxically, he could also go without taking a bath for many days unless his parents forced him. He kept the same clothes on, slept in his socks, stayed in his pajamas all day, and neglected his chores unless great pressure was exerted on him.

Throughout grade school he remained aloof from other children. Although his parents sensed he had affection for them, he never overtly expressed it. He would kiss his parents in a polite way when he had to leave them.

When Ted was 11 the family spent two years in biweekly family therapy with a psychologist with no discernible change. School officials became progressively concerned about skin irritation and chapping from his cleansing rituals; hospitalization was suggested at age 12 because he spent all his free time doing them.

In this first hospitalization he received an antipsychotic drug for a week, without effect other than sleepiness. An elaborate behavior modification system was established in which all privileges required payment in points. These were earned for time spent not performing rituals and for compliance with ward routine. Most rituals and excessive cleansing were quickly suppressed on this regime. He was slowly desensitized to water and could duck his head under water, a feat of which he was proud.

After eight weeks of hospitalization he was discharged, and his parents were asked to keep a detailed diary of his compulsive behaviors. They noticed that he was now more responsible, bathing, and doing chores without prodding. His teachers reported more participation in class activities and no time lost doing rituals. The staff of the hospital trained the parents to continue behavior modification techniques. Three weeks later they relinquished this approach as "difficult and unnatural" and Ted's compulsive activity recurred.

The family history contains no individuals with this disorder. One uncle did have repetitive facial grimacing (tics) and was severely socially isolated. At age 16 he walked out of school after giving a class presentation and "remained in bed for two years." Despite a very high IQ he remained a farm hand on the family property. He became an alcoholic in his twenties and died of it in middle age. He carried a diagnosis of schizophrenia. None of the immediate family is unusual in any way. Ted's father is rather placid but successful in a management career, and participates in community activities. One full sibling and three half siblings (from a previous marriage of his father) are without behavioral difficulties.

When examined on admission to the research ward, Ted's mental status was normal except for mild emotional flattening and quiet speech. He was friendly and likable, with a shy but attentive manner. There was no evidence of thought disorder or delusions. His compulsions were associated with a "feeling." He said he "knows" nothing will happen if his objects are rearranged, but has difficulty resisting his "feeling" indefinitely. The feeling is at first weak but increasingly compelling, turning into irritation if it is denied its outlet.

Follow-up On admission to the research ward Ted began receiving an experimental antidepressant drug that had been reported effective in adults. It helped dampen the urgency felt behind the compulsions and feelings of irritability or frustration if they are blocked. Three weeks after admission his absorption in rituals and resistance to discontinuing them for the sake of other activities had lessened. However, he still spent his spare time (2 to 3 hours per day) doing his usual routines.

A program of behavior therapy involving increasing exposure to intolerable messiness and "dirt" and the prevention of compulsive responses was planned. Despite the 75 percent chance of eventual success, Ted stated he was not willing to subject himself to such stress.

Instead, ward privileges and his money allowance were tied to the attainment of progressively more difficult goals such as decreasing tardiness because of involvement in rituals, decreasing rearranging and gesturing in public, and the toleration of disorder outside of his immediate bed area and closet space. Social skills and friendship-making lessons were added once this approach was established.

By the time of discharge, Ted was never late to classes and activities. He initiated conversations more often to socialize rather than to ask for something. He no longer gestured in public, but occasionally did so when he thought no one was looking at him. He stopped being verbally abusive when interrupted in his rituals or when his belongings were moved. He quietly rearranged them on his own.

These methods were shared with the parents, and at discharge they were referred to a psychiatric clinic in their home area. There a child psychiatrist in conjunction with a psychologist interested in behavioral techniques helped his parents extend and continue the above approach at home. His parents remarked that they preferred this behavioral program to the previous program that involved earning points for good behavior, because it made use of natural rewards, such as giving him his allowance. In addition, they appreciated the simplicity of this program, which did not require them to keep any records.

Ted returned to public school, where he did average work. The teachers were to report any tardiness or public compulsive behavior to his parents, in addition to using usual school disciplinary measures. His parents were to decrease his allowance and/ or restrict an activity in response to relapse. However, this rarely happened. By three months after discharge Ted continued doing his rituals in private in his spare time, and continually thought about them. He reported the absence of a buildup in frustration when prevented from doing so. His parents stated he was not verbally abusive when they entered his room, and he regularly did things with another boy outside of school. However, he remained aloof from most other people.

DISCUSSION

Psychopathology and Diagnosis   Ted's life is dominated by his obsessions and compulsions. Obsessions are recurrent, persistent ideas, thoughts, images, or impulses that are experienced by the individual as alien and senseless. That is, the individual recognizes that these thoughts are not voluntarily produced, but seem to invade consciousness against his will. These thoughts, as in Ted's case, frequently involve the idea of contamination. Other common obsessions involve thoughts of violence, such as of hurting one's child, and doubt about whether one has done something, for example, hurt someone accidentally, or neglected to do something, such as turning off the stove.

Obsessions frequently, as in Ted's case, are the stimulus for compulsions—repetitive and seemingly purposeful behaviors performed in a stereotyped fashion and designed to produce or prevent some future event. The compulsions are not, in fact, realistically connected with what they are designed to prevent, or they are clearly excessive in relation to their purpose. In Ted's case, the obsession about contamination leads to a variety of compulsions, all designed to avoid illness: he spends inordinate amounts of time washing his lips and mouth; he wears two layers of clothing to avoid catching pneumonia; he picks up his food with paper. His compulsions arranging his room are related to obsessions about "perfection."

Adults with obsessions and compulsions invariably recognize that the symptoms are senseless and, at least initially, make some attempt to resist them. Resisting, however, leads to increasing anxiety until eventually the symptom cannot be resisted any longer.

The word "compulsive" is often used loosely to describe any behavior that is repetitive, driven, or excessive, such as gambling, certain forms of sexual behavior, and overeating. The technical term "compulsion," however, is used only to describe behaviors that are not in themselves pleasurable (as is gambling, sex, and eating) and that are designed to avoid some future dreaded event.

Similarly, the word "obsessive" is often used loosely to describe brooding and rumination about some unpleasant thought, regardless of its content. The technical term "obsession" is used only to describe thoughts that are both intrusive and senseless. The parent who cannot help worrying about his sick child may be said to be brooding, but does not have an obsession. On the other hand, the parent who everyday cannot help having the thought that he may have run over one of his children as he backed his car out of the garage on the way to work has an obsession.

Obsessions and compulsions range from mild superstitions ("Step on a crack, you'll break your mother's back."), which normal individuals may have, to a crippling condition such as Ted's. They may also be seen as symptoms of other disorders, such as major depression or schizophrenia. When, as in Ted's case, they are the predominant disturbance and significantly interfere with functioning, the diagnosis of *obsessive compulsive disorder* is made. Obsessive compulsive disorder is considered an anxiety disorder, since the symptoms have the function of warding off anxiety, and anxiety is experienced when the individual resists the symptoms.

Etiology   Psychoanalytic theory explains the symptoms as the result of the ego's attempt to keep aggressive impulses from reaching consciousness. Thus the parent who worries that he has run over his child may be turning a wish to hurt his child into the "senseless" fear that he has in fact hurt the child. Ted's compulsion to have his room neatly arranged might be a defense against the anxiety that is caused by his wish to be defiantly messy. His refusal to bathe or change his clothes might be evidence that he is indeed ambivalent about how neat and clean he wants to be.

Learning theory proposes that an obsession originates in an association between an anxiety-producing event and a neutral thought. A compulsion develops when an individual discovers that performing a particular act is associated with diminishing anxiety. The reduction in anxiety reinforces the act, and the individual is therefore likely to repeat it. More recently, electroencephalographic and neuropsychological data suggest that subtle dysfunction of the frontal-temporal lobe of the brain may be associated with the disorder. All of these proposals are hypotheses for which conclusive evidence is not yet available.

Course and Treatment   Obsessive compulsive disorder tends to be a chronic condition. Treatments ranging from psychoanalysis to electroconvulsive therapy have been used, without notable success. In Ted's case, both drugs and behavior therapy were used. The behavior therapy consisted of techniques designed to control the symptoms, regardless of their etiology. This combination of treatments seems to have helped Ted temporarily. Whether the effects will be lasting remains to be seen.

Prognosis   Ted's history suggests that his improvement may be short-lived unless his parents are able to continue to use the behavioral approach when he returns home. Even with treatment, the early onset and severity of the symptoms do not bode well for the future.

RAPED

Mary Billings is a 33-year-old divorced nurse, referred to the Victim Clinic at Bedford Psychiatric Hospital for counseling by her supervisory head nurse. Mary had been raped two months ago. The assailant gained entry to her apartment while she was sleeping, and she awoke to find him on top of her. He was armed with a knife and threatened to kill her and her child (who was asleep in the next room) if she did not submit to his demands. He forced her to undress and repeatedly raped her vaginally over a period of 1 hour. He then admonished her that if she told anyone or reported the incident to the police he would return and assault her child.

After he left, she called her boyfriend, who came to her apartment right away. He helped her contact the Sex Crimes Unit of the Police Department, which is currently investigating the case. He then took her to a local hospital for a physical examination and collection of evidence for the police (traces of sperm, pubic hair samples, fingernail scrapings). She was given antibiotics as prophylaxis against venereal disease. Mary then returned home with a girl friend who spent the remainder of the night with her.

Over the next few weeks Mary continued to be afraid of being alone and had her girl friend move in with her. She became preoccupied with thoughts of what had happened to her and the possibility that it could happen again. Mary was frightened that the rapist might return to her apartment and therefore had additional locks installed on both the door and the windows. She was so upset and had such difficulty concentrating that she decided she could not yet return to work. When she did return to work several weeks later, she was still clearly upset, and her supervisor suggested that she might be helped by counseling.

During the clinic interview, Mary was coherent and spoke quite rationally in a hushed voice. She reported recurrent and intrusive thoughts about the sexual assault, to the extent that her concentration was impaired and she had difficulty doing chores such as making meals for herself and her daughter. She felt she was not able to be effective at work, still felt afraid to leave her home, to answer her phone, and had little interest in contacting friends or relatives.

The range of Mary's affect was constricted. She talked in the same tone of voice whether discussing the assault or less emotionally charged topics, such as her work history. She was easily startled by any unexpected noise. She also was unable to fall asleep because she kept thinking about the assault. She had no desire to eat, and when she did attempt it, she felt nauseated. Mary was repelled by the thought of sex and stated that she did not want to have sex for a long time, although she was willing to be held and comforted by her boyfriend.

Mary was very concerned about her boyfriend Joe's reaction to the assault. She said that his primary desire was to obtain revenge against the rapist, and she was afraid that Joe might try to find him and kill him. Joe would not let her discuss how traumatic the rape had been for her, but rather he was preoccupied with his own feelings. Furthermore, he was against her going for counseling and suggested that it would be best if she just "forgot all about it." Mary was concerned that their relationship might now fall apart.

Mary didn't tell her mother about the rape. Her mother was ill and hospitalized, and Mary did not want to upset her.

Therapy began with the first interview. The female therapist allowed Mary to vent her feelings of anger and fear and let her know that these feelings were appropriate. Specific suggestions for ensuring her safety were also given, such as, to check when she entered the apartment and to vary her route to and from work. The therapist also suggested that Mary and Joe enter couple counseling to help them cope with the trauma of the assault. This type of counseling provides both parties with an opportunity to express their feelings as well as maintaining focus on the victim's need for support from her loved ones. Although Mary felt that Joe would be resistant to counseling, through role playing she was taught how to approach this subject with him. Mary's strategies worked, and one week later she did enter couple counseling with Joe.

Mary was taught a way to deal with the initial sleep disturbance. She was instructed not to take naps, to go to bed at a specific time, to set an alarm to awaken at a specific time, and upon entering her bed, if she did not fall asleep within 10 minutes, to leave the bed and do something active, such as exercising. In this way, her bed again became the stimulus only for sleep, rather than for anxious rumination. Mary was also instructed in deep muscle relaxation to alleviate the physical symptoms of anxiety. She was told to actively interrupt the intrusive thoughts about the assault whenever they occurred ("thought stopping"). She was advised of the common symptoms following an assault that she had not yet experienced, such as nightmares, sexual problems, fear of men, crying spells, and some degree of phobic avoidance of situations that might remind her of the rape. Mary was informed that if these symptoms developed, they would in all probability pass with time if she continued to express her feelings and if she received adequate support from the important people in her life.

DISCUSSION

Psychopathology and Diagnosis Psychologically traumatic events that are outside of the range of usual human experience, such as rape, military combat, earthquakes, airplane crashes, or torture, evoke some symptoms of distress in almost anyone who experiences them. Usually these reactions are mild, nonspecific, and short-lived, and would not be considered psychopathological. However, sometimes, as in this case, a characteristic psychopathological syndrome develops—the *post-traumatic stress disorder*. Mary's reaction included the salient features of the disorder. She reexperienced the trauma in the form of recurrent, intrusive thoughts about the rape. Her emotional responses became constricted, as evidenced by her monotone voice and her decreased desire to go to work or be with friends. Characteristic symptoms of anxiety, such as impaired concentration, exaggerated startle response, sleep disturbance, and avoidance of situations that might arouse memories of the event (being alone in her apartment), were also evident.

Course The symptoms of post-traumatic stress disorder usually begin shortly after the event, as they did in Mary's case. More rarely there is a latency period, which may range from several months to several years before any manifestations of the illness are apparent. During this period an individual may appear to be remarkably unaffected by the traumatic experience. Such a delayed onset was commonly seen in survivors of Nazi concentration camps in World War II.

Most women who are raped experience some or all of the symptoms of post-traumatic stress disorder. As might be expected, the most frequent and marked symptoms are the recurrent thoughts of the assault. Again, these usually immediately follow the event, diminish over time, and in a majority of victims, return on the anniversary of the assault. Another common symptom is repeated nightmares about the event. Mary has been warned that she may experience nightmares in the future. (Interestingly, many victims report that during the course of successful therapy the contents of their dreams change. Early dreams of passively submitting are replaced by dreams in which they fight back and even annihilate the assailant.) Victims of rape often feel guilty about having failed to deter the assault, and guilt is a common symptom in the survivors of catastrophes in which others were injured or killed.

Treatment The treatment of post-traumatic stress disorder involves allowing the patient to ventilate painful feelings, providing behavioral techniques to alleviate specific symptoms, and mobilizing the patient's social support system. These therapeutic techniques are effective whether the trauma is rape, combat experience during the Vietnam war, or being held hostage in Iran.

SOMATOFORM
DISORDERS

PARALYZED

Eddie Evans was referred to the mental health clinic by his neurologist. His left arm and hand have been paralyzed for a year. He was able to move his fingers and hold on to objects, but could not raise his arm without assistance. Extensive neurological testing had revealed no nerve or brain damage that would account for the paralysis. He had received physical exercise therapy two times a week during the past year with little improvement. The paralysis occurred subsequent to an auto accident during which he sustained some cuts on his leg and strained muscles in his neck (whiplash). He was driving to work, experienced a "blackout," lost control of the car, and hit a highway guard rail.

Mr. Evans is 30 years old, married, and the father of two boys, ages 8 and 10. His wife, Diane, works as an administrative assistant to the manager of a large manufacturing company. Mr. Evans has a college degree in business administration, and prior to the accident worked for an electronics firm for two years. Since his accident he has not returned to work, stating that the physical therapy appointments and the paralysis make it impossible to work at a full-time job.

Mr. Evans was born in a small town in Michigan. His mother was not married at the time of his birth, but married his stepfather when he was two years old. His stepfather was a proud, angry man with a drinking problem who refused to allow the boy to remain in the home after the marriage. Therefore, his mother left him with a maternal aunt who raised him until she died suddenly when he was 15 years old. Her death was a severe blow, since she was the only relative who gave him any emotional support. After her death he lived with a succession of relatives. Mr. Evans found his aunt's death very difficult to handle and plunged himself into school activities and work. As a child, Mr. Evans endeavored to be self-sufficient. He mowed lawns and ran errands around town from the time he was 10 years old, and worked part-time jobs throughout high school and college.

In college Mr. Evans met his future wife, Diane. They dated for a year and were planning to get married when she became pregnant. This hastened their marriage plans. Theirs was a very traditional marriage. He continued to work his way through college and she helped him in whatever way she could and took care of the baby and later a second child. After college Mr. Evans tried working for several different companies, but always became dissatisfied with them. In his eyes, the companies always promised more than they could deliver. He was disappointed at the menial tasks he was given and would get into minor arguments and conflicts with supervisors. In each case, Mr. Evans quit the job and searched for a more challenging one. In his last job before the accident he was doing well; after his first year he had received a raise and a promotion. However, during the second year, a coworker whom he disliked became his supervisor, and disagreements and conflicts became more intense as the year progressed.

At the time of the accident there were also numerous marital problems. Four years ago Ms. Evans went back to work to help with the family finances. She became more involved with her work when their two boys went to school. She became more independent and developed a circle of friends that her husband did not like. There were frequent arguments about her activities and Mr. Evans was unhappy that she did not spend more time caring for the children and the home. He felt she was not being a "good mother" to their children. However, he rarely expressed his anger. Instead, he became more and more disenchanted and took an "I don't care" attitude.

When he was first interviewed at the mental health clinic, Mr. Evans was cooperative but appeared despondent and listless. He discussed the accident and his paralysis, but did not appear overly concerned about the paralysis. He also tended to minimize any conflicts at work or in the home, and did not see how psychological factors could be playing a part in this paralysis. Financial problems resulting from the loss of his job were the focus of his concern. The family was living on his wife's salary, and this caused economic hardship. However, he felt he could not return to work until his arm returned to full functioning.

Mr. Evans appeared to the psychologist to have a history of passive-dependent relationships with authority figures and with women. The abandonment by his mother and the rejection by his stepfather, as well as the sudden death of his aunt who was the only person he felt cared for him, caused him a great deal of pain. He tried to deny his frustrated dependence needs by becoming a person who worked hard and from an early age took care of himself and his family. Yet he never lost his desire to be taken care of both emotionally and financially, despite his efforts to function independently and his reluctance to ask others for support. The therapist assumed that the paralysis of his arm represented an expression of his wish to allow himself finally to be taken care of by others, and especially his wife, and a way to avoid the constant frustration he experienced in his search for a satisfying job.

Psychotherapy was begun on a weekly basis in an attempt to help him understand some of the psychological conflicts and issues that may be contributing to the paralysis. Although he has attended the sessions regularly, he has found it difficult to see any connection. He continues to view the paralysis as a physical problem, and believes that the physical exercise he is doing both at home and at the hospital offer the best chance for the return to functioning of his arm. His marital relationship has deteriorated. He reports that he and his wife talk infrequently and appear to be living separate lives. His interactions with the children have become minimal. Mr. Evans appears to have settled into the role of a helpless victim of his paralysis, unwilling to attempt any type of work, withdrawn from friends, and searching for some type of disability compensation that will see him through until his arm begins to function again. Nine months of weekly psychotherapy has failed to make any headway with the paralysis, and when the therapist suggested hypnosis, Mr. Evans refused. He also refused family therapy and has resisted any effort to explore his anger at his wife and family. He discussed his early history and the death of his aunt in a matter-of-fact manner. He has decided that his marriage is, for all practical purposes, over. However, any divorce action will have to await the resolution of the paralysis. At this point, his whole life appears to be in a state of paralysis, waiting for a dramatic resolution of his problems. Nonetheless, Mr. Evans reports that he is less depressed and anxious and feels that the therapy has helped.

DISCUSSION

Psychopathology and Diagnosis Mr. Evans has a physical complaint—paralysis of his arm and hand. Although such a symptom suggests a neurological disorder, extensive testing has not uncovered any organic basis for the symptom. It is certainly not rare for a true neurological disorder to elude discovery, but in Mr. Evans's case there is not only the absence of signs of an organic etiology, but positive evidence for the role of psychological factors in causing his symptom. For this reason, Mr. Evans is diagnosed as having a somatoform disorder, a mental disorder in which there are physical symptoms suggesting physical disorder, but for which there are no demonstrable organic findings or physiological mechanisms, and for which there is positive evidence or a strong presumption that the symptoms are linked to psychological factors or conflicts.

Mr. Evans has a classical form of one subtype of somatoform disorders, *conversion disorder*. In conversion disorder the physical symptom is a loss or alteration of a normal physical function. The most common conversion symptoms suggest neurological disease, such as paralysis, seizures, blindness, or various anesthesias. The term conversion originated in the early psychoanalytic theory that psychic energy, libido, that was blocked from expression, was "converted" into the physical symptom. The term is still used, but now implies only a psychological etiology, rather than the more specific psychoanalytic notion.

Conversion disorder, which used to be called hysteria, was apparently very common in the nineteenth century. Its prevalence has apparently decreased with the increasing sophistication of modern society, and it is now most commonly seen in this country among immigrants from less developed countries.

Conversion symptoms usually occur in response to an overwhelming stress, as in military combat. In such cases, the symptom is usually short-lived, with or without treatment. In Mr. Evans's case his symptom began after an auto accident, but it is clear that the accident only triggered the symptom, which is rooted in a personality disturbance and also allows him to be taken care of by his wife and to avoid the difficulties he always had at work. Because his conversion symptom is so effective at "solving" his life problems, the prognosis for recovery is poor.

Treatment   Mr. Evans's therapist was unsuccessful in getting Mr. Evans to acknowledge and try to understand the role of psychological factors in his paralysis. The therapist suggested hypnosis because often it is successful in treating conversion symptoms. However, because the patient was unable to accept the possibility of psychological factors playing a role in his paralysis, he refused to try hypnosis.

Prognosis   The persistence of the conversion symptom for over a year, the lack of motivation for change, and Mr. Evans's assumption of the role of a chronic victim all bode ill for the future.

LOOKING FOR BAD NEWS

Anna Karsch is a 52-year-old office manager in a large accounting firm. She was referred to one of the psychiatrists in her Health Maintenance Organization by a cardiologist after she had complained to the administrator of the organization when the cardiologist refused to schedule her for cardiac catheterization (a diagnostic procedure with definite risks). She canceled her first appointment but then called and made another one when she realized that the psychiatric evaluation was necessary if she were to have any more diagnostic tests.

Although she has been a member of the Health Maintenance Organization for only three years, her medical records already fill one large chart and half of another. In reviewing these records the most striking feature is her belief that she has serious organic heart disease. This belief has persisted despite an extensive battery of laboratory examinations, including two separate occasions when she carried a portable cardiac monitor for a 24-hour period. These examinations have not shown any evidence of organic heart disease.

Ms. Karsch describes the symptoms that trouble her in great detail. They consist of occasional twinges of pain in various parts of her upper chest which are unrelated to exercise. As soon as she experiences one of these she stops what she is doing, sits, or if possible, lies down, and listens "to my heart pounding." She claims to have heard several irregularities in her heartbeat. During these episodes she frequently has the thought "I am having a heart attack!" Over the last three years her unshakable belief concerning her heart disease has severely limited her travel, since she is afraid to be far from the medical center where her EKG records are stored. Her social life has been severely restricted, since she has stopped visiting family members and friends who live outside of her neighborhood. For the last four years she has used all her sick days at work and from one to three weeks additional unpaid sick time each year.

Ms. Karsch says she has been having trouble with her heart for about ten years. She herself does not report any significant life changes preceding the onset of her symptoms, but on inquiry it emerges that her problems began shortly after the second of her two children left home for college. She reports that her marriage is a happy one and that her husband "knows there is something really wrong with me and that I am not crazy."

Ms. Karsch grew up in a poor immigrant family that discouraged physical displays of warmth. Her father took a genuine interest in his four children and would always spend Sundays with them. Her mother spent the last five years of her life bedridden with what Ms. Karsch describes as the "late effects of tuberculosis." Ms. Karsch proudly describes the devoted care that her father gave to her bedridden mother in her mother's final years. This care by her father included gently bathing her mother daily with a sponge, and feeding her mother specially prepared nutritious foods.

Unfortunately for Ms. Karsch, her mother's illness and death left her, as the eldest child, with a heavy burden of household responsibilities and little time to play. The family could not afford to hire anyone to help in the home and her father never remarried. She was expected to watch over the younger children, prepare the meals, and handle the family shopping and laundry. As her siblings matured, they began to help more in these tasks, but by this time Ms. Karsch was already in high school. She did not have time for extracurricular activities, but she was an excellent student. She attended two years at a local nonresidential college, taking business courses, and says that she would have liked to have finished, but had to leave in order to go to work. She met her husband, an accountant, at one of the offices where she worked.

The Karschs have had a stable marriage focused around providing financial security for themselves and for their two children, both of whom have finished college now and are working successfully. Ms. Karsch describes their careers with considerable pride, but voices some regret that they have moved to different cities. Her fears concerning heart disease have restricted her social life and also affected her marriage. Her husband does the shopping so that she will not have to carry any bundles. Recently, he has taken a course in cardiopulmonary resuscitation at her suggestion.

At the conclusion of the first interview Ms. Karsch wanted to know if the psychiatrist thought she was "crazy." She did not really seem to be reassured emotionally by statements on this issue, however, and instead launched into a diatribe concerning what she experiences as the unfair and prejudiced medical treatment she has received in the Health Maintenance Organization. It is with some difficulty that the psychiatrist convinced her to return for a second interview.

Ms. Karsch brings a xeroxed copy of an emergency room visit record with her to the second interview, insisting that the psychiatrist look at it. The intern's note includes the report of an episode of chest pain and shortness of breath, a normal physical examination, and the note "R/O M. I." (M. I. stands for myocardial infarction, the technical term for a heart attack.) Ms. Karsch says that she feels this was one of the few times she has been taken seriously by the medical establishment. She asks, "Even though you're a psychiatrist, you know what 'M. I.' means, don't you?" The psychiatrist used this opportunity to explore the nature of her reasoning concerning her heart disease. It is clear that she has done a good deal of reading in the medical field, but she appears to have remembered the information she has gathered selectively. Thus, she emphasizes that even relatively mild chest pains may be the warning signs of a serious heart attack. She does not go into any detail as to what the other causes of occasional mild chest pains might be, nor does she seem at all interested in this. She omits any mention of features of her pain (e.g., lack of relationship to exercise) that might suggest other causes than organic heart disease. In short, she is much more focused on the "M. I." than on the "R/O" (which means "rule out" and indicates that the diagnosis is uncertain but must be considered due to its seriousness). Rather than searching for reassurance and hoping for negative results of diagnostic procedures, as most people do in their transactions with physicians around physical symptoms, she seems to be actually looking for bad news.

In speaking about her medical history, Ms. Karsch becomes defensive and even hostile when the accuracy of her own beliefs is questioned, even by implication. She is able to consider the possibility that she might not have severe organic heart disease, but dismisses it with the comment, "that won't do much good after I'm dead." Her thinking about what is going on inside her body, though more detailed and conscious than most people's, does not have any bizarre qualities.

Near the end of the second session the psychiatrist begins an exploration of Ms. Karsch's expectations for future care within the Health Maintenance Organization. He indicates that he feels that some future psychological explorations might be useful for her and that they would be supported by the organization. He tries to emphasize that her suffering is real, whatever the results of the diagnostic and physical examinations she has undergone, and that she deserves both understanding and relief. Despite these efforts, Ms. Karsch makes it clear that she has come to see the psychiatrist only to get his "approval" for a cardiac catheterization. The psychiatrist indicates that his mind is not closed on this issue, but that he himself does not understand her or her problems well enough to make any recommendation yet on this matter. After he makes this statement, she becomes polite but distant and avoids looking straight at him. He schedules another appointment and concludes the interview by saying, "I know you are not happy with what has happened here today. I still think it's worth your while to come back at least one more time. I believe you could feel better than you do now."

Ms. Karsch does not show up for her next appointment. The psychiatrist calls her at home and she says that she "forgot." He calls her again when she does not show up for the second appointment, and this time she says, "I really don't want to see you, and I don't want to talk about it." At the end of the contract period, Ms. Karsch and her husband withdraw from the Health Maintenance Organization.

DISCUSSION

Psychopathology and Diagnosis   Ms. Karsch believes that her physical symptoms indicate a disease that should be investigated and treated by physical means. The cardiologist was satisfied that her symptoms were not the result of organic heart disease, and the psychiatrist felt he had evidence that psychological factors were linked to her symptoms and her persistent search for physical treatment. This combination of symptoms suggesting a physical disease, the absence of organic findings adequate to explain the disturbance, and evidence that psychological factors or conflict are linked to the symptoms indicate a somatoform disorder.

In Ms. Karsch's case, the predominant disturbance is not the particular sensation (occasional chest pains and pounding heart) that she has; these are not uncommon in the general population of "healthy" persons. Her problem lies in the persistent, unrealistic interpretation of the sensations as abnormal, leading to the belief that she has serious heart disease. This is the typical pattern of *hypochondriasis.*

Patients with hypochondriasis are much more common in the offices of nonpsychiatric physicians than in those of mental health professionals. As in Ms. Karsch's case, referral for psychiatric evaluation or treatment is often greeted with resistance and hostility. This is not merely due to the patient's fantasy that psychiatric referral means that "there's something wrong with my head"—it also implies, to the patient, that "there's nothing wrong with my body." The nonpsychiatric physician is also likely to be resistant to treating such patients, since in a physical sense, their complaints are not justified. A major challenge for the nonpsychiatric clinician is to accept and feel comfortable with hypochondriasis as a bona fide mental disorder that is as deserving of treatment as any other.

Etiology In addition to the deterioration of affection and trust within the physician-patient relationship, patients with hypochondriasis may suffer negative effects from repeated invasive diagnostic procedures, and may also risk alienating their medical care system to the extent that genuine physical disease is missed. Hypochondriasis and true physical disease in the same individual are not incompatible. In fact, a past experience with true organic disease in oneself or in a family member may predispose an individual to the later development of hypochondriasis. We can see this in Ms. Karsch's case in the report of her mother's long illness. Her description of how she remembers her mother also provides us with some clues concerning the development of her current problem. It may be that Ms. Karsch, consciously or unconsciously, associates the right to receive tenderness and loving care with the presence of severe illness. The burdens imposed upon her by her mother's death may have heightened this impression, since she experiences herself as having missed much of the fun and play of childhood. Psychosocial stressors may also predispose to the development of hypochondriasis, and the onset of Ms. Karsch's symptoms was associated with the departure of her remaining child for college. She utilizes her "heart disease" to exert control over relationships—in this case, with her husband.

Although Ms. Karsch marshals her data selectively to support her belief that she has severe heart disease, she is still able to entertain the possibility that she does not. Thus, her irrational belief is not a delusion. In addition, her descriptions of her symptoms do not have the bizarre quality that usually characterizes somatic (body) delusions in psychotic disorders such as schizophrenia and major depression with psychotic features. If there is any characteristic "flavor" of hypochondriasis, it is the patient's recitation of his or her medical history and symptoms in profuse detail and in a tone that sometimes borders on relish, along with the impression that he or she is disappointed on hearing negative findings and appears to be "looking for bad news."

Course and Treatment Ms. Karsch's story is, unfortunately, not an unusual one for patients with hypochondriasis. It is only because she is "trapped" by the closed system of the Health Maintenance Organization (a prepaid total care medical clinic) that she came for psychiatric consultation in the first place. In an open-care system the hypochondriacal patient typically seeks a new internist or cardiologist as soon as the previous one suggests that psychiatric consultation might be appropriate.

Hypochondriasis is usually chronic, and when severe, it can lead to invalidism and illness as a permanent way of life. However, many patients with hypochondriasis work regularly, as Ms. Karsch does, and manage to limit their impairment to leisure time, social life, or only moderate losses of productivity in their work. The challenge for the psychotherapy of patients with hypochondriasis is to establish a therapeutic alliance between therapist and patient that grants the reality and validity of the patient's suffering but does not involve the therapist in a tacit affirmation of the patient's pathological beliefs. The psychiatrist in Ms. Karsch's case tries, but does not succeed in doing this. Although the intervention described here failed to help Ms. Karsch with her symptoms or with her basic psychological problem, future efforts at intervention may be more successful. She will surely be back in a doctor's office before too long.

DISSOCIATIVE DISORDERS

TOO MANY PEOPLE IN MY HEAD

Sue Ellen Wade was admitted to the county psychiatric hospital for the first time when she was 37 years old. She complained of depression over her inability to control "impulses to self-destruct" that were forced upon her by someone she referred to as "Ellen." Over the previous six months Ellen had tried to kill her on more than one occasion, once making her swallow a large quantity of tranquilizers, and another time making her fall down the stairs of her house. Ms. Wade complained that she had been struggling for many years against Ellen, whom she described as "another self." Ellen periodically "took over" the patient's "real self" and made her do "horrible things." Ms. Wade said that Ellen had been going out with other men, spending afternoons away from the home in motel rooms, and flaunting her promiscuity in front of her husband. Ms. Wade said that her real self, Sue, was a very diligent and conscientious mother, homemaker, and part-time secretary. Although she felt on many occasions overwhelmed by the sheer number of responsibilities she had, on the other hand, she willingly accepted them as "her lot in life." Ms. Wade had been in psychotherapy for the previous two years due to her problems in controlling the promiscuous behavior of Ellen and her chronic depression with intermittent thoughts of suicide and suicide attempts.

Ms. Wade had had two previous brief contacts with psychotherapists. When she was 27 years old she was seen for several months by a therapist because she felt Ellen was trying to talk her into stabbing her second son, who was then two years old. Five years later she was seen briefly by another therapist, due to her husband's insistence that she do something about her promiscuity. Neither treatment lasted long. The patient claimed that each therapist had made sexual advances toward her.

When interviewed in the hospital, Ms. Wade usually appeared diffident, depressed, passive, submissive, and fearful. She was primarily concerned with her husband and her two sons, ages 14 and 12, and her responsibilities at home. She lacked appetite, had lost about 10 pounds over the preceding two months, was sleeping unevenly, felt tired most of the time, and wanted to die. In her own words, "I have tried to commit suicide four times. I can't cope. All the pulling in my head back and forth in different directions. Too many people in my head trying to do different things."

When asked about the people in her head, Ms. Wade referred to Ellen, whom she said she hated, and a little girl, "Sue-Sue," who was 6 years old and who was very fearful, weak, and shy.

During the initial evaluation, in order to have direct contact with Ellen, the therapist decided to induce a hypnotic trance.

Therapist: Ms. Wade, I'd like to try something now that will enable me to speak with Ellen directly. Okay?

Ms. Wade: If you have to.

Therapist: I want you to roll your eyes up toward the ceiling, looking as high up toward your forehead as you possibly can. That's right. Now I want you to take a deep breath and close your eyes and let yourself float on down through the chair. Let your body feel very, very light, like it's floating right on down through the chair and go into a trance. Very relaxed. That's good. Now, when I count backwards from three to one, Ellen is going to speak with me. Ellen should stay seated in the chair, not do anything physical or violent, and should go back to Sue when I say so. Three, two, one. Ellen?

Suddenly the patient was bright and smiling, appearing strikingly self-confident. She sat on the edge of her chair and held her head up and shoulders back. In response to questions about herself, she described her mood as "terrific" and explained that she loved her life, and enjoyed experiencing it to the fullest. She said she liked to dance, liked to ride horses, liked to stay out late at night, and liked to experience sex with a variety of men. She said she was glad she was not Sue because Sue was so guilty and so miserable all the time. She said that she did not have guilt about anything and had no responsibility except for her own pleasure. She said perhaps Sue wanted to be here in the hospital, but she, Ellen, would prefer being outside enjoying herself.

After having talked with Ellen for about 10 minutes, the therapist told her to turn back into Sue, and with that request her demeanor suddenly changed into that of her former self.

In later psychotherapy sessions, Ms. Wade explained her early history. She was the fifth of seven children. The family was quite poor. Her father was an oil-rig worker, and her mother took in laundry to make extra money. When the patient, nicknamed Sue-Sue, was 6 years old, her mother had died unexpectedly of a stroke. Her father was not able to afford a housekeeper and therefore was forced to make other living arrangements for some of his children. The oldest two children, 13 and 11, were relatively self-sufficient and remained with him. The next three, ages 9, 8, and 6, were placed in an orphanage. The two smallest children, ages 4 and 2, were sent to the father's brother who lived in the next county.

The patient spent two years at the orphanage where she complained of severe mistreatment at the hands of the staff. She claimed she was beaten, had her head held under water in the bath, was forced to sit on her knees with her arms held in the air for hours at a time, and was frequently locked in a dark closet. Her father visited her on weekends when she would complain to him, but if he reported her complaints to the orphanage staff, she would only be even more severely punished.

During this time Ms. Wade developed an imaginary "friend" whom she called "Ellen." While Sue-Sue was very timid and shy and took her punishment stoically, Ellen was able to resist in ways that Sue-Sue was not. Ellen frequently yelled at and hit back at her tormentors when they tried to touch her. From this point on, Ellen was an alternative personality.

When the patient was 9 years of age, her father remarried a woman who had three children of her own. The family was reunited, but due to the large number of children, there was little affection or attention to be had. Her stepmother was very businesslike and never allowed her to enjoy herself. She would always be assigning her some chore or task to do rather than allowing her to play with games or read a book. The patient was very obedient, never protested, and never got angry. Her stepmother frequently said to her, "If you're not good, you'll go back to the orphanage."

The patient married a car salesman when she was 21. Before her marriage her sexual history was limited to a few brief encounters, which she would disown the next day by telling herself that Ellen had done it. Shortly after her marriage to her husband, a kind, considerate man and a good provider, the patient began her pattern of sexual escapades. Approximately one afternoon per week, she would switch into Ellen, pick up a strange man at a bar in a neighboring town, and spend the afternoon in a motel with him. Typically, she would disparage his performance afterward and would always refuse to see him again. She sometimes had the fantasy that she would like to stab these men to death with a knife after having had intercourse with them. At approximately 5 P.M. she would become uneasy, switch back to Sue, and hurry home to cook dinner.

Ms. Wade felt guilty and was angry at Ellen who, on several occasions, would "come out" at home and tell her husband about the affairs. When Ms. Wade felt particularly overwhelmed by her burdens at home, she would curl up on the floor in the corner of a room and become Sue-Sue, who would daydream of dolls or tremble and sob because of fear of being beaten again. The switch to the Sue-Sue personality was much less common than that to Ellen.

During the course of her six-week hospitalization, treatment was very difficult. Most of the time, in her Sue personality, Ms. Wade was extremely self-disparaging, to the point of sometimes banging her head against the walls of the ward when she felt overwhelmed by her guilt and depression. Occasionally Sue-Sue appeared after these episodes. At other times, while she was Ellen, she was uninterested in therapy and merely wished to escape the hospital. After additional explorations of her different personalities with hypnosis, the treatment team decided not to encourage the emergence of the personalities via the hypnotic trances but rather to teach Ms. Wade to hypnotize herself and use the vehicle of the trance state to gain control of the switches from one personality to another. By teaching her that she could control the various parts of herself that she experienced as different people, she might begin to learn that these personalities were really different parts of herself and not really different people. Therapy also involved pointing out to her repeatedly that each personality represented a part of herself that she did not want to face or that she wished were not her. Thus, the promiscuous Ellen was a part of herself that desired to be free of all responsibility and to be able to lead an unrestricted life, including limitless sexual indulgence without feeling pangs of guilt or remorse afterward. Sue, of course, represented another part of her that was overly conscientious and allowed herself little or no pleasure. As a result of the therapist's constantly reinforcing the wholeness of the personality of Ms. Wade, and his teaching her that she could exercise control over herself, the switching to the various personalities began to decrease in frequency. By the time she was discharged from the hospital, she was no longer suicidal, and she was at least somewhat optimistic that, with continuing therapy, she would be able to control her behavior and alleviate her depressed mood.

In the two years of twice-weekly psychodynamically oriented psychotherapy that followed her hospitalization, Ms. Wade learned to recognize and accept the many facets of her single, though complex, personality. She recognized the struggle between the punitive side of her self-concept and the impulsive self-satisfying side. She came to realize that she needed to be able to gratify herself to a certain degree without necessarily indulging her every desire. She also needed to be able to reduce the burden of her responsibilities by allowing others to share them and take over some of the functions that she had always felt obliged to carry out herself. After two years she was no longer depressed. She was seeing friends and had begun to take courses at a local college. Her husband received an offer for a better job, and the family moved to another town. About a year and a half later, she called her therapist and said that she had been feeling a little depressed again and asked if he could recommend someone for her to see near her new home. She insisted, however, that she was no longer bothered by switching into other personalities.

DISCUSSION

Psychopathology and Diagnosis Ordinarily, by the time one has become an adult, there is a relatively clear sense of self or identity. This enables the individual to perceive himself or herself as an integrated whole person with continuity over time, even when there are aspects of one's personality with which one is uncomfortable or dissatisfied. Some difficulty in achieving a clear sense of self or identity, particularly during adolescence or early adult life, is well within the range of normality. Severe disturbance in identity does indicate psychopathology and may take several forms. There may be uncertainty about a variety of issues relating to identity, such as severe conflicts over goals, group loyalties, and moral values that cause such subjective distress that social functioning is impaired (see Case 42, "Who Am I?"). There may be a persistent feeling of discomfort about one's anatomic sex and a desire to be of the other sex (see Case 18, "John or Nancy?").

In Ms. Wade's case her inability to reconcile different aspects of her self takes a bizarre and extremely unusual form: she experiences parts of her self as separate personalities, each of which determines her behavior at different times. Her normal personality, which she refers to as "Sue," is the overly conscientious and guilt-prone housewife. In marked contrast is "Ellen," who is carefree, sexual, and hedonistic.

Finally, there is "Sue-Sue," the timid and defenseless girl of her childhood who is always fearful of being abused by others.

The existence within the individual of more than one personality, each with its own fully integrated behavioral patterns and memories, is called *multiple personality disorder.* This diagnosis is classified within a larger group of disorders called dissociative disorders. Dissociative disorders all involve disturbance in consciousness, identity, or motor behavior. Other dissociative disorders are psychogenic amnesia, psychogenic fugue, and depersonalization disorder. In psychogenic amnesia the disturbance is limited to the sudden inability to recall important personal information—in excess of ordinary forgetfulness. In psychogenic fugue there is, in addition, sudden unexpected travel away from one's home and the assumption of a new identity. In depersonalization disorder there are recurrent periods of alteration in the perception or experience of the self so that the usual sense of one's own reality is temporarily lost or changed. For example, the individual may feel as if he is observing himself from outside of his own body or as if he were in a dream.

Usually in multiple personality disorder the dominant personality is unaware of the existence of the other personalities. In Ms. Wade's case, however, Sue, the dominant personality, was aware of the existence of both Ellen and Sue-Sue. On the other hand, the fact that her two main personalities, Sue and Ellen, are polar opposites of one another is quite characteristic of the disorder.

Etiology Ms. Wade was placed in an orphanage when she was 6, following the sudden death of her mother. The abuse that she suffered in the orphanage is characteristic of the severe emotional trauma in childhood that is often found in patients with this disorder. Obviously, it is unclear why only in rare instances the psychopathology that often develops later takes the form of multiple personality disorder.

Treatment Ever since multiple personality disorder was first described by Prince in 1905, the treatment has involved hypnosis. Hypnosis enables the therapist to gain access to the various personalities in order to better understand them and the nature of the conflicts with which the patient is struggling. In Ms. Wade's case hypnosis was a useful tool for evaluation, and later self-hypnosis helped her to achieve greater control over the switches. However, the therapist directed most of his activity to increasing the patient's ability to tolerate the conflicts within herself without having to resort to expressing them as separate personalities. Although this approach seemed useful in her case, because such cases are so rare, there is little information regarding the efficacy of other treatment approaches.

Prognosis Ordinarily, multiple personality disorder lasts for many years even with treatment. The follow-up period in Ms. Wade's case is less than two years, so it is too early to make any firm prediction about the long-term outcome of her case.

POSSESSED

Victor Hennigan was a 28-year-old white male who lived in the southwest. He was of medium height, overweight but muscular, with a thick neck and massive forearms. He was a Jehovah's Witness who had been married for five years to a Mexican American woman some thirteen years his senior. He had four children, three of them girls, his wife's by a previous marriage. Victor was referred to an outpatient community health clinic after extensive neurological examinations had failed to disclose any organic reasons for a four-month history of episodes involving bizarre and violent behavior for which he had no memory, and that witnesses had described as "berserk."

He apparently had no emotional problems prior to the first of these episodes. He came home from his job as a taxi driver, showered, and went into the bedroom to dress. He began feeling a cold "prickling" at the back of his neck, and a sensation as of a great weight on top of his head. The next thing he knew, some 2 hours had passed and he was three blocks from his house, in the midst of a heated confrontation with two policemen, his clothes torn, his hands cut and bleeding. He is said to have screamed and either fainted or convulsed at that point, with some frothing at the mouth.

The written report prepared by the policemen indicated that when they first encountered him, in response to his wife's frantic telephone call for help, "he had a wild glare in his eyes." According to his wife, before the police arrived he had, in a frenzy, smashed furniture, glassware, and decorations in his home, and had shredded some of his clothing. The police transported Victor to the county's inpatient neuropsychiatric unit, where a mental status examination found him to be alert, well-oriented, with no evidence of psychosis, no deficits in memory (other than for the period of berserk behavior), concentration, or attention, and no impairment of judgment. Victor denied any ongoing anxiety or depression and any chronic sources of environmental or interpersonal stress. However, earlier that day a passenger had attempted to commandeer his taxi to Mexico, at gunpoint. Victor had finally managed to convince the passenger to leave with his day's receipts instead.

The examining physician referred Victor to a private facility for neurologic and general medical evaluation for the possible presence of a seizure disorder, though Victor's fainting or convulsion had not involved loss of bowel or bladder control and there seemed to be no ensuing clouding of consciousness, all features characteristic of true seizures. The neurologic workup, which took place over the next several months, was negative, and a referral was made to the county mental health clinic.

The patient's second episode of violent behavior, for which he also has no memory, again began with sensations of coldness and prickling at the back of the neck and weight on top of the head. He "came to" to find himself in the process of strangling his wife, who told him later that he had also tried to throw her down the stairs.

In the third episode, which occurred the day before his first contact with the outpatient clinic, he was at a meeting of his Jehovah's Witnesses congregation when he experienced the usual preepisode symptoms and awoke to find several of his fellow Witnesses prying his hands from around his own throat. A Jehovah's Witnesses elder, who accompanied Victor to his first outpatient session, confirmed that it had looked as if Victor were making a serious effort to strangle himself, and said that he had in fact turned quite blue in the face before the combined strength of four or five men thwarted his efforts.

Though Victor presented himself as a plodding, unimaginative sort of fellow, sober, serious-minded, and lacking any conspicuous flair for the dramatic, he shared with the psychologist to whom his case had been assigned at the outpatient clinic certain other experiences, thoughts, and feelings of an unusual nature that he had been having since the first episode. For instance, he reported that there was a certain room in his house about which he had a "bad feeling." He could not even pass the doorway of this room without feeling a chill, and more than once when in the room it had seemed to him that he could see out of the corner of his eye a "black cloud" or "dark shadow" that was somehow ominous. He spoke also of feeling that "someone" was "inside" him, someone bad and evil, and he told of situations in which he had been aware of doing things he didn't want to do but that he felt powerless to stop himself from doing, as when sometimes, on looking at himself in a mirror, he would begin to utter the vilest of blasphemies. He had also, with the experience of no volitional control, squirted shaving cream on some of the clothing and lingerie of his three stepdaughters.

The Witness elder accompanying Victor suggested to the treating psychologist the possibility of Victor's being under the influence of one or more wicked, discarnate entities, a possibility recognized in the Witnesses' belief system.

Victor had a stable employment history, having worked in aircraft maintenance for eight years following his graduation from high school. He had been driving a taxi for about two years, after the firm for which he had been working went out of business. Following his first episode of berserk behavior, he was advised to give up driving, and when seen in the outpatient clinic he and his family had been supported by public assistance for about four months.

Victor's present marriage is his first. His Mexican American wife, Constancia, speaks very little English, but Victor is fluent in Spanish. Victor professed his marriage to be happy and problem-free, though he did evince some concern about his three oldest stepchildren, all said to be unusually attractive young ladies, who range in age from 13 to 17, and who seemed to be pressing, often energetically, for some freedom from the behavioral restraints imposed because of the parents' religious and cultural backgrounds. Victor also shared the fact that in his heart of hearts he wasn't certain how sincerely he subscribed to the Witnesses' belief system. He himself had been raised in the Roman Catholic faith but, despite a strict parochial school education, or perhaps because of it, had found that faith emotionally unsatisfying. After a brief flirtation with various charismatic, evangelical, and pentecostal sects in which speaking in tongues and being rendered cataleptic by the spirit of the Lord were common experiences for others, if not for him, he had drifted into the Witnesses. It was at a Witnesses meeting that Victor first met the woman who became his wife.

The psychologist who examined and eventually treated Victor in the outpatient clinic found him to be oriented to time, place, and person. However, his reports of feeling that there was someone bad and evil inside of him, and of seeing a black cloud in a particular room in his house, suggested that he had had brief psychotic experiences. Victor's conversation, however, once one took into account the strangeness of some of its content, was relevant, coherent, organized, and lucid. Abstract thinking was unimpaired. General cognitive functioning seemed to be in the normal range. Victor was clearly anxious and depressed, partly because of four months of living on public assistance and partly due to the recurrent upsetting experiences which, despite the explanations offered him by his church, he could not understand. The more comforting possibility that the experiences were organically based, rather than that they were caused by psychological factors or perhaps even the result of demonic possession, had been eliminated by the negative neurologic findings. Victor had an image of himself as a stolid, solid hardworking man, kind, responsible, full of good thoughts and good deeds, trying hard to live up to the behavioral ideals of the Witnesses faith; but he had begun to fear that he might, against his will and possibly without his conscious knowledge, seriously harm or kill some other person or himself, though in the same breath he vehemently denied being either homicidal or suicidal. There was no history of alcohol or drug abuse.

During Victor's second outpatient session, when the psychologist asked him to talk in detail about the involuntary blasphemies that he had reported, Victor suddenly began to breathe heavily, making harsh, gasping sounds, his face contorted, his eyes bulging and wild. His voice deepened and took on an unmistakably Irish accent, and he began berating the psychologist, calling him "bastard" and "black nigger," and asking threateningly, "What are you people trying to do?" The psychologist at this point asked him who he was, and he said, "I'll tell you who I am! I'm the devil! I've got him now, and I'm going to keep him!" Meanwhile, Victor had been rising from his chair, and seemed to be reaching for the psychologist's throat. When the psychologist, without thinking, crossed his forearms in front of his face to protect himself, Victor's face went slack, his eyes closed, and he crashed heavily forward to the floor, making no attempt to break his face-first fall. He seemed to be unconscious for a minute or two, then came to with amnesia for events during the episode. His voice and limbs were tremulous. He complained of a dry mouth, and of muscular stiffness and soreness.

The next time the "devil" appeared, during a later session, it was the result of deliberate provocation by the therapist. The psychologist found that the "devil" could be induced to become manifest by the psychologist's threatening to touch Victor with a crucifix or to put "holy water" (ordinary tap water) on him. Once the devil appeared, unconsciousness could be brought about by the simple expedient of the psychologist's making the sign of the cross—apparently the expectations of the personality system that called itself "the devil" were drawn from the same sorts of grade B movies that had formed the expectations of the psychologist.

Victor was successfully treated by means of a quasihypnotic approach, "quasi" because his religious community held hypnosis to be a satanic phenomenon. The treating psychologist hypothesized that the period of apparent unconsciousness that followed the manifestation of the "devil" during the second session actually represented a state like that of hypnotic trance, and as such could be considered a period during which Victor was particularly open to suggestion. Once Victor was "unconscious," the psychologist directly suggested the departure of the devil "in the name of Jehovah God" from Victor "forever," and the devil's return to his underworld domain, which the psychologist took care to specify as being outside of and a long way from Victor. In the session following the use of "exorcism" Victor reported feeling like his old self, as he had felt before he had ever had his first attack, and that the room in his house had lost its sinister quality, and the black cloud was no longer seen. The treating psychologist now found that he could no longer provoke the appearance of the devil.

Victor was followed for six subsequent weekly sessions, during which no further use was made of quasihypnosis or "exorcism." During these sessions, Victor discussed issues related to his feelings of anger and resentment. Interestingly, he began spontaneously remembering and reporting past behaviors of his, motivated primarily by anger, that were not congruent with the image he liked to hold of himself; he seemed to go through a process of becoming able to acknowledge his capacity for consciously experiencing and expressing anger.

The therapist suspected that Victor was also having difficulty with sexual feelings aroused by his stepdaughters and that the incident in which he squirted shaving cream on his stepdaughters' clothing might have symbolically represented ejaculation. However, Victor was not particularly psychologically minded, and attempts to obtain further information that would support this hypothesis were unsuccessful.

After the last face-to-face contact, Victor was followed by telephone calls, irregularly spaced, over a three-year period. At the time of the last telephone contact there had been no recurrence of the problems that had brought him to the attention of mental health professionals, nor had any new behaviors indicative of psychopathology appeared. He had returned to his job as a cab driver, and reported himself satisfied with the progress of his life.

DISCUSSION

Psychopathology and Diagnosis Although popular fiction might suggest that states of "possession" are a common symptom of emotional disturbance, patients with symptoms like Victor's are rarely seen by mental health professionals. Victor's disturbance consisted of discrete episodes of violent and bizarre behavior, following which he seemed to lose consciousness and for which he had no memory. In between these episodes he had unusual thoughts (a bad feeling about a certain room, someone bad and evil inside him), strange perceptions (felt a chill, saw a black cloud), and odd behavior (uttered blasphemies).

In certain religious subgroups it is accepted that at times individuals may exhibit peculiar behavior because they come under the influence of deities or devils. Usually such phenomena, as "speaking in tongues," occur during religious ceremonies. Generally, such behavior, because it is understandable in terms of subcultural beliefs, is not regarded as psychopathology, no matter how bizarre it may appear to the outsider. Although Victor is a Jehovah's Witness, his behavior was regarded as deviant, even by the elders of his church.

In rare forms of epilepsy, seizures may take the form of episodes of bizarre behavior. This is the reason that Victor was first referred for a neurological and general medical workup. In the absence of an organic cause for the disturbance, Victor was then referred to a mental health clinic.

Victor's bizarre behavior suggests a psychotic disorder, such as schizophrenia. However, the abrupt onset and extremely brief duration of each episode, with complete return to his normal state between episodes, is never seen in schizophrenia or, for that matter, in any of the other psychotic disorders such as major depression, bipolar disorder with psychotic features, or paranoia.

The sudden and temporary alteration in identity and behavior is evidence of a dissociative disorder. The emergence of the devil during a therapy session suggests that during the episodes of going berserk Victor becomes the devil. Although this raises the possibility of multiple personality, Victor's devil does not seem to have a complex and integrated personality, but is characterized only by fragmentary aggressive behavior. It would also be quite unusual for multiple personality to appear for the first time in an adult. Almost invariably it begins in preadolescence.

Since Victor's illness does not meet the criteria for any of the other specific dissociative disorders, such as psychogenic fugue or psychogenic amnesia, he would be diagnosed as having an *atypical dissociative disorder.*

Treatment   The therapist demonstrated great flexibility and ingenuity in the various stages of the treatment. By getting Victor to discuss behavior that was unacceptable to him (the blasphemies), he induced the dissociated state. His instinctive, defensive gesture when Victor accosted him apparently was interpreted by Victor's "devil" as a sign of the cross, and had the effect of aborting the dissociative episode. The therapist then used a standard treatment for dissociative disorders, hypnosis, in an ingenious manner. He assumed that the period of unconsciousness following the episode was like a hypnotic trance and he used posthypnotic suggestion to exorcise the devil. Apparently, during this trance, the patient was particularly receptive to the premise that the states of possession or dissociative episodes could be controlled by human mental capacities, initially the therapist's, but ultimately his own.

Etiology   Beginning with Freud, dissociative disorders have been understood as resulting from the inability of the individual to tolerate awareness of unacceptable impulses. Because of Victor's religious background as a child and his current involvement with a strict religious subgroup, it is understandable that he might have more difficulty dealing with aggressive and sexual impulses than someone raised in a more permissive environment.

Prognosis The prognosis for dissociative disorders is variable. Psychogenic amnesia and fugue usually are brief and do not recur. Depersonalization disorder and multiple personality tend to persist for many years. It is hoped that Victor's therapy has made it easier for him to accept aspects of his personality that were formerly unacceptable and that could only find expression in the persona of the devil. Post-hypnotic suggestions in many cases are known to "last" for many years. The fact that Victor has been well for the three years following therapy bodes well for the future.

PERSONALITY DISORDERS

LONG-SUFFERING

ACoA

A 30-year-old secretary entered therapy because she was chronically unhappy, unable to find satisfaction in her relationships with men, and worked far below her potential. The immediate precipitant to her entering treatment was the breakup of a long and tumultuous love affair with a boyfriend who had mistreated and exploited her. He had openly gone out with other women and yet expected her to be immediately available at his request, criticized her dress and appearance, and would disappear and reappear unpredictably.

She was pessimistic about life, felt and acted as if she were living under a cloud, and expected the future to bring no relief. She would spend long hours brooding and was irritable and withdrawn from friends. She often had difficulty falling asleep and would frequently awake from nightmares in which she would be shamed or attacked. The patient's depressed mood had characterized her functioning for as long as she could remember, although she also retained an ironic sense of humor and could experience pleasure when things went well. Nonetheless, she never went for more than a few days at a time without crying and periodically would consider suicide. She denied other symptoms of depression, such as impaired concentration or decreased appetite.

The patient's mother had been puritanical and long-suffering, and her father had been warm and giving, but also alcoholic, unreliable, and hedonistic. Her associations to early memories often involved themes of punishment or physical injury. Her mother had developed cancer and died after a prolonged illness when the patient was 12. The patient felt vaguely to blame and prematurely burdened by the responsibility of bringing up younger siblings. She felt singled out for unhappiness and punishment. During her adolescence, she was hardworking, self-denying, scrupulously careful, and very lonely.

She was ashamed of her body and of her sexual feelings, expected others not to like her, and was shy and retiring.

The patient was able to maintain several long-standing and mutually supportive relationships with childhood girl friends which persist to this day. Her relations with men were much more problematic and repeatedly followed the same pattern. She was easily infatuated, would quickly become subservient, unable to stand up for her rights, unhappy, and victimized. Her work history was similar in that she would stay in jobs far below her capacity and ambition, feeling exploited by the boss but also very attached to him. She became especially depressed on vacations and would feel that she was indulging herself.

The patient avoided winning in all competitive situations. At parties she would stay away from the men she felt most attracted to or introduce them to her girl friends and then devote herself to preparing food and drinks. She felt guilty if a man seemed to prefer her and worried that other women would become jealous. On several occasions she had passed up a better job so that a coworker could have it. Afterward, however, she was angry that other women had more fun with men and got better jobs.

The patient had received an inheritance after her mother's death. She felt very guilty about the unexpected windfall, refused to spend any of it on herself, and managed to give it all away. She dressed in a drab and matronly style. On the rare occasions when she treated herself to more expensive and attractive clothing, she inevitably found herself spilling greasy food on these and ruining them.

At the conclusion of the initial consultation, both the evaluating psychiatrist and the patient agreed that some form of psychiatric treatment was indicated, with the goals of alleviating the patient's depressed mood and altering her repetitively self-defeating attitudes and behaviors. In choosing a particular format and orientation for the psychotherapy, they agreed upon an individual (rather than group or family) treatment that would be primarily exploratory (rather than supportive or directive). Depending upon the patient's goals, motivation, and circumstances, this might have taken the form of brief psychodynamically oriented therapy, longer term, more open-ended psychotherapy, or psychoanalysis. The patient had both the psychological characteristics and the finances to attempt characterological change through psychoanalysis. She was comfortable dealing with psychological concepts, was interested in becoming more aware of her unconscious motivations, and was able to see when, as a result of her emotional problems, she was reacting to the therapist in an irrational way. (In psychoanalysis, this is called transference.) She was also able to tolerate frustration and control her impulses to act without thinking. She was also sufficiently distressed to be motivated to attempt this ambitious treatment. Medication was withheld (at least initially) because the patient had no symptoms of melancholia (see Case 23, "Weeping Widow"), and her depressed mood seemed clearly related to characterological and situational difficulties.

The patient presented many clear signs of transference during the early phases of treatment. Most often, she experienced the male therapist as extremely critical and felt vulnerable to what she perceived to be his savage attacks. This was repeatedly interpreted by the therapist as a projection of her own intense self-criticism and also as a continuation of aspects of her relationship with her mother. At other times during sessions she experienced the therapist as a tempter (much like her father) and would become sexually excited, but also frightened. She frequently felt overwhelmed by angry, depressed, and excited feelings, would cry helplessly, or be very withdrawn and silent. Over several years, in a gradual and steady way, these and other intrapsychic conflicts were explored as they manifested themselves in the transference, in her outside life, and in her memories of earlier life experiences. As her sexual and competitive feelings became more conscious and acceptable, her heretofore severe and puritanical prohibitions against pleasure and victory gradually became less intense and peremptory. Her chronic depression disappeared. She felt free to indulge a taste for finer things without having to ruin them or experiencing guilt. She also became less self-effacing and no longer tolerated abuse in her relationships with men. She no longer avoided competition with other women and in fact entered the business world, tripled her salary, and enrolled in a graduate program in business administration. She seemed more physically attractive and alive.

In many areas of personality functioning this patient has experienced profound changes, and her functioning is no longer so impaired that a diagnosis of a mental disorder is warranted.

DISCUSSION

Psychopathology and Diagnosis Most patients seek treatment following the development of an episode of illness that represents a distinct change in their subjective experience or functioning. Other patients, such as this one, seek treatment for long-standing problems that may have only recently been exacerbated. Although this patient's many problems are obviously intertwined, it is diagnostically useful to conceptualize them into two areas: her pattern of relating to herself and to others in her environment, and her mood.

There is abundant evidence that she had distorted views about herself and had a longstanding pattern of maladaptively relating to people. As an adolescent she had a negative view of herself (she was ashamed of her body and of her sexual feelings, expected others not to like her). This persisted into adult life and was evident in work (she stayed with jobs far below her capacity), in her presentation of herself (wouldn't buy attractive clothes), and in her relations with men (allowed men to mistreat her and avoided desirable men who showed an interest in her). Such enduring maladaptive patterns of behavior indicate a personality disorder. Since the most conspicuous feature of this patient's personality disturbance is her self-defeating view of herself and interaction with others, this disorder has been called *masochistic personality disorder.* (This is not a specific personality disorder in DSM-III because self-defeating features are present in most personality disorders, and it is therefore controversial whether these features constitute a separate personality syndrome. Thus, in DSM-III such a case would probably be classified as other personality disorder.)

Apparently, for many years she has had a depressed mood (felt unhappy, pessimistic about life, as if she were living under a cloud) with associated symptoms of the depressive syndrome (difficulty falling asleep, crying, guilt and suicidal thoughts). Significantly, she does not appear to have had a sustained episode of depression with more severe symptoms, such as loss of appetite and weight, psychomotor change, and impaired concentration. This rules out a major depressive episode. As in Case 24, "Learning to Cope", mild depressive symptoms, present most of the time, for several years, are called dysthymic disorder.

Treatment   Psychoanalysis involves an exploration with the patient of childhood wishes and fears as manifest in current unconscious conflicts and behavior, and in recurring life patterns. In this case, the patient's relationship with a "puritanical and long-suffering" mother and an "unreliable" and "alcoholic" father evidently led to unconscious conflicts about self-assertion and experiencing pleasure. A crucial element of psychoanalysis is the reliving of these conflicts in the context of the relationship with the therapist (transference). In addition, the patient is encouraged to look at the ways in which these unconscious conflicts interfere with current relationships outside of treatment.

Since the untreated course of both dysthymic disorder and masochistic personality disorder tends to be chronic, apparently this patient benefited greatly from her treatment. However, the relative efficacy of psychoanalysis as a treatment remains controversial. This is due in part to the absence of well-designed studies in which psychoanalysis is compared to other treatment modalities with a comparable patient group. On the one hand, some psychoanalysts argue that for patients with personality disturbance, such as this one, psychoanalysis is the treatment of choice and perhaps the only treatment likely to succeed in achieving fundamental personality change. On the other hand, other clinicians who subscribe to alternative treatments, such as behavioral or cognitive therapy, argue that psychoanalysis is lengthy, costly, and not as effective as focused brief therapies.

THE PERENNIAL PARIAH

Two years ago, when Saul Levine was 28, he consulted a psychologist who was well-known for his willingness to make use of any mode of treatment that seemed to offer the greatest likelihood of success for a particular patient. Saul's chief complaint was that he was always "staring out at a world full of goodies that I can never have." He felt lonely and isolated, unlovable, undeserving, and unable to experience pleasure. Ten years of a variety of therapies had done nothing to alleviate these feelings.

Raised in a middle-class home, the only child of a somewhat reticent father who worked as a librarian and a more extroverted mother who was a social worker, Saul had been in all respects a "normal" child who did well at school, made friends, and displayed no signs of psychopathology. He was a placid child who required no disciplining. According to his father, "Saul was always extremely polite." His mother emphasized that he was "a bright, lovable child who received lavish praise from his father and from me, as well as his aunts and uncles." Saul stated: "When I was about 12 years old, I began to get the feeling that I was not like other people . . . , I felt that I was repulsive." He started withdrawing from people and became more and more of a social isolate. By the time he completed high school he had no friends, kept almost entirely to himself, and developed a variety of rituals. For example, he would place his clothes in a specific order, facing a given direction, and he would double-check almost everything he did. Although such rituals have persisted, they have never been particularly prominent or interfered with his functioning.

When Saul turned 18, his parents realized that he would not simply outgrow his patterns of interpersonal avoidance. They urged him to be more sociable and outgoing, but to no avail. Saul enrolled in college but dropped out after two years and then spent most of his time alone in his room, rarely joining his parents at the dinner table. When he was 21, his parents sent him to a psychoanalyst, who saw him three times a week for the next six years. His social isolation persisted, and during one period he slept at least 18 hours a day. Consonant with his increased self-contempt, he invented various "tortures" and subjected himself to them, one at a time. For example, for several years he starved himself to the point that he was 40 pounds under his ideal weight. Intermittently he indulged in binge eating, followed by self-induced vomiting. He stated that he felt he was not entitled to the joys of intimacy, and that he did not deserve to eat normally and experience everyday pleasures.

After six years of psychoanalysis, he emerged no better. When asked what insights he had acquired, he replied, "None!" The best explanation he could offer for his condition was, "When I entered puberty, my brains were biochemically scrambled."

Two years ago he consulted a behaviorally oriented psychiatrist who admitted him to a university hospital. During two separate in-patient experiences over the course of a year, Saul found that he functioned extremely well on the ward. He socialized with other patients, took leadership roles, ate normally, and adapted so well to the structured environment that many people wondered why he had been admitted as a patient. Upon leaving the hospital, however, there were no generalized gains. Saul retreated to the safe confines of his parents' home and spent most of his time in his bedroom.

Next, he was treated by a biologically oriented psychiatrist who placed him on several medications, including antidepressants and an experimental drug intended for "obsessive depressives." At the same time, he consulted the above-mentioned psychologist, who endeavored to work with Saul and his parents in the hope of perhaps helping him by altering the family system. However, there seemed to be nothing particularly pathological about the family interactions. Saul and his parents were all excessively deferential, if not obsequious, but the psychologist could discern no significant collusions, triangulations, double-binding communications, or pathogenic dynamics. During the course of these meetings, Saul spoke openly about his perceptions of himself as a "born victim" having no niche in the "fierce competition of the world." He discussed his irrational feelings of being repulsive and undeserving. When asked to describe himself, Saul said that he realized he is a man of average height, slimly built, quite ordinary in appearance, "perhaps even more attractive than average." Nevertheless, his *feelings* about his body and his general being did not accord with reality.

Overtly, Saul always appeared affable. He smiled readily and appropriately, appeared attentive to what was said, but he was consistently overly polite and expressed no overt anger; he never raised his voice. His posture was tense. He spoke with difficulty—forcing out his well-chosen words. An avid reader, Saul's vocabulary was impressive. Yet his tense posture and staccato speech suggested an automaton—a humanoid computer. The psychologist referred him to an expert in bioenergetics, who endeavored to loosen his "character armor" through a variety of procedures such as bending, stretching, pounding, kicking, and emotional ventilation. Meanwhile, the psychologist continued seeing Saul and his parents.

The combination of the experimental drug, bioenergetic ventilations, and family discussions seemed to yield some positive results. Saul spoke of "a ray of hope," and obtained gainful employment as a clerk in a bookstore. Nevertheless, Saul continued to talk about his overwhelming loneliness. He wrote the following:

The feeling that I have as I walk through the world filled with people, wanting so much to be in contact with them and yet always remaining apart, can scarcely be described. I couldn't possibly tell you how it feels to live all my life without ever feeling the touch of a human hand. To have to live all my life in this utterly cold and barren way is a source of pain and anguish that I could never express. Every single day of my life is like this, filled with bitterness and despair. It hurts! It hurts! And worst of all is the knowledge that for me there is no reprieve, that I will have to live in this horrible way all my life on this earth. A life sentence with no parole.

The family therapy sessions included a range of specific risk-taking assignments for Saul. He continued to work in the bookstore and appeared to make further progress, as evidenced by his attending a family function (he had avoided all social gatherings for more than ten years). On one occasion he took what was for him an enormous risk—he asked a young woman out on a date. Perhaps his greatest fear was of male-female involvement, especially the thought of any sexual intimacy. In therapy he said he still felt like an outcast, and numerous strategies were devised to enable him to become a member of the human race. Instead of avoiding people, he began a systematic series of approach-responses, making social contacts, step by step. This was shortlived. Saul quit his job ("I just found it too demanding!"), retreated back to his room, and resumed binge eating and throwing up. He sent the psychologist another letter:

To be honest with you, I feel that life for me is utterly hopeless. If my life is to be a tale of never ending loneliness, I don't want to live. Loneliness is the worst thing in the world. What are the prospects that my isolation will end? Virtually nil. *13 YEARS* of therapy have not had the slightest effect on my irrational and self-destructive behavior. What conclusion does this lead to? The conclusion is that when my parents are no longer living I will be totally alone for the rest of my life. Better to be dead . . . My thought at the moment is that I must prepare myself for either a lonely life or an early death. Of the two choices, I prefer the second. In short, I'm like a condemned man on death row. It makes me very sad. But I must accept it, because there is nothing anyone can do to change it.

At this juncture, the psychologist is of the firm opinion that formal psychotherapy will achieve very little. Saul's exposure to diverse methods ranging from psycho-analysis to psychotropic medication made no iota of difference. The main clue to an approach that has some chance of success is that he functioned well in the structured environment of a psychiatric hospital. A different milieu might enable him to achieve a sense of belonging. The quest now is to find a setting in which Saul can function as he did on the psychiatric ward.

DISCUSSION

Psychopathology and Diagnosis   This unfortunate man has suffered through-out his life from feelings of alienation from other people, inability to experience plea-sure (anhedonia), and self-reproach. He is virtually always depressed, and most recently, reviewing his long but unsuccessful therapy, concludes that an early death is preferable to continued loneliness. Despite the severity of his chronic depression, it does not appear as if he has ever had a full depressive syndrome with such symptoms as decreased concentration, impaired appetite, and psychomotor retardation. Therefore, a diagnosis of dysthymic disorder is appropriate (see also Case 24, "Learning to Cope," and Case 25, "Death of a Family").

The "tortures" that Saul inflicts on himself and the binge eating are probably related to his depression and low self-esteem. However, not all of his symptoms can be attributed to his affective disorder. He has a strange sense that he is different from all other human beings and is completely isolated from all social relations. He exhibits poor emotional rapport during the interview and speaks in a noticeably stilted manner. He has rituals, which are not sufficiently prominent or incapacitating to justify a diagnosis of obsessive compulsive disorder, but which do suggest magical thinking. These peculiar symptoms are often seen in individuals with schizophrenia who have recovered from the psychotic phase of the illness. When such symptoms are chronic and occur without a history of overt psychotic periods, as in Saul's case, this is called *schizotypal personality disorder*. Previously, such cases were called borderline schizophrenia, and there is evidence that these individuals have a higher than expected number of relatives with schizophrenia, suggesting a genetic relationship between the two disorders.

Treatment   This case illustrates that certain deeply ingrained maladaptive patterns of behavior and emotional response are extremely resistant to all available therapies. Saul has had psychoanalysis, behavior therapy, antidepressants and other medications, family therapy, and bioenergetics—all with no or minimal effect. Psychoanalysis is considered by many to be the treatment of choice for altering basic personality functioning. However, Saul's poor interpersonal relations and overall level of psychological functioning make him a far-from-ideal candidate for this form of treatment. Antidepressants and behavior therapy are often useful for dysthymic disorder. However, when the disturbance in mood is so intertwined with basic personality disturbance, as in Saul's case, these treatments are far less effective.

In spite of the poor prognosis in this case, the treating psychologist continues to look for an individually tailored treatment approach that might be helpful. Even a small change that will result in some relief from the suffering that Saul experiences will be well worth the effort.

ANGRY YOUNG MAN

Philip Berman, a 25-year-old single unemployed former copy editor for a large publishing house, was referred for private outpatient therapy after he had signed out against medical advice following a two-week hospitalization. Mr. Berman had been hospitalized after a suicide attempt in which he deeply gashed his wrist with a razor blade. He described to the outpatient therapist how he had sat on the bathroom floor and watched the blood drip into the bathtub for some time before he telephoned his father at work for help. He and his father went to the hospital emergency room to have the gash stitched, but he convinced himself and the hospital physician that he did not need hospitalization. The next day when his father suggested he needed help, he knocked his dinner to the floor and angrily stormed to his room. When he was calm again he allowed his father to take him back to the hospital.

The immediate precipitant for his suicide attempt was that he had run into one of his former girlfriends with her new boyfriend. The patient stated that they had a drink together, but all the while he was with them he could not help thinking that "they were dying to run off and jump in bed." He experienced jealous rage, got up from the table, and walked out of the restaurant. He began to think about how he could "pay her back."

Mr. Berman had felt frequently depressed for brief periods during the previous several years. He was especially critical of himself for his limited social life and his inability to have managed to have sexual intercourse with a woman even once in his life. As he related this to the therapist, he lifted his eyes from the floor and with a sarcastic smirk said, "I'm a 25-year-old virgin. Go ahead, you can laugh now." He has had several girlfriends to date, whom he described as very attractive, but who he said had lost interest in him. On further questioning, however, it became apparent that

Mr. Berman soon became very critical of them and demanded that they always meet his every need, often to their own detriment. The women then found the relationship very unrewarding and would soon find someone else.

During the past two years Mr. Berman had seen three psychiatrists briefly, one of whom had given him a drug, the name of which he could not remember, but that had precipitated some sort of unusual reaction for which he had to stay in a hospital overnight. Another gave him three treatments with electroconvulsive therapy (ECT) because he complained that he was suicidal. These had no effect on his mood but, according to him, caused significant memory loss. He saw the third psychiatrist for three months, but while in treatment he quit his job and could no longer afford the therapy. When asked why he quit, he said, "The bastards were going to fire me anyway." When asked whether he realized he would have to drop out of therapy when he quit his job, he said, "What makes you think I give a damn what happens to therapy?" Concerning his hospitalization, the patient said that "It was a dump," that the staff refused to listen to what he had to say or to respond to his needs, and that they, in fact, treated all the patients "sadistically." The referring doctor corroborated that Mr. Berman was a difficult patient who demanded that he be treated as special, and yet was hostile to most staff members throughout his stay. After one angry exchange with an aide, he left the hospital without leave, and subsequently signed out against medical advice.

Mr. Berman is one of two children of a middle-class family. His father is 55 years old and employed in a managerial position for an insurance company. He perceives his father as weak and ineffectual, completely dominated by the patient's overbearing and cruel mother. He states that he hates his mother with "a passion I can barely control." He claims that his mother used to call him names like "pervert" and "sissie" when he was growing up, and that in an argument she once "kicked me in the balls." Together, he sees his parents as rich, powerful, and selfish, and, in turn, thinks that they see him as lazy, irresponsible, and a behavior problem. When his parents called the therapist to discuss their son's treatment, they stated that his problems began with the birth of his younger brother, Arnold, when Philip was 10 years old. After Arnold's birth Philip apparently became an "ornery" child who cursed a lot and was difficult to discipline. Philip recalls this period only vaguely. He reports that his mother once was hospitalized for depression, but that now "she doesn't believe in psychiatry."

Mr. Berman had graduated from college with average grades. Since graduating he had worked at three different publishing houses, but at none of them for more than one year. He always found some justification for quitting. He usually sat around his house doing very little for two or three months after quitting a job, until his parents prodded him into getting a new one. He described innumerable interactions in his life with teachers, friends, and employers in which he felt offended or unfairly treated, and frequent arguments that left him feeling bitter and resentful. He currently had no one he regarded as a friend and spent most of his time alone, "bored." He was unable to commit himself to any person, he held no strong convictions, and he felt no allegiance to any group.

The patient appeared as a very thin, bearded, and bespectacled young man with pale skin who maintained little eye contact with the therapist and who had an air of angry bitterness about him. Although he complained of depression, he denied other symptoms of the depressive syndrome. He seemed preoccupied with his rage at his parents, and seemed particularly invested in conveying a despicable image of himself. When treatment was discussed with Mr. Berman, the therapist recommended frequent contacts, two or three per week, feeling that Mr. Berman's potential for self-injury, if not suicide, was rather high. This judgment was based not so much on the severity of Mr. Berman's depression as on his apparent impulsivity, frequent rages, childish disregard for the consequences of his actions, and his pattern of trying to get other people to suffer by inflicting injury on himself. Mr. Berman willingly agreed to the frequent sessions, but not because of eagerness to get help. "Let's make it five sessions a week," he said. "It's about time my parents paid for all that they've done to me."

The patient was seen in insight-oriented psychotherapy for approximately four months. (In this type of therapy, the therapist tries to make the patient aware of the conflicting motives behind his or her maladaptive emotions, thoughts, and actions. The resulting insights enable the patient to resolve some conflicts and to find more adaptive ways of dealing with those that remain.) The treatment was extremely difficult, both for the therapist and for Mr. Berman. Although many of Mr. Berman's perceptions of himself and others seemed to the therapist to be rather clearly distorted, even the most minimal challenging of his perceptions met with obstinate resistance and anger. His intense rage at his ungiving, unnurturing mother, his attempt to destroy her by destroying himself, his overwhelming feelings of guilt about his rage, and his need to punish himself for such feelings—all were readily apparent. Nevertheless, even a gentle suggestion by the therapist regarding the source of either his intense anger or his own self-hatred was met with impatient sighs and sarcastic gestures. For example, he would roll his eyes to the ceiling or get out of his chair and walk to the window to look out at the traffic. Conversely, if the therapist refrained from making remarks that could be interpreted as criticism and merely tried to convey empathy for how Mr. Berman was feeling, Mr. Berman would consider this evidence of the therapist's weakness and incompetence. This would be followed by sarcastic remarks apparently designed to provoke the therapist to treat him harshly. He ignored any attempt to show him that he dealt with his therapist in many of the same maladaptive ways that he dealt with other people in positions of authority who could be of some assistance to him. Mr. Berman was apparently unable to budge from his deeply ingrained ways of reacting to others.

Finally, abruptly during one session, Mr. Berman stood up and stormed out of the office when the therapist made a routine comment about something he had said. In retrospect, it seemed to the therapist that Mr. Berman had for some weeks been waiting for an opportunity to break up the therapeutic relationship. The preceding month had shown some slight signs of his improving, which could have meant that the treatment was both becoming important to him and, at the same time, his relationship with the therapist was necessarily becoming more frightening and threatening. Therefore, he seemed to seize an opportunity to feel abused by the therapist, thus justifying his interrupting treatment and his rejection of the therapist.

DISCUSSION

Psychopathology and Diagnosis   Mr. Berman enters therapy after a serious suicide attempt and he gives a history of frequent brief periods of depression over the past several years. Although this raises the question of an affective disorder, the disturbance in mood is neither sufficiently sustained nor associated with other symptoms of the depressive syndrome to warrant a diagnosis of an affective disorder. Rather, his disturbance in mood, together with his inability to control his anger, indicates a general instability of mood that is part of a more pervasive pattern of instability in a variety of areas. These include not only mood, but also interpersonal relationships, his sense of identity, and impulse control.

His interpersonal relationships are characterized by his constantly trying to use other people for his own ends and his constant disappointment in others. No one can do enough for him. His sense of himself does not include any strong feelings about future goals, values, or identification with others. He feels chronically "bored." His abrupt leaving of jobs, his suicide attempt, and his sudden termination of therapy all indicate a problem with impulse control.

The patient clearly demonstrates a number of symptoms characteristic of individuals with *borderline personality disorder:* difficulty with impulse control, manipulation of other people and generally unstable interpersonal relationships, instability of mood, and lack of a sense of occupational or social identity. The term borderline was originally intended to describe a level of personality organization and functioning that was between neurotic and psychotic. Now, when used to refer to a specific personality disorder, it describes a particular constellation of maladaptive personality traits, and there is no necessary implication that such a personality disturbance is on a continuum with a psychotic disorder, such as schizophrenia.

As is the case with many of the personality disorders, individuals who have borderline personality disorder are often also diagnosed as having another personality disorder. The personality disorders most commonly associated with borderline personality disorder are narcissistic personality disorder, schizotypal personality disorder, and histrionic personality disorders. Mr. Berman, although he has some narcissistic personality traits, seems to have a rather pure case of borderline personality disorder.

Treatment   The treatment of borderline personality disorder is of great interest to psychoanalysts, and various modifications in the standard application of psychoanalysis have been proposed. One of the principal difficulties, as with Mr. Berman, is the difficulty in establishing a working alliance between the patient and the therapist. Without it, therapy inevitably fails.

[handwritten margin notes: "Kernberg describes narcissism as feature of borderline" "Diagnoses don't = borderline may II?" "no guilt, no anxiety — Kellee"]

UPTIGHT

Ronald Lewis is a 32-year-old accountant who is "having trouble holding on to a woman." He does not understand why, but the reasons become very clear as he tells his story. Mr. Lewis is a remarkably neat and well-organized man who tends to regard others as an interference to the otherwise mechanically perfect progression of his life. For many years he has maintained an almost inviolate schedule. On weekdays he arises at 6:47, has two eggs soft-boiled for 2 minutes, 45 seconds, and is at his desk at 8:15. Lunch is at 12:00, dinner at 6:00, bedtime at 11:00. He has separate Saturday and Sunday schedules, the latter characterized by a methodical and thorough trip through *The New York Times*. Any change in schedule causes him to feel varying degrees of anxiety, annoyance, and a sense that he is doing something wrong and wasting time.

Orderliness pervades Mr. Lewis's life. His apartment is immaculately clean and meticulously arranged. His extensive collections of books, records, and stamps are all carefully catalogued, and each item is reassuringly always in the right and familiar place. Mr. Lewis is highly valued at his work because his attention to detail has, at times, saved the company considerable embarrassment. He is often asked to look over final drafts of documents to ensure that nothing has been overlooked. His perfectionism also presents something of a problem, however. He is the slowest worker in the office and probably the least productive. He gets the details right, but may fail to put them in perspective. His relationships to coworkers are cordial, but formal. He is on a "Mr. and Ms." basis with people he has known for years in an office that generally favors first names.

Mr. Lewis's major problems are with women and follow the same repetitive pattern. At first, things go well. Mr. Lewis is tall and handsome, and his courtly respect is something women initially find endearing. His sexual technique is somewhat studied, but effective, and he has no trouble getting women interested in him. Soon, however, he begins to resent the intrusion upon his schedule a woman inevitably causes. This is most strongly illustrated in the bedtime arrangements. Mr. Lewis is a light and nervous sleeper with a rather elaborate routine preceding his going to bed. He must spray his sinuses, take two aspirin, straighten up the apartment, do thirty-five situps, and read two pages of the dictionary. The sheets must be of just the right crispness and temperature and the room must be noiseless. Obviously, a woman sleeping over interferes with his inner sanctum and, after sex, Mr. Lewis tries either to have the woman go home or sleep in the living room. No woman has put up with this for very long.

Mr. Lewis's emotional life shows a paradox. He can feel things deeply—cry at movies or while reading a novel—and he maintains close ties to his parents and to two old friends. On the other hand, in most relationships he seems constricted, unspontaneous, and aloof. He wavers in how he regards himself. At times he believes that he is the last bastion of sanity and good sense in an otherwise poorly organized world. At other times, he accepts the criticism one woman made of him—that he is "uptight and should learn to loosen up."

Mr. Lewis comes from a lower-middle-class background with an ambitious and fastidious mother and a "sloppy Joe" father whom both he and his mother looked down upon. As a child he had problems with bedwetting and soiling. He was severely chastened by his father for this and became very ashamed and embarrassed. He recalls playing "doctor" with a neighborhood girl and being fascinated by pretending to take her rectal temperature. In the early grades of parochial school he developed a reputation as a raconteur of "dirty jokes" until he was caught by a nun and severely reprimanded. He then became a model student who never used dirty words.

The therapist believed that the patient needed psychodynamically oriented psychotherapy in order to help him evolve a less rigid way of conducting his life and relating to others. He recommended twice-a-week sessions, but Mr. Lewis was unwilling to commit himself to more than one per week.

During the initial sessions, he spoke at length and mechanically from extensive notes he had prepared so as not to miss any important topic. He was controlling, constricted, stubborn, and acted somewhat superior (he cast a jaundiced eye on the upheaval of papers on the therapist's desk). The therapist did not often confront this issue directly; when he did, it led to a pointless power struggle. Instead, he restricted his interventions to those moments when Mr. Lewis seemed to be feeling some strong emotion, and focused on his difficulty in expressing it. The sessions gradually became more spontaneous and less adversarial.

At the present time, Mr. Lewis has been in treatment for two years. Although he does his best to deny that the treatment is meaningful to him or has changed his life, the evidence to the contrary seems pretty clear. He can now sleep in the same bed with a woman, be late to work, not read *The New York Times* on Sunday; he gets his work done faster but with less precision—all without much anxiety. He has even begun occasionally to come late for sessions, whereas previously he always managed to be early or on time. He has changed jobs twice and is making three times his previous salary. He treats the therapist with less formality and contemptuous respect. He can now openly challenge interpretations the therapist makes, and can tease and be teased. He is having more fun with sex, has been dating a woman seriously, and may soon get married. On the other hand, he still has problems and would probably strike a new acquaintance as uptight, although much less so than before. People in his life comment on the change—they find him more cheerful, accessible, and fun to be with.

DISCUSSION

Psychopathology and Diagnosis Mr. Lewis comes into therapy because his life is not going well. More specifically, he has been unsuccessful with women. He does not have any symptoms such as excessive anxiety or depression that would indicate the presence of an "illness." In fact, his problem is a consequence of the exaggeration of personality traits that are in themselves not pathologic. (For example, some degree of orderliness and perfectionism is adaptive.) It is only in the last few decades, and primarily in the United States, that mental health professionals have approached problems of this nature as psychopathology and amenable to treatment.

It is obvious that Mr. Lewis is extremely orderly and perfectionistic. He is aloof, formal, and unbending in his relationships with others. This constellation of personality traits is referred to as compulsive. Because these traits are so severe that they interfere with Mr. Lewis's effectiveness, comfort, and ability to experience pleasure, they indicate a *compulsive personality disorder.*

Etiology and Associated Features Compulsive personality disorder is apparently more common in males than in females, and also seems to occur more frequently in some families. Whether these differences are due to biological factors, or have more to do with differential reinforcement of compulsive traits by society or in certain families is unknown. The severe punishment Mr. Lewis received for his childhood infringements of the rules of cleanliness and proper behavior may have contributed to the development of this particular personality disorder.

Impairment Among the personality disorders, compulsive personality disorder is relatively benign, in that it is rarely associated with marked impairment in social or occupational functioning. Mr. Lewis, for example, was by no means a failure at work, and his social functioning was at least superficially adequate. In contrast, other personality disorders, such as antisocial, paranoid, and borderline personality disorders, often make it impossible for an individual to have even a semblance of a normal life.

Treatment The rigidity of the compulsive personality makes the psychotherapeutic process difficult. However, in Mr. Lewis's case, there is ample evidence that significant improvement has occurred, and the expectation is that, with continued treatment, more improvement can be expected. Why did Mr. Lewis get better? We asked the therapist, and he replied, "Who knows? Probably many things together— a little bit of insight, a little bit of identification with a very sloppy therapist, a little bit of permission and direction for behavioral changes, a little bit of spontaneous remission as he got older, and so forth."

GARY GILMORE

Gary Gilmore, a 36-year-old prison parolee, was admitted to the hospital on August 10, 1976, pursuant to a court order to determine his competency to stand trial. He was charged with two counts of first-degree murder in connection with the shooting deaths of two young men, one at a motel registration desk and the other at a gas station. The following is based on the report of the psychologist responsible for the evaluation.

The patient grew up in a family that consisted of his father, his mother, and a brother one year older than the patient. He indicated that his family was "a typical family, but there wasn't much closeness in it. I was always left to fend for myself and I got in trouble very early."

Though the patient was obviously bright, he received poor grades in school because "I just wasn't interested." He started "sluffing" school at a young age and at least on two different occasions was temporarily suspended from school for his truancy and for alleged thefts from his schoolmates. At the age of 14 he was sent to a youth correctional center for stealing a car and was at the reform school for eighteen months. Almost immediately after being released, he started burglarizing and was in the county jail on three different occasions, the last two for one year each time.

When Gilmore was 20 years of age, he was sent to Oregon State Penitentiary for eighteen months for burglary and robbery. Following this, he spent two years in a city jail for a "long string of traffic offenses including reckless driving and drunk driving. I started drinking before I was 10 years old." In prison, Gilmore gained a reputation for brutality to other inmates and was known as "the enforcer" and "hammerhead." He also was known as a talented artist and tattoo expert. On a number of occasions, he tattooed obscene words and pictures on the backs and forearms of ineffectual and disliked inmates: "I thought it was a good way to get back at the snitches. I would tattoo them on their bodies where they could not watch what I was doing. It wasn't until they looked at their tattoo in the mirror that they saw what I had done to them."

After he was released from jail he committed armed robbery several times within the next month. He was then sent to Oregon State Penitentiary where he stayed for eleven years, and then was transferred to a federal prison in Illinois, where he stayed for another year and a half.

Gilmore indicated he has used almost all types of illicit drugs including heroin, various types of amphetamines, cocaine, and psychedelics. In more recent years he quit using drugs, partly because they were not as available in prison, and just smoked marijuana. He drank whenever he had the opportunity in prison, but said that since he was released he has mainly been drinking just beer.

His first heterosexual experience occurred when he was 13 or 14 years old. He says "I tried to have sex as much as I could after that, but I've been locked up for so long, I have not had a very active sex life." He denied any homosexual activities.

He was released from federal prison in April of 1976 and came to Utah to work with his uncle in a shoe repair shop. This did not turn out well, so he briefly tried painting signs, and just before his arrest was insulating houses.

He met a woman on May 13, and the very next day moved in with her. He indicated that this was "probably the first close relationship that I ever had with anyone. I just didn't know how to respond to her for any length of time. I was very insensitive to her. I am more accustomed to violence and fighting. I was thoughtless in the way I treated her. She didn't like me to drink and even offered to quit smoking if I would quit drinking, but I never did quit drinking. Also, her two children bugged me and sometimes I would get angry at them and slap them because they were so noisy. And I always ended up in a fight with some other guy whenever we went to a party."

With an attitude of desperation that was in marked contrast to his usual unfeeling manner of talking about himself, he indicated, "I found out that I just couldn't make it on the streets and I was unwilling to go back to prison." He violated his parole initially by leaving Utah and traveling to Idaho where he drank an excessive amount and visited a brothel. He called his parole officer the next morning and told him where he was and what he had done. The parole officer urged him to come back to Utah so they could work out the situation. The parole officer decided not to report him. Shortly thereafter, after an argument with his girl friend, Gilmore went to a large store, picked up a stereo, held it over his head, and walked out. Two security guards followed him and tried to arrest him, so he shoved the stereo at one of them and jumped in his car and drove off. The other guard hung onto the door handle but soon let go after the car began to accelerate. Gilmore then went to a tavern on the outskirts of town and apparently was followed by the police but managed to elude them. The next day he talked to his parole officer and the police and was able to persuade them not to bring charges against him. He then returned to his girl friend's house, but she ordered him out, drawing a gun to make him leave.

On July 19, just before midnight, "I pulled up near a gas station. I told the service station guy to give me all of his money. I then took him to the bathroom and told him to kneel down and then I shot him in the head twice. The guy didn't give me any trouble but I just felt like I had to do it."

The very next morning, Gilmore left his car at a service station for minor repairs and walked to a motel.

> I went in and told the guy to give me the money. I told him to lay on the floor and then I shot him. I then walked out and was carrying the cash drawer with me. I took the money and threw the cash drawer in a bush and I tried to push the gun in the bush, too. But as I was pushing it in the bush, it went off and that's how come I was shot in the arm. It seems like things have always gone bad for me. It seems like I've always done dumb things that just caused trouble for me. I remember when I was a boy I would feel like I had to do things like sit on a railroad track until just before the train came and then I would dash off. Or I would put my finger over the end of a BB gun and pull the trigger to see if a BB was really in it. Sometimes I would stick my finger in water and then put my finger in a light socket to see if it would really shock me.

Despite Gilmore's anger at being locked up, he was quite willing to tell me the events of his life and the circumstances that led up to his being charged with the two murders. Though he said he was sorry that he killed the two victims, it was said without depth of feeling, and he appeared actually to be indifferent.

The patient is functioning in the superior range of intelligence with a verbal IQ of 140, a performance IQ of 120, and a full-scale IQ of 129. His general fund of knowledge is surprisingly good considering his sporadic schooling. Gilmore indicated he is an avid reader of both fiction and news magazines; he is quite proud of his vocabulary. His orientation to time, place, and person is intact, and his memory for both remote and recent events is very good, except that "I can't remember those things around the time they gave me shock treatment. They gave it to me in the prison trying to control my behavior." The two perceptual motor tests that he completed were done in a very careful and meticulous manner. His defective judgment is related to a personality disorder, and there is no evidence of an organic cerebral dysfunction.

Gilmore denies any perceptual distortions or unusual or bizarre thoughts at any time in his life "except when I was on drugs." He indicated several times that he was tired of living in prison and convinced that he could not live in society. Though he complained of frequent headaches, he reported sleeping soundly: "I've always slept well even in jail and prison. Nothing disturbs my sleep." He has a good appetite. His spirits are in the normal range: "I almost never get blue. Though I've made a mess of my life, I never stew about the things I have done." Personality tests, both objective and projective, failed to disclose any disturbance in thinking or mood.

Gilmore clearly understands the "nature of the proceedings against him" and the "punishments specified for the offense charged." There is no "inability to assist his counsel in his defense."

Postscript

Following the thirty-day evaluation period at the hospital, Gary Gilmore was returned to jail, found competent, tried, convicted, and on October 7, 1976, he was sentenced to death. He gained considerable notoriety by insisting that Utah carry out the execution without undue delay. He refused to appeal his conviction: "You sentenced me to die. Unless it is a joke or something, I want to go ahead and do it." Despite his desire to be executed, a total of three different stays of execution were issued; one each by the Utah Supreme Court, by the Governor of Utah, and finally by the United States Supreme Court. Frustrated in his efforts to be executed, he twice tried suicide by drug overdose. The newspapers continued to give extensive coverage to his "fight for the right to be executed"; from October 7, 1976, until January, 1977, he received approximately 5000 letters from people living in more than twenty countries throughout the world. He read nearly 1500 of these letters and responded to many of them. He received letters covering a multitude of themes, including requests for advice on how to rear children, requests for him to will various organs in his body to the writers, pleas for him to become interested in religion and repent of his sins, inquiries from schoolchildren wondering what it would be like to die, and expressions of love, devotion, and sexual attraction from women ranging in age from their late teens to over forty.

On January 17, 1977, he was executed, becoming the first person to be executed in the United States since 1966. In his book, *The Executioner's Song,* Norman Mailer depicts much of his life and the circumstances surrounding his crimes and execution.

DISCUSSION

Psychopathology and Diagnosis This case illustrates the way in which behavior that violates social norms becomes the province of both the mental health and the legal professions. The mental health professional, evaluating an individual who has committed a criminal act, wants to know whether the criminal act is symptomatic of a mental disorder. However, some criminal acts are better understood as an expression of subcultural norms (for example, some group delinquent behavior, politically motivated terrorism, and much "professional" criminal behavior). In such cases the individual may commit a heinous crime with no compassion for the victim, but have a sense of loyalty and caring for the members of the subgroup to which he or she belongs. Other criminal acts may represent isolated responses of an individual to a desperate situation (for example, a woman on welfare who steals a snowsuit for her child because she has no money for clothing).

Antisocial behavior may be symptomatic of a variety of psychological disorders. For example, acts of violence are sometimes committed by individuals with psychotic disorders, or with drug-induced organic mental disorders. Bad checks are sometimes written by an individual whose judgment is impaired during a manic episode. A pattern of antisocial behavior may also be the primary manifestation of a mental disorder. In kleptomania, for example, the individual is unable to resist the impulse to steal items that are of no apparent use or value to him or her. The case illustrates a much more common disorder in which there is a pervasive and life-long pattern of antisocial behavior, *antisocial personality disorder.*

Gary Gilmore's life exemplifies the characteristic unfolding of an antisocial personality disorder. Beginning in childhood, there were gross violations of basic social norms. He disobeyed family rules, was truant from school, and was eventually suspended for stealing from his schoolmates. He began drinking at age ten and went on to abuse a variety of illegal drugs. (Alcohol and drug abuse are disorders commonly associated with antisocial personality disorder.) By the time he was 16 he had been arrested for burglary and car theft. As an adult his illegal activities escalated to include armed robbery and eventually murder. He was known for his cruel and violent behavior in prison. He was never able to maintain steady employment or to sustain a close relationship with another person.

Mr. Gilmore also demonstrated a callous and guiltless disrespect for other people's rights that is characteristic of individuals with antisocial personality disorder. Evidence for this is his repeated tattooing of obscene words on inmates' backs without their consent, and his indifference about the two murders he committed. Many regard this lack of sympathy for others and the absence of the capacity to experience guilt as the most salient features of antisocial personality disorder. According to this view, these are the features that are most useful in distinguishing criminal behavior that is symptomatic of antisocial personality disorder from similarly appearing behavior that is an expression of identification with certain subcultural norms.

Etiology   Studies of the etiology of antisocial personality disorder have indicated the importance of environmental and genetic factors. The presence of a genetic factor is indicated by the research finding that the children of fathers with the disorder are more likely to have it, even if they are raised from infancy by adoptive parents who do not have the disorder. Environmental factors are demonstrated by the higher incidence of antisocial personality disorder among children whose adoptive fathers have the disorder but whose biological fathers do not.

The legal profession approaches issues of criminal behavior with an entirely different set of questions, to which the diagnosis of antisocial personality disorder turns out to be irrelevant. The court may ask for a psychiatric evaluation, as in Gilmore's case, to determine whether the individual is able to understand the nature of the charges brought against him and to cooperate with his counsel in his defense. In other cases, an evaluation may be requested because the defense claims that a criminal act was committed when the individual's sense of reality was so disturbed that he did not appreciate the nature or consequences of the act, and therefore cannot be held responsible. None of the features of antisocial personality disorder exclude an individual from standing trial or enable him to avoid criminal responsibility for his acts.

Treatment   Unfortunately, no treatment has been demonstrated to be effective for antisocial personality disorder, particularly in its more severe forms. For this reason, society responds to the disorder entirely through the criminal justice system.

THE MOST NATIVELY TALENTED ACTOR IN THE ENGLISH-SPEAKING WORLD

A 30-year-old actor, Robert Graham, sought consultation in order to improve his capacity to express emotion on stage. At a rehearsal of a play, he had difficulty portraying a character afflicted with a painful depression following the death of his beloved wife. His performance was perceived as shallow by his colleagues. Exasperated after repeated readings, he commented that he had trouble becoming "a character who was so involved with a woman that his life essentially ended simply because she died." Mr. Graham was surprised that his lack of empathy startled and even horrified his fellow actors. He availed himself of the advice of friends who had profited from psychotherapy and sought consultation immediately after his frustrating acting experience.

In the initial session he related in a friendly and engaging manner. He quoted poetry and was facile with words, ideas, and psychological constructs. Disarmingly depreciatory about his own plight, he pointed out that it might appear that he suffered from "pathological narcissism." However, he noted that "we live in a narcissistic period of history" and that it was an asset to be "tuned in to the times." He had long recognized that he felt a "special sense of entitlement," but he attributed this to his view of his real assets and accomplishments. "I don't wish to be immodest, but I *am* uniquely talented." Already successful, he had appeared in many films and TV shows. He felt that it was "inevitable" that he would become "the next Olivier or Gielgud, the dominant actor of our age." He realized that success in the acting world depended on luck as well as on ability. He observed that "lady luck is always on my side" and confided that as a child he believed that "through willpower" he could influence events to "work out" favorably for him.

Mr. Graham recognized that his difficulty with empathy on stage was a "flaw," even as he described himself as being "possibly the most natively talented actor for my age in the English-speaking world." He requested a series of consultation sessions to determine whether psychoanalysis was indicated in his case. He observed that analysis was "trendy" and that "one shouldn't seek treatment simply to improve one's ability to act."

Mr. Graham was the older of two children. His mother was an internationally famous opera singer, his father a successful impressario. From his earliest years he was told that he was "uniquely cute." He could recite poetry and act out scenes from plays he had written himself. At soirees his parents conducted regularly, he was told that he was "gifted" by his parents' friends, many of whom were active in the theater.

His mother, attentive and indulgent when with him, traveled extensively. His early caretakers were maids who were "pleasant." For reasons he never learned, his mother would always find something unacceptable about a maid's performance within a year, and replace her with someone "just as good." He denied any strong feelings about this. "They were all nice, but I didn't care that much about any of them really." Despite her indulgent manner when with him, his mother was actually not affectionate. He had no early memories, for example, of being hugged, put to bed at night, or comforted when upset. "I took care of myself."

Mr. Graham perceived his father as being "soft" and "weak," but financially successful and well respected in his field. His father was subservient to his mother at home, ingratiating, and even obsequious. His father tried to gratify her needs and avoid frustrating her. Mr. Graham remembers feeling "amused" by his father's posture toward his mother, but also felt "contempt" for him from his earliest years. Like his mother, his father admired his son's capacities to perform at parties, and "in general to be glib and charming."

When Mr. Graham was 7 years old, a sister, his only sibling, three years younger, was killed in an automobile accident. His memories of his sister were "fond," although he was unable to remember his feelings following her death: "It's all a blur." He related in passing that he had played with his sister regularly, and that following her death there had been no single person he played with on a regular basis during the remainder of his childhood.

Following his sister's death, his mother buried herself in her work. Despite her protestations of love for him, she saw him less frequently, and as the years passed was only involved in the superficial details of his life. She remained interested in his "performances," however, when he began to act during grade school. She sent him gifts on opening night—a practice she kept up until her death from a stroke five years before the patient presented for consultation. "I felt saddened by her loss," he said, but denied experiencing a prolonged or painful period of grief and mourning.

Mr. Graham's father, always a heavy drinker, drank even more after he lost his daughter. When intoxicated he would become tearfully depressed, which his son found "embarrassing." Mr. Graham spoke with disdain of his father. He recalled his feelings of "disbelief" during childhood at how "spectacularly undignified" his father was in public situations. His father attempted to establish a warmer, closer relationship with him. "I role-played caring for him in order to be civil, but I felt disgusted." He "drifted away" from his father in early adolescence and had little subsequent contact with him. When his father died of cirrhosis the year after his mother's death, he felt "nothing."

Mr. Graham attended a series of private schools and summer camps. He was graduated from an Ivy League college, having majored in theater, and immediately began a successful career on the New York stage. He was "discovered" by a film producer and success followed success until the present consultation.

The patient's pattern of adaptation had become clearly established by his early adolescence and remained constant thereafter. He was perceived by others as charming and entertaining. As a child, he was always invited to parties and was "one of the most popular kids in my class." He had a facility, both with peers and with adults, to make people feel that they were "special." He recognized this capacity during adolescence and subsequently used it consciously to further his ambitions. He responded to the appreciation of others with pleasure, on the one hand, yet with an inner feeling of contempt. He noted that people were gullible and "easily taken in by appearances."

He had "pseudointimate" relationships with many people, but never experienced a deep and durable relationship with anyone. Others perceived him as being exceptionally well integrated socially and wished that they could be part of his inner circle. There was no "inner circle," however. Rather, there was an entourage of rotating admirers.

In school he was outstanding in subjects in which he was interested. His grades in other areas, for example, science courses, were generally average. However, occasionally he did poorly in subjects requiring sustained study. He would always experience a sense of rage stemming from his belief that he was entitled to a higher grade on the basis of "ability" rather than objective performance. Frequently he felt that the reason that teachers gave him poor grades in these subjects was that they felt angry at him, "jealous or threatened" in some way. This reaction to evaluation of his performance was typical in other situations as well. He greatly appreciated approval but responded to criticism with fury. He reacted to objective feedback about poor performance as if it were unfair criticism. Because of this trait, he had difficulty learning skills in areas in which he was not innately talented. He tried to learn tennis, for example, but broke his racket in a rage following a private lesson when he was an adolescent, and never played again. Although he was known as a temperamental actor, his acting gifts were great enough so that he had not yet had the experience of feeling more criticized than approved of. He admitted, however, that he could not think of an occasion when he and a director disagreed on an interpretation, and when he felt that the director was correct. He had noted that, for reasons unknown to himself, he was perceived by colleagues, audiences, and critics to be emotionally cold. This had not proven to be a problem in his career thus far, but he did wish to "tune up" his personality to be better able to convey warmth. He felt that if he could accomplish this he would be an "ideal" actor.

Mr. Graham began to date in early adolescence. His first sexual intercourse occurred at the age of 16, and subsequently regular sexual activity occurred with many partners. His feelings about women puzzled him. He would become apparently deeply involved in romantic liaisons with women whom he initially found appealing in every way. After a period of weeks to months, however, he would gradually lose interest in his partner. Usually he would start an affair with another woman before breaking up with the first. His partners would often become depressed when they lost him, sometimes suicidal. During recent years he had lived with several different women, sometimes taking the father role with their children. Despite the solicitous and caring behavior that he manifested when with them, he gave them "little thought" after he left. He never experienced a sense of grief or depression following termination of a relationship. He felt that psychoanalysis might help him "understand" why women who initially fascinated him rapidly became unaccountably "boring." Although he felt no real sense of distress, he realized that his interpersonal and sexual relationships differed from those of anyone he knew. "It is almost as if people are playthings and I need lots and lots of new toys."

Mr. Graham was told that he did need treatment, and psychoanalysis was recommended. He felt both amused and irritated that the consultant actually believed that his behavior was pathological. He deliberated about beginning analysis for many months. After yet another breakup of a romantic relationship and many hours of discussions with anyone he could find who had also been in psychotherapy or analysis, he decided to begin treatment.

The therapist's view was that the patient's psychobiography revealed characteristic types of developmental interactions that resulted in a profound disorder of interpersonal relationships. His mother had related to him during early childhood and subsequently in a way that rewarded performance success and exhibitionistic role playing, but without sustained reciprocity of understanding or affection. The patient's father was perceived as weak, and efforts he made to relate to the patient positively were devalued. Early in life the patient developed a sense of grandiose entitlement and the generalized expectation that he should be treated by everyone as his mother had treated him. Simultaneoulsy, he viewed people as worthy of contempt similar to his early feelings toward his father. (It emerged in the analysis that the patient also felt contemptuous of his mother because of her ability to be easily taken in by his role playing.)

Narcissistic entitlement, grandiosity, and exhibitionism began to emerge in a setting in which there were deficits of sustained affectionate caretaking. The early death of the patient's sister resulted in the loss of one interpersonal tie that might have grown into a truly caring one. In addition, both parents retreated even more from intimacy with the patient at that time. Furthermore, the patient now had no competitors to keep him from being center stage in family scenarios. The patient's attitude toward his sexual partners was similar to his mother's attitude toward their maids, although this was not consciously appreciated by him at the beginning of treatment.

One important observation about this patient at the beginning of treatment was the fact that apparently he had never during the course of his life experienced grief or depression. The closest he had ever come to manifesting a painful reaction to loss had been after his mother's death. Nonetheless, his feelings of sadness at that time were ephemeral and were not associated with a true mourning reaction. The absence of grief and depression is a significant historical feature.

The analyst considered three possible meanings of this ominous finding:

1 The patient *had* in fact experienced grief at key points in his life. These painful feelings had been repressed and would emerge in analysis. The capacity to experience depression would similarly emerge.

2 The patient had never experienced grief or depression during development. Absence of these affects reflected absence of the capacity for mature interpersonal relations and also impairment in superego development (the development of conscience and other internal standards of behavior). Nonetheless, through the experience of psychoanalysis, restoration of normal psychological functioning would be possible.

3 The patient had prolonged chronic impairment in interpersonal relations, and the capacity for healthy psychological functioning to such a degree that psychoanalysis would be of no assistance. The patient would simply relive his problems in analysis and leave treatment unchanged.

At the beginning of psychoanalysis it appeared that the latter possible outcome might well occur. Initially, the patient found the psychoanalytic situation "fascinating." He engaged in the novelty of all aspects of the beginning phases. Most early sessions consisted of the patient reporting details of his acting performances, or of his manipulative interactions with others. He related dreams, freely associated and commented on his condition with apparent intellectual understanding, but nonetheless without a sense that he and the analyst were cooperatively involved in an enterprise that was deeply meaningful to him. After some months he complained of losing interest in the treatment process. "Motivation depends on interest," he said. "If I lose interest and motivation, how can I change?" He began to complain about the analyst, and soon sessions became full of devaluing commentary. The central theme of these criticisms was that the analyst "collected patients" for financial reasons and had no real interest in the people he worked with. Paranoid trends were manifested by his intermittent suspicion that the analyst might in fact be motivated by even darker forces. He suspected, for example, that the analyst was jealous of his good looks and of the adulation he received from his fans.

In response to the analyst's comments the patient was at times irritable, at times overtly rageful. He usually conveyed a sense of being aloof, although pseudoinvolved. Although he spoke of breaking off the process, he only missed sessions when seriously physically ill. When the analytic work was interrupted for vacations, he experienced only a sense of relief that his daily schedule was now less burdensome.

After three years of psychoanalysis, however, Mr. Graham suffered his first serious professional disappointment. He auditioned for a role which he felt "perfect for," but which was given to a competitor. Rather than manifesting his usual rageful response, he burst into tears on the couch. Subsequently he became progressively depressed to the point that he had suicidal fantasies. He now revealed for the first time that such fantasies had been present during childhood, particularly when he felt lonely. He responded to vacations with deepening of the depression and expressed feelings of confusion and "hurt" that the therapist could leave when he was suffering so much. He noted during this phase of treatment that he had never truly cared for a woman and wondered whether this was attributable to his own problems.

Shortly thereafter, he began a relationship with a woman that was different in quality than any he had ever engaged in previously. Rather than being an actress or model, expressive, dramatic, flamboyant, this woman was a rather quiet graduate student in her early twenties. This relationship has deepened and persisted and has been characterized by a new-found concern for his partner's personality, rather than the degree to which she could satisfy his immediate needs. Coincident with the development of this relationship, he began to speak in sessions more and more about the painful time he had as a child as a result of the loss of his sister. At one point he commented that she was the only person he had ever loved. This was the first time he had mentioned the word "love."

DISCUSSION

Psychopathology and Diagnosis   Mr. Graham enters treatment ostensibly to improve his functioning as an actor. Because he is not suffering from any recognizable symptom, like depression or anxiety, he does not understand why the therapist believes that he has psychopathology. However, Mr. Graham's pattern of relating to himself and the world reveals numerous maladaptive characteristics that are now subsumed within a broad concept of psychopathology.

Perhaps the most striking feature of Mr. Graham's personality is his inflated sense of self-importance and uniqueness. Although he undoubtedly is talented, he is convinced that he "inevitably" will become "the dominant actor of our age." He is preoccupied with fantasies of his future successes. From early childhood he was the center of attention, always performing for others, and he grew to need constant admiration. Whenever he met with a failure, in school as a child or later when criticized for his acting, he reacted with rage.

In his relations with people he demonstrated entitlement—the expectation of special treatment by others. For example, he expected to be given good grades in school for his "ability" rather than for his objective performance. He was adept at exploiting others: he knew how to make people feel special and used this capacity to further his own ends. His romantic involvements with women, although they began with a period of idealization, always ended with his finding them totally "boring." Finally, both in his acting and in his obliviousness to the feelings of the women that he abandoned, he demonstrated a profound lack of empathy.

As Mr. Graham himself partially recognized, he suffered from "pathological narcissism." In fact, when the constellation of psychopathology described above is so pervasive and severe that it interferes with social and occupational functioning, as in Mr. Graham's case, it is called *narcissistic personality disorder.* Although narcissistic forms of psychopathology have been of major interest to psychoanalysts for several decades, the diagnostic category has only recently, with DSM III, been included in the standard nomenclature of mental disorders used in this country.

Although Mr. Graham seems to have an almost pure form of narcissistic personality disorder, frequently patients with the disorder also show some or all of the features of other personality disorders. The most commonly associated personality disorders are borderline personality disorder (see Case 12, "Angry Young Man") and histrionic personality disorder (overly dramatic, craving for activity and excitement, overreacting to minor events, superficial, and self-indulgent).

Treatment   The kinds of personality problems that Mr. Graham had have been primarily of interest to psychoanalysts. His psychoanalyst was concerned that Mr. Graham's early development was so distorted that he did not have the capacity to form genuine relationships with others, since such a relationship with the therapist is necessary for a successful psychoanalysis. He was also concerned that Mr. Graham did not have sufficiently healthy psychological functioning to be able to introspect, tolerate the frustration of the analytic situation, and expose himself to the scrutiny of the analyst. On the other hand, Mr. Graham had many assets which augered well for psychoanalysis as a therapy: he was verbal, intelligent, and had exhibited various personality strengths necessary for his professional success.

In the course of his treatment, as expected, Mr. Graham exhibited his characteristic interpersonal psychopathology. He began by being fascinated by the treatment, but soon lost interest. He devalued the analyst and reacted with rage to his comments. A turning point in the therapy came when he, for the first time, became depressed. This reawakened childhood memories of loneliness and depression and seemed to lead to an emotional tie to the therapist that had previously not been present. Following this phase of treatment, he developed a relationship with a woman that seemed to involve genuine feelings of concern for her and less preoccupation with satisfying his own needs for attention and admiration.

Prognosis Fundamental personality change is not easily accomplished. It took three years of psychoanalysis for Mr. Graham to show signs of developing a new capacity for relating to others. It may take several more years of therapy for such a change to be pervasive and enduring. This positive outcome is dependent on Mr. Graham's willingness to persist in treatment and the continued skill and dedication of the analyst.

SUBSTANCE-USE
DISORDERS

MY BEST FRIEND

Dr. Arnie Rosenthal is a 31-year-old white male dentist, married for ten years with two children, who has been living at his parents' home for the past week following a "temporary separation" from his wife. He had been referred for treatment by his wife's psychotherapist because of uncontrolled use of cocaine, which over the past year had made it increasingly difficult for him to function as a dentist. During the previous five years he used cocaine virtually every day, with only occasional periods of abstinence of one to two weeks. For the past four years he wanted to stop cocaine use, but this desire was overridden by a "compulsion" to take the drug. He estimates having spent twelve to fifteen thousand dollars on cocaine during the past year. He had stopped taking cocaine two months ago, when he was admitted to a hospital for a hernia repair, but had not returned to work.

During the past four years he had been in treatment with three different psychiatrists for his drug problems and feelings of depression, and was continuously on various psychotropic medications, including antidepressants and lithium. At one point he was taking seven different medications concurrently. He reports no beneficial effects from any of these medications on his depressed mood or pattern of cocaine use.

The patient's wife, who accompanied him to the interview, complained primarily about her husband's lack of energy and motivation that started with his drug use five years ago and was now continuing despite his having taken no drugs for the past two months. She complained that "he isn't working; he has no interests outside of me and the kids—not even his music—and he spends all of his time alone watching TV." She is also bothered by his occasional temper outbursts, but that is less troubling to her.

An unsolicited letter from the patient's mother stated that she was "extremely perturbed" because of his "bad habits" such as smoking pot, drinking alcohol, and constantly using nose drops and eye drops. She described her son as being extremely lovable, kind, and considerate and stated her wish for the day when he would "function without a crutch." There is "not a day that goes by" that she's not worried about his health and well-being, describing herself as "a mother pouring out her heart and crying for help for her child," and requesting the therapist to "not breathe a word" to him about her letter.

The patient's chief complaints were feeling chronically tired and weak. He said that he was first aware of feeling depressed about a year after getting married and that there were many unresolved issues and conflicts in his marriage from which he characteristically would "just back off." He said he hated both his mother and his mother-in-law and described them both as "overpowering intrusive bitches who never see me as a person," and he felt very intimidated by them. He had a profoundly depressed affect, speaking softly and slowly. He said that for the first time he allowed himself to express anger toward his wife about a week ago, when she suddenly decided that she wanted a marital separation. He said "previously it seemed to me to be wrong to be angry at her," but when she broke the news about separating, "I felt like killing her."

During childhood he suffered nightmares, nail biting, temper tantrums, anxiety about school and schoolwork, was an underachiever, and spent a lot of time daydreaming. He remembers often longing for his mother's attention, which he felt she gave only when he was sick. Throughout school and the first two years of college he slid by with minimal work and barely passing grades. From the age of 14 he intermittently dated only one girl, who later became his wife, and whom his parents thought to be "perfect."

His main interest, from the age of 8, was music. He would spend hours every day practicing the saxophone. In junior high school he was invited to play with a rock band, an experience he describes as being "the highest high of my life until that point." Music was the career he wanted, and while in college he began writing original songs and playing professionally. Though it diminished his school grades, he was happy with the time spent in music and stated, "the high I got from playing was equal to no other." His parents wanted him to go to medical school and disapproved of his musical pursuits. He was offered a lucrative record contract and national tour with his band, but was unable to accept them since, as a minor, it required his parents' consent. Their refusal to consent stimulated his fantasy of running away from home under an assumed name. He went so far as to procure falsified identification papers. A turning point came when he saw three close friends burn to death in a fire at the age of 19. The trauma and guilt that he had survived led him to quit the band, to propose to the girl he had been dating, and to decide to pursue dentistry because his low grades during the first two years in college precluded acceptance to medical school. He was on the dean's list each semester thereafter and was accepted to every dental school to which he applied.

During his second year in dental school he got married, while being supported comfortably by his in-laws. After having been married one year he began using marijuana, smoking a joint each day upon coming home from school, and spent the evenings "staring" at TV. When he graduated from dental school his wife was pregnant, and he was "scared to death" at the prospect of being a father. His deepening depression was characterized by social isolation, increased loss of interests, and frequent temper outbursts. He needed to be intoxicated with marijuana, or occasionally sedatives, for sex, relaxation, and socialization. Following the birth of the child he "never felt so crazy," and his marijuana and sedative use escalated. Two years later, a second child was born. He was financially successful, had moved to an expensive suburban home with a swimming pool, had two cars and "everything my parents wanted for me." He was 27 years old, felt he had nothing to look forward to, felt painfully isolated, and the drugs were no longer providing relief.

He tried cocaine for the first time and immediately felt good. "I was no longer depressed. I used cocaine as often as possible because all my problems seemed to vanish, but I had to keep doing it. The effects were brief and it was very expensive, but I didn't care. When the immediate effects wore off, I'd feel even more miserable and depressed so that I did as much cocaine as I was able to obtain." He now was continuously nervous and irritable. Practicing dentistry became increasingly difficult. He did not seek therapy for a year because of fear that he would be institutionalized and because he "did not want to give up my best friend, cocaine."

The patient was seen by a psychiatrist for weekly psychotherapy over the next three years. For the first six months he was given a standard dose of antidepressant for his profound lethargy and other depressive symptoms. He remained separated from his wife and lived with his parents. He spent his time moping about the house, sitting, and staring out of the window. When his energy improved after having taken phenelzine for two to three weeks, he spoke of long pent-up anger toward his mother and wife. The psychotherapeutic effort focused on enabling him to identify and to express intense emotions, mostly with regard to rage toward his mother stemming from both childhood and current life circumstances.

He saw his mother as a person who attended to his physical but who neglected his emotional needs. He vividly recalled instances when he was terrified by her screaming at him for situations over which he had no control and for which he felt he deserved to be comforted, such as dropping a toy or falling down when running. He described his father as a person who was passive in the face of these onslaughts by his mother, but with whom his relationship was warmer and more stable, albeit more distant than he would have preferred.

Although he was able to speak freely with the therapist about his feelings toward his mother, he continued to be too intimidated by her to be able to change his behavior other than to avoid her. A telephone call from her in the morning would be cause for him to walk around the entire day with a "knot in the pit of my stomach." After seven more months of treatment, during a joint session with him and his mother, he clearly stated his wish to be regarded as an individual whom she must "accept or not accept," but she must not expect that he would automatically behave in accordance with her needs or expectations. He asserted his intention to assume autonomy—control over the choices and directions he would make in his life. Saying that to her appeared to have a beneficial effect on their relationship. He later reported that he felt fortified by observing his mother more terrified at answering the therapist's questions than he had felt having to answer hers.

Another issue during the first year of treatment was his preoccupation with re-conciling with his wife, a desire motivated mostly by his wish to function fully as a father to his children. He was deeply in debt, was being sued by creditors, and was falling behind on payments for the mortgage on his home and promissory notes on his dental practice. After a separation of five months, he and his wife resumed living together, although there was no emotional reconciliation. They declared personal bankruptcy, sold their home, moved into an apartment, and he began working on salary for other dentists.

During the second year of treatment he was seen with another patient who had a similar drug history and psychodynamics. They formed a two-patient "minigroup" that met weekly for six months and then sporadically. Both individuals found that in these sessions they could help each other put their most pressing problems into a clearer perspective: for the other patient, his relationship with cocaine; for Dr. Rosenthal, his relationship with his wife.

The patient and his wife lived together for the next eighteen months. During this time their relationship was distant, tense, and characterized by his feeling "guilty and intimidated." He felt that he had to submit to various demands imposed upon him by her. He smoked marijuana after work every day in an attempt to relieve his inner turmoil when they were together. Meaningful communication between them was non-existent. During a joint session it became apparent that the distance between them could not be bridged. By the end of the second treatment year they again separated, this time obtaining a divorce.

During the three months between the second separation and agreeing on a divorce settlement, Dr. Rosenthal was again given medication because of increased depression, which he attributed to his concerns about "leaving" his children and bitterness over his wife's "unfairness" in the legal negotiations concerning money and visitation. Several sessions were held jointly with his wife in order to work out areas of conflict, especially issues concerning the children. Since both parents had a strong desire not to use the children as pawns in resolving their differences they were both responsive to these sessions, where the therapist acted as an advocate for the children.

After signing the separation agreement, the patient moved into his own apartment, developed new social relationships, and renewed some old friendships. The therapist continued to help him to learn to be "true to himself" in regard to family, work, and social relationships. Dr. Rosenthal occasionally did resort to taking minor tranquilizers and marijuana to reduce his discomfort in social situations, but never took cocaine. "I had to take a tranquilizer or smoke a joint in order to join a group of people whom I didn't know. If I didn't know the person to whom I was talking, I had so very little confidence. My feelings of inadequacy prevented me from ever letting myself go."

Over the last treatment year the patient learned and was encouraged to use techniques of meditation, in addition to psychotherapy, to help him gain a greater sense of personal value, more objectivity toward his emotions, and a feeling of being more centered. (The therapist suggested meditation because he had recently found it personally helpful and felt it might be a beneficial adjunct to the more traditional psychotherapy he was administering.)

Dr. Rosenthal now developed a new level of awareness and functioning. In his words, "The past year has been the roughest and the most gratifying of my life. I had to deal with growing up, with responsibilities, and with a new perspective on relationships." He approaches life with greater joy and has more admiration for himself than ever before. His work as a dentist has become more productive and satisfying because of his greater empathy for patients. In contrast to his previous view that dental work is merely mechanical, he now appreciates it as being healing and as helping to improve the quality of peoples' lives.

In social situations he is more at ease, outgoing, and confident. He does not use marijuana, alcohol, or other drugs. He has had two relationships with girl friends, each lasting four to six months, in which he felt warmth, closeness, and compassion that he had never experienced before. With his parents he can detach himself in ways that "allow me to watch their actions and take them for what they are really worth, without reflexly getting sucked into the emotions they trigger in me."

Treatment continues weekly, with the current focus being on uncovering and working through feelings of anger toward his father for failing to protect him from the physical and emotional cruelty inflicted by his mother. He feels that although he has accomplished much, he is not yet ready to "go it alone."

DISCUSSION

Psychopathology and Diagnosis When Dr. Rosenthal entered the therapy described in the follow-up, he was no longer using cocaine, and the focus of therapy was on his other long-standing problems: depression, difficulties in interpersonal relationships, and pervasive feelings of inadequacy. The long-standing depressed mood accompanied by lethargy, but apparently not involving the full depressive syndrome, indicates dysthymic disorder (see Case 24, "Learning to Cope"). Whether or not this diagnosis still applies to him currently is not clear.

The pervasive disturbance in his interpersonal relationships and in his feelings about himself strongly suggest a personality disorder. Although there are features suggesting avoidant personality disorder (his apparent discomfort in social situations) and dependent personality disorder (his reluctance to stand up to his mother), his personality disturbance does not conform to any of the specific recognized subtypes. Therefore, a diagnosis of mixed personality disorder would be made.

Dr. Rosenthal's history of difficulties associated with the use of cocaine should also be given diagnostic consideration. In our society, the use of certain substances that affect mood or behavior under certain conditions is considered normal. Examples are the recreational use of alcohol, smoking tobacco, and drinking coffee. However, when the use of a substance to modify mood or behavior is so excessive that it interferes with social or occupational functioning or the individual cannot function without it, this is evidence of a substance-use disorder.

The immediate effect on the central nervous system (CNS) of the maladaptive use of a substance is called intoxication. An example is the acute effects of alcohol, which are well known and need no description. Cocaine intoxication causes the individual to feel a sense of well-being and confidence, and there may be elevated mood, grandiosity, psychomotor agitation, and talkativeness. Physical symptoms may include rapid heart rate and dilated pupils. It is easy to see how this patient used the pleasant effects of cocaine as a self-prescribed treatment for his chronically depressed mood.

This patient's use of cocaine (and of other drugs in the past) was clearly pathological. His whole life, at least until shortly before starting therapy, revolved around the use of cocaine; he had developed a very expensive habit, was unable to work, had separated from his wife, and was uninterested in former pursuits.

Substance-use disorders are divided into two types: abuse and dependence. Excessive use of most of these substances, such as alcohol, barbiturates, or heroin, leads to the development of tolerance (the need for increasing amounts to achieve the desired effect) and withdrawal (the development of an unpleasant and sometimes dangerous syndrome following cessation or reduction in substance use). Tolerance and withdrawal indicate a physiological dependence, and when either is present, a substance dependence is diagnosed. Cocaine use, even when excessive, is apparently not associated with the development of tolerance or withdrawal. Therefore, this patient's drug problem is diagnosed as *cocaine abuse,* which indicates a pathological pattern of use and psychological dependence. Because he is not using cocaine at present, this disorder is currently "in remission."

A variety of social and economic factors have a role in determining which substances an individual will abuse. Cocaine in recent years is the drug of choice of the affluent and well educated, whereas heroin and other opioids tend to be used by individuals from economically deprived urban communities. Ethnic factors may also be involved, as evidenced by the rarity of alcoholism among Jews.

It is not uncommon, as with this patient, for cocaine abuse to be associated with the maladaptive use of other drugs, such as marijuana and sedatives. It is not clear in this case whether these drugs were sufficiently abused to warrant separate additional diagnoses.

Course Dr. Rosenthal's three disorders—cocaine abuse, dysthymic disorder, and mixed personality disorder—all tend to have a chronic course. Perhaps because there is no physiological dependence on cocaine, cocaine abuse does not tend to have as prolonged a course as other substances of abuse, such as alcohol and opioids.

Treatment Ordinarily, the treatment of individuals with substance-use disorders involves the medical treatment of the specific effects of the substance, either symptoms of the acute intoxication state or symptoms of withdrawal. In cocaine abuse the intoxication state rarely requires medical attention, and there is no physiological dependence, hence no withdrawal syndrome. When Dr. Rosenthal began his current treatment, he had stopped taking the drug and the therapy dealt with his underlying personality disorder and affective disorder. In the therapy it became clear that he was using cocaine and other drugs to treat the symptoms of these disorders.

It is hard to label Dr. Rosenthal's treatment. He received an antidepressant, was seen individually, in a minigroup, and with his family, and was taught how to make use of meditation. During periods of his therapy the focus was on solutions to pressing reality problems (his separation and divorce), while at other times he explored the origins within his family of those maladaptive patterns of relating to people that had caused him so much pain. The constant factor in his treatment was the working alliance with his therapist, who in a flexible way was willing to make use of whatever kind of treatment seemed most appropriate at that time.

I AM DUNCAN. I AM AN ALCOHOLIC

"I am Duncan. I am an alcoholic." The audience settled deeper into their chairs at these familiar words. Another chronicle of death and rebirth would shortly begin. The Fellowship of Alcoholics Anonymous would reaffirm its mission, celebrate again the saving of a life.

The tall, carefully dressed man continued. "I know that I will always be an alcoholic, that I can never again touch alcohol in any form. It'll kill me if I don't keep away from it. In fact, it almost did." Smiling as he recognized the familiar effect of his words on his audience, Duncan went on. "Some of you know what I'm talking about, don't you? And I think my story'll ring a few bells as well." It was a well-known story to all of them. "I must have been just past my 15th birthday when I had that first drink that everybody talks about. And like so many of them—and you—it was like a miracle. With a little beer in my gut, the world was transformed. I wasn't a weakling anymore, I could lick almost anybody on the block. And girls? Well, you can imagine how a couple of beers made me feel, like I could have any girl I wanted. So, like so many of you, my friends in the Fellowship, alcohol became the royal road to love, respect, and self-esteem. If I couldn't feel good about myself when I wasn't drinking, if I felt stupid or lazy or ugly or misunderstood, all I had to do was belt down a few and everything got better. Of course, I was fooling myself, wasn't I, because I was as ugly and dumb and lazy when I was drunk as when I was sober. But I didn't know it."

Duncan paused, wiped his brow, took a deep breath, then started in again. "Though it's obvious to me now that my drinking even then, in high school, and after I got to college, was a problem, I didn't think so at the time. After all, everybody was drinking and getting drunk and acting stupid, and I didn't really think I was different. A couple of minor auto accidents, one conviction for drunken driving, a few fights—nothing out of the ordinary, it seemed to me at the time. True, I was drinking quite a lot, even then, but my friends seemed to be able to down as much beer as I did. I guess the fact that I hadn't really had any blackouts and that I could go for days without having to drink reassured me that things hadn't gotten out of control. And that's the way it went, until I found myself drinking even more—and more often—and suffering more from my drinking, along about my third year of college."

Duncan paused again, took a long draw from his coffee mug, then recalled those earlier days. "My roommate, a friend from high school, started bugging me about my drinking. It wasn't just because I was coming in at all hours or that I was getting sick in the room, and it wasn't even that I'd have to sleep it off the whole next day and miss class, it was that he had begun to hear other friends talking about me, about the fool I'd made of myself at parties. He saw how shaky I was the morning after, and he saw how different I was when I'd been drinking a lot—almost out of my head was the way he put it. And he could count the bottles that I'd leave around the room, and he knew what the drinking and the carousing was doing to my grades. So, at his demand, I went to the counseling center, where I was assigned a counselor who totally turned me off to anything a mental health worker could do. All he would say was that my drinking was a sign of deep emotional problems and that I'd have to agree to get into my past and my feelings about my parents and things like that, or I wasn't going to change my drinking. I was totally disenchanted. Partly because I wanted to show this person he was wrong, and partly because I really cared about my roommate and didn't want to lose him as a friend, I did cut down on my drinking by half or more. I only drank on weekends—and then only at night. And I set more-or-less arbitrary limits on how much I would drink, as well as where and when I would drink. And that got me through the rest of college and, actually, through law school as well. I'd drink enough to get very drunk once or twice a week, but only on weekends, and then I'd tough it out through the rest of the week.

"Shortly after getting my law degree, I married my first wife, and with establishing myself in practice and then, a little later, starting a family, I became so preoccupied with interesting things in my life that, for the first time since I started, my drinking was no problem at all. I would go for weeks at a time without touching a drop, so involved was I in my growing practice and family. Then, I'm sorry to say, things got worse again, a lot worse."

Duncan lowered his eyes, sat back a moment, then reached into his coat pocket for a cigarette, which he lit, drew deeply on, then stubbed out. He took another deep breath, then began talking again.

"My marriage started to go bad after our second son, our third child, was born. I was very much career-and-success oriented, and I had little time to spend at home with my family. Part of that was because my wife and I had grown apart during the eight years of our marriage. She had gotten very involved in local school-related activities and with the children and the family, and I had begun to see how attractive making it in corporate law could be. My traveling had increased a lot, there were stimulating people on those trips, and, let's face it, there were some pretty exciting women available, too. So home got to be little else but a nagging, boring wife and children I wasn't very interested in. My drinking had gotten bad again, too, with being on the road so much, having to do a lot of entertaining at lunch when I wasn't away, and trying to soften the hassles at home. I guess I was putting down close to a gallon of very good scotch a week, with one thing or another.

"And as that went on, the drinking began to affect both my marriage and my career. With enough booze in me and under the pressures of guilt over my failure to carry out my responsibilities to my wife and children, I sometimes got kind of rough physically with them. I would break furniture, throw things around, then rush out and drive off in the car. I had a couple of wrecks, lost my license for two years because of one of them. Worst of all was when I tried to stop. By then I was totally hooked, so every time I tried to stop drinking, I'd experience withdrawal in all its horrors. I never had D.T.'s, but I came awfully close many times, with the vomiting and the "shakes" and being unable to sit still or to lie down. And that would go on for days at a time." Several heads nodded in solemn agreement that the pains of withdrawal were one of the worst consequences of alcoholism. "The trouble, too, was that the more I drank, the more I built my tolerance, so I could drink more and show it less. Many a time I'd be driving perfectly, without a swerve or a needless extra movement, when I had twelve or fifteen drinks in me. If I'd been stopped, I would have spoken without slurring a word and walked a straight line without missing the mark. Only my blood level would have given me away.

"Then, about four years ago, with my life in ruins, my wife given up on me and the kids with her, out of a job, and way down on my luck, the Fellowship and I found each other. Jim, over there, bless his heart, decided to sponsor me—we'd been friends for a long time, and I knew he'd found sobriety through this group. I've been dry now for a little over two years, and with luck and support, I may stay sober. I've begun to make amends for my transgressions, I've faced my faults squarely again instead of hiding them with booze, and I think I may make it." With that, Duncan looked downward, neither to the right nor to the left, walked over to his seat in the third row of the hall, and sat down, saying nothing to those who clustered around him, patting him on his back. He'd told his tale of suffering, retribution, and redemption; he hoped it would inspire others with fewer months of sobriety than he.

DISCUSSION

Psychopathology and Diagnosis In his candid self-disclosure Duncan describes a common progression from heavy social drinking in adolescence to a severe form of *alcohol dependence*. Duncan, like many others, first used alcohol to boost his low self-esteem. Although when intoxicated he felt better about himself, he soon began to show the maladaptive effects of alcohol—intoxication. Impairment in judgment, attention, coordination, and reaction time due to the effect of alcohol in the brain (alcohol intoxication) caused him to have automobile accidents. Other evidence of maladaptive behavior due to excessive alcohol use included fighting and foolish behavior at parties when intoxicated, missing classes because of hangovers, and falling grades. Initially, there was a strong tendency for him to minimize his difficulties, as is often the case in individuals with alcohol problems. This was followed by a period during which, recognizing the increasingly harmful effects of alcohol, he attempted to set limits on his drinking. This was reasonably effective for a number of years, but then he lapsed into an even more destructive pattern of alcohol use.

When the illness was at its most severe point, he exhibited the essential features of alcohol dependence. He had a pathological pattern of use in that he drank excessively every day, and needed to drink in order to function. His social functioning was impaired: he fought with his wife and children, broke furniture, and wrecked his car. He eventually lost both his family and his job. Physiological addiction to alcohol was present, as evidenced by the need to consume increasing amounts of alcohol to become intoxicated (tolerance), and the development of the "shakes" after stopping drinking (withdrawal). One of the most surprising features of individuals with alcoholism, illustrated well by Duncan, is their willingness to continue drinking in the face of the disastrous marital, vocational, economic, and physical consequences of alcohol. Duncan lost a wife and children, a career, financial security, self-respect, and—nearly—his life before he was able to stop drinking. Why did he persist in his alcoholic course? In truth, no one has explained this phenomenon satisfactorily, even though many complicated theories have been offered. What seems to make the most sense is that the reinforcing properties of the drug—its capacity to generate feelings of relaxation, well-being, and self-satisfaction, and to block out competing negative feelings and memories, albeit for only brief periods of time—are sufficient to compensate the individual for the ultimately severe penalties he or she pays for the excessive drinking.

Alcohol dependence is a technical term for alcoholism. A milder form of the illness is alcohol abuse, in which the individual has a pathological pattern of use and some functional impairment, but does not drink enough over a sustained period of time to develop physiological tolerance or withdrawal.

Alcohol is classified with other potential drugs of abuse, such as amphetamines, marijuana, and cocaine in the diagnostic class, substance-use disorders.

Etiology There is evidence of both environmental and biological factors in the development of alcoholism. The prevalence of alcoholism is far higher in economically deprived urban communities than in affluent suburban communities. Evidence for a genetic factor is the higher prevalence of alcoholism among first-degree relatives of individuals with the disorder than in the general population, and the increased prevalence of the disorder in offspring of parents with the disorder who are adopted during infancy by parents without alcohol problems.

Interesting, as well, is the obvious importance of sociocultural factors in the development of alcoholism. It is well known that high rates of alcoholism characterize certain cultural groups, while low rates characterize others. What is less widely known is that groups with high alcoholism rates also tend to have high rates of abstention, while those with lower alcoholism rates often include relatively few teetotalers (abstainers). Some social psychologists have interpreted these data, which seem to be in conflict, as evidence of the ambivalence with which groups with high alcoholism rates view alcohol, its effects, and the concept of moderation. Others speculate that low rates of alcoholism occur in cultures that "teach" their members how to drink socially in moderation.

Course Alcoholism and other substance-use disorders generally begin in adolescence or early adult life. Substance-use disorders tend to be chronic illnesses, although often there are long periods of abstinence interspersed with binges of heavy use. Duncan recognizes that alcohol dependence is a chronic illness and that although there has been a remission for two years, there is a significant likelihood of a recurrence. It is for this reason that Alcoholics Anonymous insists that even during a long period of remission, the individual who once was dependent on alcohol recognize that he or she is still "an alcoholic."

Complications   In his recital, Duncan referred to one of the most common serious complications of chronic alcohol dependence, delirium tremens (D.T.'s). This is a delirium due to withdrawal from alcohol; it is characterized by confusion, disorientation, and often terrifying illusions and hallucinations (see Case 51, "The Innkeeper"). Less common complications include alcohol amnestic disorder, in which the major disturbance is loss of recent memory, and alcoholic hallucinosis, in which there are hallucinations without any confusion or disorientation. Irreversible widespread deterioration of intellectual functioning (dementia) may also occur.

Treatment   The approach taken by the college counselor, relating Duncan's drinking to early life experiences and feelings about his parents, was not helpful. And, in fact, insight-oriented psychotherapy is not now considered as effective a treatment for alcoholism as are other approaches that focus more specifically on the alcohol problem itself, such as Alcoholics Anonymous or behavior therapy. Duncan finally got help from Alcoholics Anonymous.

Although firm data are not available, it is widely believed that the almost 20,000 Alcoholics Anonymous groups active in the United States provide treatment for alcoholism to more individuals than any other treatment approach. Even so, AA has been estimated to reach and help but one person in twenty who have alcohol problems, which means that there is a great deal of room for other effective treatment methods.

One of the most controversial alternative approaches to the abstinence-oriented mission of Alcoholics Anonymous is treatment, usually behavioral in nature, that focuses on efforts to teach controlled—nonproblem—drinking habits. Despite promising initial data, first published in the early 1970s, controlled drinking treatment is not widely accepted today because of later data that were not nearly so encouraging. As a secondary prevention strategy to teach early problem drinkers moderation in their drinking, however, controlled drinking treatment may be more effective and is more widely employed.

The reason alternatives to existing treatments for alcoholism continue to proliferate is that no single approach, including Alcoholics Anonymous, has been studied thoroughly enough to draw conclusions about comparative efficacy. For example, although Alcoholics Anonymous is probably the predominant treatment for alcoholism in this country (which is why we chose to portray it here), virtually no data on its overall effectiveness have ever been reported. Consequently, the search for alcoholism treatment methods of proven effectiveness continues.

PSYCHOSEXUAL DISORDERS

JOHN OR NANCY?

John T., a 23-year-old computer programmer, was referred to a sex therapy specialist by a social worker because of marital problems that had started when his wife discovered that he often secretly dressed in women's clothes. They had been married for two years when his wife came home unexpectedly and discovered him dressed in female clothing that included a dress, panties, and women's shoes. His wife stared at him in shock and disbelief. He decided to tell her "the whole story," at which she panicked and insisted on their seeking marital counseling.

The story John told his wife, and later recounted to the therapist, was that as far back as he could remember, at least to age 4, he had not felt "like the other boys." He had instead felt "like one of the girls," like his sister, both in his interests and in his preference for female clothing. On occasion throughout childhood, he dressed in his mother's or sister's clothes, although by age 6 or 7 he was very aware that this was unacceptable behavior and only to be done briefly and secretly. As a child John was not comfortable with other boys; he had little interest in sports and the rough way they liked to play. He was not excluded from boys' games, but tended to drift toward the girls' games, feeling more comfortable with them.

John's father died when he was 4 years old, and he was raised by his mother, who was caring and devoted, and by his older sister. In general, despite relatively little income, the family was reasonably happy. John received average grades through school; he was skilled in math and preferred technical subjects. However, by adolescence he was well aware that he was "different," and became increasingly convinced that he was not a boy, but rather a girl. He felt anxious and ashamed of this and kept the secret from everyone. When he was about 12 he heard news reports of people who had had "sex change surgery." He felt an immediate understanding of such people, but discussed it with no one.

John's belief that he was a girl was based on a variety of factors: he spent a lot of time thinking about girls' activities, clothing, and makeup; he disliked his body and wanted a feminine one; he was becoming sexually attracted to boys. He had one brief homosexual contact which he found very exciting, but for which he felt guilty. His sexual fantasies, during rare masturbation, were of himself as a woman, being made love to by a man. He was almost always ill at ease until he discovered, at age 14, that he felt comfortable when cross-dressing in secret at home. To do so more easily he bought his own women's clothes and hid them. He felt unable to discuss any of these problems with anyone.

At age 21 John met his future wife, and they quickly became good friends. Although he was unable to tell her his problem, he felt somehow she might be able to help him. As a result, in a few months, as their relationship deepened, John proposed marriage. He believed that if he forced himself to make a commitment to marry someone he loved, he might grow more comfortable with himself as a male.

For a brief period John was happily married. However, his sense of himself as a woman remained, and he continued to have the urge to dress as a woman. He hid some female clothes in his closet, and when his wife was away he would wear them and feel at peace with himself. His sexual feelings toward his wife were more like a "woman toward a woman." He was able to function well sexually, and could have intercourse, but only with the fantasy that his wife had the penis and it was he who was being penetrated.

The patient initially arrived for therapy with his wife. She said that she felt he was "sick," that "he was a man, and a very lovable one, but that he had a crazy idea that he was really female." John was quite calm and agreed, for the sake of marital harmony, to try to defer cross-dressing and thoughts of sex change while his psychiatric evaluation was still in progress. However, he continued to feel uncomfortable as a man and intermittently gave in to the impulse to cross-dress.

On examination, there were no unusual thoughts, feelings, or behavior other than those associated with his feeling that he was really a woman. After several months of psychotherapeutic exploration, the persistence of his problem convinced the therapist that a sex-change operation might be appropriate. He was therefore referred for hormone therapy and group therapy discussions with others who had gender identity conflicts.

Over the next two years John's wife came to understand the strength and depth of his conflict, and finally, by mutual agreement, they divorced. John then received estrogen hormone treatments, electrolysis for removal of facial hair, and "lessons" to teach him feminine mannerisms and grooming. When last seen, John had been comfortably living as a woman for two years. He was dressing daily in women's clothes, had had his name changed to "Nancy," and was perceived by most strangers as a woman.

Nancy T. is currently awaiting male-to-female gender reassignment surgery. "Her" attitude is optimistic but realistic, with an educated awareness of what complications the future may bring, both physically and socially. Yet, since the original marital crisis that led to the full revelation of the problem and subsequent plan to move toward gender reassignment, John/Nancy T. has been more at ease and sure of herself than ever before in her life.

DISCUSSION

Psychopathology and Diagnosis   Although it is very common for men and women to be concerned with their adequacy in fulfilling the expectations associated with their sexual roles, it is very unusual for someone to feel a discrepancy between their anatomic sex and their subjective sense of being a man or woman. John, from a very early age, always felt that he was more female than male. This disturbance in gender identity was pervasive, and persisted unchanged into his adult life. He could only feel comfortable when the incongruity was temporarily reduced by cross-dressing.

The sense of discomfort and inappropriateness about one's anatomic sex and a desire to live as a member of the opposite sex, in the absence of physical intersex or genetic abnormality, is called *transsexualism*.Although the insistence that one is actually a member of the other sex might seem to be a delusion, the patient with transsexualism is actually speaking metaphorically— that is, that he or she feels like a member of the opposite sex, rather than asserting that he or she is anatomically or biologically a member of the opposite sex. For this reason, transsexualism is classified as a gender identity disorder, rather than as a psychotic disorder. (Gender identity disorders are mental disorders in which there is discomfort and a feeling of inappropriateness about one's anatomic sex, as well as persistent behaviors generally associated with the other sex.)

Cross-dressing is also seen in other conditions. Certain effeminate male homosexuals may dress in "drag" as part of courting behavior, but there is no desire to *be* a female. While the sexual attraction of a male transsexual (such as John) to men may suggest homosexuality, to the person with transsexualism it is heterosexual, since he perceives himself as a female. Interestingly, in John's case, while having sex with his wife he was able to experience it as heterosexual, but only by reversing the sexual roles in fantasy (imagining himself being penetrated by his wife's penis).

Cross-dressing is also seen in transvestism, a mental disorder seen only in heterosexual men. Here the cross-dressing is for the purpose of sexual excitement, and there is no wish to be a member of the oposite sex. (John's cross-dressing comforted him rather than sexually arousing him.) In rare instances, transvestism may evolve into transsexualism.

Etiology   Transsexualism invariably begins in childhood. Searches for a specific biologic cause have so far been unsuccessful. While the etiology of the disorder is not known, in many cases of male-to-female transsexualism there seems to be evidence of an unusually close relationship between the mother and the child, and parental encouragement of feminine behavior. Although John was raised only by his mother and older sister after the age of 4, this by itself can hardly explain the development of John's gender identity disturbance.

Treatment   Because psychotherapeutic attempts to reverse the gender identity of patients with transsexualism generally fail, programs to allow the individual to assume, as completely as possible, the role of a member of the opposite sex have been developed, even including surgical removal of the penis and the construction of an artificial vagina (in the case of men) and surgical construction of an artificial phallus (in the case of women). Because of the drastic and irreversible nature of sex-change surgery, strict criteria for suitability have been developed, such as that the individual has lived successfully as a member of the other sex for at least two years. Although initial follow-up studies indicate that most individuals with transsexualism who had had sex-change surgery were better adjusted following the surgery than before, recently other studies have reported less positive outcomes. For that reason, several major centers for such surgery have discontinued this treatment.

TWO'S COMPANY,
THREE'S A CROWD

A 44-year-old physician, Vladimir K., came to therapy mainly because his wife insisted that unless he change his sexual proclivities and stop insisting that she have intercourse with other men while he watched, she was going to reluctantly, but very definitely, divorce him. He could have good erections and enjoyable sex with his wife only for several weeks after he watched her go to bed with other men. Otherwise, he was undesirous and impotent. Also, although his wife was very well proportioned and hardly a pound overweight— two years before she had won a local beauty contest for married women—he consistently complained that she was too fat, and he plagued her to acquire an emaciated body—as he had also insisted with his three previous wives.

He had been and still was succeeding in virtually all other aspects of life: carrying on a thriving general practice, with many patients and friends who loved him, having an unusually good marriage (aside from their sexual incompatibility), and being devoted to his 2-year-old son and 1-year-old daughter. Both he and his wife (she was present during the first session) agreed that they shared many interests, agreed on child-rearing practices, enjoyed each other's company, and were both quite culturally and intellectually sophisticated. He treated her as an equal, was something of a feminist himself, and always supported her equal rights. He did not generally dominate her, bar her from any pursuits of her own, or put her down in any way. They rarely had fights, except about his continual urging of her to engage in "threesomes."

His previous three marriages had failed for the same reason as his present one seemed about to end: because all his wives were sexually liberal women who had agreed before marriage to copulate with other males in his presence, but had actually found this kind of sex repulsive, had only engaged in it a few times, and had steadfastly refused to continue to do so. The only woman he had ever met who seemed willing to keep participating in threesomes with him was a 40-year-old divorcée in Florida, whom he described as being "completely out of her skull," and with whom he would never consider living.

Fascination with the idea of watching others have intercourse began in adolescence, but he only arranged to have threesomes shortly after his first marriage at age 22. Over the years the circumstances under which the threesome sex encounters have occurred have varied, depending on what his wives have been able to arrange. He generally encourages his wife to find a man to whom she is attracted, and to arrange to have sex while he is watching. The encounter usually takes place in their own home, but may be in a hotel or other place if they are away on vacation. The sex encounter is usually brief, as he does not want a long encounter for fear that his wife will become emotionally involved with the other man. On the other hand, he does want frequent encounters, since he will be sexually aroused for only a few weeks after each encounter.

During a typical encounter he becomes aroused as he thinks of how much more attractive he is than the other man, and how much better he can make love to his wife. He imagines himself having passionate intercourse with his wife as he watches. As he sees the other man ending the encounter "wilted and deflated," no longer of any interest to her, he thinks of himself being adored by her and needed more than ever.

The client's history was quite in the "normal" range, in that he got along well with both his mother and father, who were both kind and loving parents, and who in turn got along well with each other. He did well in school, had friends, and had no unusual difficulties during his childhood or adolescence.

The client had had five years of psychoanalysis for similar problems, which had emphasized his great hostility to his mother and his supposed consequent latent homosexuality, but he had made no improvement. Recently, he had had a year of therapy that was based on the theories of Wilhelm Reich. In this therapy, an attempt was made to help him overcome inhibitions in the expression of "orgone energy," a hypothesized life energy. This therapy also had not helped. He was quite disillusioned with all psychotherapy because of these experiences, and he only came to see the present therapist after his wife had heard about the effectiveness of rational-emotive therapy (RET) and insisted that he try it. Vladimir was seen for only eight sessions of RET, although at first it seemed that a much longer period would be required to overcome his sexual problems.

In RET it is assumed that people with emotional problems, such as Vladimir, have rigid and extreme standards that they feel they must live up to in order to feel adequate as people. In this case, several such beliefs were easily brought to his awareness. By asking him several questions about what he was thinking and feeling when he watched his wife and another man make love, it was clear that he believed the following: "I *must* show sexual superiority over other men and therefore show (to myself and my wife) that I can make love better than they can and thereby prove I am a *real man!*" By asking him to introspect about his complaint that his wife was too fat, he was able to see that he believed "I *must* have a wife who is weak enough (and who *looks* frail enough) to worship me and do everything I ask her to do, no matter how outlandish! Then and only then will I be *securely* loved!" (Curiously, he did not seem to have a need to be worshipped by anyone other than his wife.)

Other inflexible beliefs that he held became apparent during the process of treatment: "Sex and other pleasures must come *easily* to me! Now that I have acclimated myself to be turned on by watching my wife screw other men, she *has to* arrange to go along with my being spontaneously aroused in this manner and *must not* balk or make it *too hard* for me to enjoy myself! I *shouldn't have to* go through such arduous retraining. Let my wife change rather than my having to go through the great trouble of doing so."

The unusual requirements that Vladimir made of his wife were thus seen as a consequence of his rigid and illogical beliefs. When his wife would not satisfy his whims he felt worthless and became impotent. Therapy consisted of a variety of cognitive, emotive, and behavioral methods in which his irrational *musts* were revealed to him and he was shown how actively to dispute them by challenging the antiempirical and absolutistic statements. Thus he was encouraged to persistently ask himself, "Why *must* I show superiority to other men by proving that I can screw my wife better than they can?" "Where is the evidence that I *need* a weak, frail-looking wife who will worship me and do everything I ask of her?" "Where is it writ that sex pleasure *must come easily,* as I have trained myself to make it come up to now?" "Why must I prove that I *should not have to* work at therapy to change myself and thus lead a better sexual and marital life?" Answering these questions many times, Vladimir soon saw that he could fully accept himself as a "real man" without proving sexual superiority to others; that he could easily do without a weak, worshiping wife; that he could enjoy sex "unspontaneously," even when he had to work somewhat at doing so; and that he had also damned well better work at therapy if he really wanted to change himself.

Another cognitive technique that worked very well with this intelligent but stubborn client was the therapist's helping him to see, to write out, and to review regularly the clearcut disadvantages of retaining his symptoms and not striving to surrender them. He was helped to see, for example, that as long as he remained addicted to threesomes and to the ego-salving that presumably went with this addiction he would lose his wife and virtually all other healthy women; he would only gain false ego-bolstering and never fully accept himself in his own right; he would remain a self-indulgent baby forever; etc. The therapist seriously and humorously showed him what his real gains and losses were, and had him steadily review these till he became quite convinced that the pains of his present thoughts and behaviors far outweighed their gains.

Emotively, Vladimir was given dramatic-evocative RET exercises, including rational-emotive imagery, in the course of which he imagined himself being bested by other males sexually and worked on his feelings until he made himself feel disappointed and sorry rather than inadequate and depressed.

Disappointment, in RET, means telling yourself, "It's too bad or unfortunate that something bad, such as a failure, is occurring"; feeling inadequate means, "I not only caused that bad thing to happen, but am an inadequate *person* for having that deficiency or weakness." This distinction was illustrated to Vladimir as follows:

Therapist: You say that you have not really found another man who has been better than you sexually, but suppose you did. How would you then tend to feel?

Vladimir: Awful! I would feel quite inadequate.

Therapist: Because you would be telling yourself—what?

Vladimir: I'm not as good a lover as I thought I was—and therefore a pretty weak, inadequate person!

Therapist: Right! Because you're telling yourself, "I *must* be great as a lover, or else I'm no damned good as a *person*."

Vladimir: I guess you're right about that.

Therapist: But you could, if you wanted to, choose to make yourself feel *only* disappointed and not at all self-downing when that kind of sex failure, if you want to call it that, occurred.

Vladimir: How could I?

Therapist: By convincing yourself that although *it* is bad and disappointing that you relatively failed at this time, *you* are never *it*. *It* is only one of your *behaviors*, and *you* are all the behaviors that you have done, are doing, and will in the future do. In RET, we show people how to steadily rate *it*, their behavior, but how to avoid rating *themselves*, the living process that creates these behaviors. If you can see that *you* are never a worm but that your performance is often below the level you would like it to be, you will then make yourself distinctly disappointed about *it* but not disappointed or self-downing about *you*.

Vladimir was also given a shame-attacking exercise, where he got himself to confess some of his "failings" (e.g., having a fairly small penis) to male friends and was able to make himself feel *un*ashamed and *un*humiliated as he did it.

Behaviorally, Vladimir was directed to do several kinds of activity homework assignments, including looking at many well-proportioned and plump women and imagining having enjoyable sex with them—until he started to become easily aroused at the sight of and the images of this type of woman. He also forced himself to have sex at least twice a week with his wife (instead of almost always avoiding it as he had been doing at the beginning of rational-emotive therapy) and to use the sensate focus and other procedures developed by the sex research team of William Masters and Virginia Johnson.

At first Vladimir was reluctant to carry out these homework assignments. The therapist pointed out that without hard work in therapy he simply was not going to improve and conquer his problems:

Therapist: How come you didn't do the homework assignment of having sex with your wife regularly, as you said you would?

Vladimir: Well, uh, to tell the truth, uh, I really didn't feel like doing it.

Therapist: Who the hell asked you what you *feel* like doing? Do you feel like being married and getting along with your wife and living with your children?

Vladimir: Oh, yes!

Therapist: Well?

Vladimir: You mean, getting what I want out of marriage is contingent on my changing sexually, whether I want to or not?

Therapist: Well, *isn't* it?

Vladimir: Well—uh, I guess so.

Therapist: What are you telling yourself, exactly, when you don't feel like making love to your wife and you know that you'd better try to do so, in order to change?

Vladimir: It's too damned hard! Why should I *have* to do so?

Therapist: To change! No matter *how* hard it is. And don't forget this: isn't it much harder *not* to change, and remain the way you are?

Vladimir: Yes, in some ways.

Therapist: Right! But you mean, I hear you saying implicitly, in some ways it's easier to goof and, at any one moment when you are about to go to bed with your wife, to avoid the situation and remain the way you are. Well, it is easier—temporarily! But your low frustration tolerance or short-range hedonism, which tells you strongly that you shouldn't *have to* work at changing, that therapy and what you do in between sessions *should* come easily and not be *so* hard, *too* hard, where is that going to get you?

Vladimir: Nowhere, I guess.

Therapist: You'd better say that much more strongly: Utterly nowhere! And *seeing* that you have low frustration tolerance won't help too much either. Only, as we say in RET, work and practice, work and practice, to give up your nonsense and to force yourself to act against it, only that is likely to get you better and to get you the results that you say you want.

Vladimir: Mmmm. I'm afraid you may be right.

Therapist: Damned right!

As a result of these RET procedures, Vladimir improved considerably and decided to quit therapy after eight sessions, which took place over a twelve-week period. At the time therapy ended, he was having sex regularly with his wife, enjoying it, and looking forward to further regular participation. He only thought of threesomes once in a while and when he did, he imagined himself participating with his wife and another woman, and not passively watching while his wife copulated with other males. He began to love watching his wife's body instead of being turned off by its "fatness"; and, for the first time in his life, he even thought of having affairs with two other women he knew who were, if anything, a bit overweight.

One year following his treatment with RET, Vladimir is free of the symptoms that brought him into treatment. He is getting along beautifully in his marriage and is happy with the results of his treatment. When asked what elements of RET were most helpful to him, he replied:

> First, the realization that it was exceptionally stupid of me to go for the ego satisfaction of beating out other men sexually instead of the much more solid satisfaction of enjoying my relations with my wife. Second, you showed me that rating myself in any way, as either a good or a bad person, amounts to a ridiculous overgeneralization and is inevitably anxiety-producing. Now instead of looking frantically for self-esteem I look for life's enjoyment. A hell of a better choice!

DISCUSSION

Psychopathology and Diagnosis According to the patient and his wife, Vladimir's problems are essentially limited to his unusual sexual requirement: he can only function sexually with his wife if he has recently observed her having intercourse with another man. In all other areas of his life, including his nonsexual relationship with his wife, he describes his functioning as superior.

When an individual requires unusual or bizarre imagery or acts in order to be sexually excited, this is called a *paraphilia* (from Greek *para*, abnormal, deviant, and *philia*, love). In the past, such conditions were referred to as perversions or sexual deviations. Although there are numerous specific paraphilias that have been described, there are three common types. In the first, the individual uses a nonhuman object for sexual stimulation, for example, a shoe fetish. In the second, the individual causes the partner to suffer or be humiliated, or the individual him- or herself suffers or is humiliated. Examples include sexual sadism, in which the individual is excited by beating the partner as part of the sexual act, and sexual masochism, in which the individual is excited by being bound and humiliated. In the third, sex acts are with nonconsenting partners. Examples are a man who exposes himself to unsuspecting women in subways (exhibitionism) or who watches with binoculars while unsuspecting women undress (voyeurism).

Vladimir's need to observe his wife having intercourse with other men in order for him to be aroused is certainly unusual and indicates that he suffers from a paraphilia. However, since his specific requirement does not conform to any of the typical forms of the disorder, it would be called an atypical paraphilia.

Vladimir does acknowledge one additional problem. He cannot help but regard his well-proportioned wife as overweight and unreasonably complains that she lose weight. This quirk seems related to his sexual problem in that they are both related to his need to feel superior and secure.

Treatment   The typical paraphilias tend to be chronic and very resistant to all forms of treatment, although recently special behavioral programs for reconditioning the stimuli for sexual excitement have been developed which seem promising when applied to sex offenders, such as repeated rapists. Rational emotive therapy was apparently successful in this case of atypical paraphilia; we do not know how effective it would be in general for individuals with more typical paraphilias.

RET, as illustrated in this case, is similar to cognitive behavior therapy (see Case 25, "Death of a Family") in that the patients' usual ways of thinking about the world and themselves are directly challenged and, in addition, patients are given many assignments to practice new ways of responding to formerly difficult situations. This therapist's interactions with the patient during RET were considerably more blunt and direct than is usually the case in psychotherapy, and the therapist seems comfortable with this kind of confrontation. Such a therapist might feel quite uncomfortable being as passive as is often necessary in psychoanalysis; conversely, a therapist who by nature is more passive might have difficulty optimally employing RET.

LATIN LOVER

Carlos Domera is a 30-year-old dress manufacturer who came to the United States from Argentina at age 22. He is married to an American woman, Phyllis, also age 30. They have no children. At the time of evaluation they were separated. Mr. Domera's problem was that he had been unable to have sexual intercourse for over a year due to his inability to achieve or maintain an erection. He had avoided all sexual contact with his wife for the prior five months, except for two brief attempts at lovemaking which ended when he failed to maintain his erection.

The couple separated a month ago by mutual agreement due to the tension that surrounded their sexual problem and their inability to feel comfortable with each other. Both professed love and concern for the other, but had serious doubts regarding their ability to resolve the sexual problem. Mr. Domera was only moderately successful in business, and felt somewhat frustrated as he was very ambitious and perfectionistic. He was depressed both about business disappointments and his sexual and marital problem. Four months earlier he had sought psychiatric help and had been given an antidepressant by another therapist which had helped relieve some difficulties he had sleeping and his depressed mood, but which had not affected his erection difficulties.

Mr. Domera conformed to the stereotype of the "macho Latin lover," believing that he "should always have erections easily and be able to make love at any time." Since he couldn't "perform" sexually, he felt humiliated and inadequate, and he dealt with this by avoiding not only sex, but any expression of affection for his wife.

Ms. Domera felt "he is not trying; perhaps he doesn't love me, and I can't live with no sex, no affection, and his bad moods." She had requested the separation temporarily, and he readily agreed. However, they had recently been seeing each other twice a week.

The couple came together for a sex therapy evaluation predominantly at the wife's insistence, since she had read that her husband's problem could be helped. On the other hand, her husband was pessimistic, convinced that he was sexually "crippled." He strongly suspected a biological cause or "rapid aging."

During the evaluation he reported that the onset of his erectile difficulties was concurrent with a tense period in his business. After several "failures" to complete intercourse, he concluded he was "useless as a husband" and therefore a "total failure." The anxiety of attempting lovemaking was too much for him to deal with.

He reluctantly admitted that he was occasionally able to masturbate alone to a full, firm erection and reach a satisfying orgasm. However, he felt ashamed and guilty about this, from both childhood masturbatory guilt and a feeling that he was "cheating" his wife. It was also noted that he had occasional firm erections upon awakening in the morning. Other than the antidepressant, the patient was taking no drugs, and he was not using much alcohol. There was no evidence of physical illness.

At the end of the evaluation session the psychiatrist reassured the couple that Mr. Domera had a "reversible psychological" sexual problem that was due to several factors, including his depression, but also more currently his anxiety and embarrassment, his high standards, and some cultural and relationship difficulties that made communication awkward and relaxation nearly impossible. The couple was advised that a brief trial of therapy, focused directly on the sexual problem, would very likely produce significant improvement within ten to fourteen sessions. They were reassured that the problem was almost certainly not physical in origin, but rather psychogenic, and that therefore the prognosis was excellent.

Mr. Domera was shocked and skeptical, but the couple agreed to commence the therapy on a weekly basis, and they were given a typical first "assignment" to do at home: a caressing massage exercise to try together with specific instructions not to attempt genital stimulation or intercourse at all, even if an erection might occur.

Not surprisingly, during the second session Mr. Domera reported with a cautious smile that they had "cheated" and had had intercourse "against the rules." This was their first successful intercourse in more than a year. Their success and happiness were acknowledged by the therapist, but they were cautioned strongly that rapid initial improvement often occurs, only to be followed by increased performance anxiety in subsequent weeks and a return of the initial problem. They were humorously chastised and encouraged to try again to have sensual contact involving caressing and non-demanding light genital stimulation, without an expectation of erection or orgasm, and to avoid intercourse.

During the second and fourth weeks Mr. Domera did not achieve erections during the love play, and the therapy sessions dealt with helping him to accept himself with or without erections and to learn to enjoy sensual contact without intercourse. His wife helped him to believe genuinely that he could please her with manual or oral stimulation and that, although she enjoyed intercourse, she enjoyed these other stimulations as much, as long as he was relaxed.

Mr. Domera struggled with his cultural image of what a "man" does, but he had to admit that his wife seemed pleased and that he, too, was enjoying the nonintercourse caressing techniques. He was encouraged to view his new lovemaking skills as a "success" and to recognize that in many ways he was becoming a better lover than many husbands, because he was listening to his wife and responding to her requests.

By the fifth week the patient was attempting intercourse successfully with relaxed confidence, and by the ninth session he was responding regularly with erections. If they both agreed, they would either have intercourse or choose another sexual technique to achieve orgasm. Treatment was terminated after ten sessions, and follow-up three months later verified that the improvement had persisted and the couple was again living together.

DISCUSSION

Psychopathology and Diagnosis Patients with sexual problems will often avoid or defer seeking help due to embarrassment, a hope that things will change without professional help, a lack of awareness that help is available, or a lack of agreement that help should be sought. Often patients may have their first sex therapy evaluation when their relationship is in a crisis stage with one saying, "Get help, or our relationship is over." This case was somewhat in that category, with the tension jeopardizing the couple's ability to stay together.

It is important for a diagnosis of sexual problems that the clinician rule out transitory disturbances, such as the failure of a man to achieve an erection during a brief period of extreme stress. It is also important, particularly with women who are having problems with sexual excitement or orgasm, to determine that during sexual activity there is stimulation that is adequate in focus, intensity, and duration. Furthermore, certain physical disorders that may interfere with sexual functioning, such as diabetes and other endocrine diseases or neurological diseases, must be ruled out. Mr. Domera's ability to masturbate to orgasm and his morning erections rule out a physical cause, and thus he was spared the need for extensive medical tests such as hormonal studies, studies of penile blood flow, and sleep studies (in which spontaneous erections persist in cases of psychogenic impotence but are absent when the cause is a physical disorder). Finally, sexual dysfunctions may be a symptom of a major mental disorder, such as major depression. Although Mr. Domera is depressed, he does not have the full depressive syndrome necessary for the diagnosis of major depression, and his depressed mood appears to be secondary to his sexual difficulties.

Psychosexual dysfunctions are classified according to the stage of the sexual response cycle during which the disturbance occurs: appetitive (desire for sex), excitement (erections in males, vasocongestion and lubrication in females), and orgasm. Mr. Domera's problem is in the excitement phase in that he either cannot be physically aroused, or maintain sexual arousal (erection) until completion of the sexual act. Technically this is referred to as *inhibited sexual excitement.* Although Mr. Domera is also unable to have an orgasm during sexual intercourse, this is because of the disturbance in the excitement phase. The additional diagnosis of inhibited male orgasm is not given, but is reserved for those rare cases in which the individual maintains an adequate erection, but is unable to have an orgasm or has a markedly delayed orgasm.

Etiology A few decades ago sexual problems were generally thought to have deep-seated psychological origins involving "castration anxiety" and "penis envy." Although Mr. Domera has some maladaptive personality traits, such as perfectionism, there is no evidence that he suffers from a pervasive personality disturbance, and in this respect he is typical of the kinds of patients who seek treatment for sexual dysfunctions.

Regardless of the original cause of this disorder, however, once the problem has begun, the man generally becomes anxious that it will happen again. This "performance" anxiety, then, often has an inhibitory effect on arousal the next time intercourse is attempted. This, in turn, further enhances the anxiety, and a vicious cycle eventually results. This undoubtedly is the case with Mr. Domera.

Treatment The fact of the patient's occasional firm erections and positive response to masturbation justified the dramatically optimistic reassurance given during the evaluation of this couple, despite their year-long problem. In fact, the positive reassurance was a therapeutic technique to help reduce the anxiety associated with long-term pessimism. The therapy further focused on teaching the patient to enjoy sex without intercourse and that a male can be a good lover without an erection. This knowledge is often enormously helpful, especially to men with a traditional sense that the male must "perform" intercourse or be ashamed, an idea that is very prevalent. In addition, this man's perfectionistic success drive was redirected toward the goals of relaxation and pleasing his wife without intercourse, rather than insisting he have a "perfect erection." Thus he was able to relabel what he could do as "successful" and maintain a sense of mastery.

This couple was greatly helped by the wife's ready acceptance of nonintercourse means of stimulation and her easy reassurance of her husband that he was indeed pleasing her with or without erection. As he relaxed, their verbal communication improved, and he was predictably likely to respond with erections as he was no longer demanding himself to produce them.

As is common in sex therapy, success leads to further success, and although slightly unusual, this couple was able to make very rapid progress and learn techniques to deal with future "setbacks." If the treatment had not progressed so rapidly, either a slower paced, lengthier sex therapy or more exploration of the patient's ambivalence or conflicts in the relationship, fears of intimacy or success, or deeper anxiety about sexual pleasure might have been addressed. However, in this case, these more complex issues were bypassed, and the sexual symptom was the sole target.

Other approaches have been used for the treatment of psychogenic inhibited sexual excitement, including individual psychoanalytic approaches, behavioral relaxation techniques, couples marital therapy, group therapy with others with sexual problems, placebo hormone treatments, and numerous folklore remedies. However, current sex therapy approaches with couples have had the highest success rate by a substantial margin.

AFFECTIVE DISORDERS

AGITATED ACTOR

Daryl Jacobson, a 25-year-old married man, was seen in an emergency office consultation at the request of his wife. She had made two dozen phone calls to doctors listed in the yellow pages before she reached one able to refer her to a psychiatrist who could see her husband that same day.

The couple lived on the West Coast but were staying with friends back east while the patient, a professional dancer, tried out for a Broadway show. Mr. Jacobson had been attending acting school and performing part-time until approximately a month previously, when his agent presented him with the possibility of a role in a show in New York that was being produced by one of the agent's friends.

At first it seemed likely that Mr. Jacobson had been given the part. About two weeks before the emergency office visit, however, he began to come home at the end of a day of rehearsal making critical and disparaging remarks about the way the sessions were run and the leadership of the director. One week later, a fellow performer called the wife and asked her to tell her husband to "cool it," reporting that her husband had been trying to "take over" the rehearsals, giving unsolicited advice to both the director and the other performers as well. At this point, his wife realized that there had been a definite change in his usually easygoing demeanor; he had become tense, irritable, and had made several nasty comments about her figure and their recent sex life.

Three days later Mr. Jacobson was escorted out of the theater after he had an angry outburst and began shouting obscenities at other performers. Although calmer at home, his wife reported that she could not follow much of what he was saying, that he was talking "a-mile-a-minute" and pacing the room incessantly, dressed only in his underwear, and denying that he needed to eat or sleep. The following day he went out and bought $75 worth of baseball cards.

Mr. Jacobson's family lived in Connecticut. Following a frantic phone call from his wife, the patient's mother drove into the city, and after a great deal of coaxing, brought him to a local community hospital where he was admitted. He received one dose of an antipsychotic, tranquilizing medication, spent most of the night disrupting the ward, and signed out against medical advice the next morning. It was at this point that his wife began to search for an emergency consultation. Her husband agreed to see another psychiatrist, but refused to consider hospitalization.

During the consultation the patient maintained control but was visibly tense and agitated. He stood throughout the interview, wandering about the room, looking out the window at the traffic, looking at the pictures on the wall, and touching the plants. He gave a nearly continuous stream of commentary about his predicament. Although he spoke rapidly and moved quickly from topic to topic, his account was mostly understandable and to the point. It was difficult to question him, but when possible, he answered appropriately. When asked if he would prefer sitting down he replied: "I can't sit; I need to stand, to walk, to move around, you know, like I have this energy, this feeling that keeps me going. I'm a dancer, you know; I'm into movement, moving, like I think I could go on forever."

Concerning the possibility that something might be wrong with him, he acknowledged that he had lost his job, but he felt it was primarily the director's fault and not his. When confronted with his wife's fear of him, he agreed that he was acting differently and had been cruel, and that she didn't deserve such harsh treatment. He denied feeling elated or cheerful, stating only that he had been feeling "nervous" and "tense."

In the course of the conversation Mr. Jacobson mentioned that this experience was similar to what his father had gone through several times. His father, it turned out, was an unsuccessful salesman who spent nearly twenty years going from job to job, usually being fired after episodes in which he became excited and had confrontations with his bosses. Five years ago an episode of hostile and argumentative behavior resulted in a brief psychiatric hospitalization during which he was started on lithium. The ensuing five years had been free of these outbursts.

Mr. Jacobson responded favorably to the notion that he and his father seemed to have similar problems and that he, like his father, possibly needed lithium. He agreed to take the drug, to have his blood tested regularly for the level of lithium (a necessary precaution with this drug), and to return to the office every other day until his condition subsided. He was told to take three capsules the first two days, get a blood test, and then increase the dosage to four capsules. He also agreed to take a moderate dose of an antipsychotic tranquilizer at bedtime since he had not been sleeping.

On the next two visits, the patient and his wife agreed that his speech and general activity level had decreased somewhat, but he complained of "restlessness" in the muscles of his arms and legs that was different from his earlier state, and tolerable only if he kept his extremities moving, such as by walking or doing calisthenics. These symptoms were recognized as a relatively common side effect of the antipsychotic mediation. Another medication was prescribed to counteract this side effect. His blood test revealed a therapeutically effective blood level of lithium after several days of treatment. The restlessness was relieved within 24 hours, and after one week the medications other than lithium were discontinued since Mr. Jacobson was now calm, coherent, sleeping, and eating. He was aware that he had been through a dramatic change in his usual behavior and mood, was embarrassed by much of what he had done over the preceding weeks, and was appreciative that his wife and others had exerted such efforts to get help for him.

DISCUSSION

Psychopathology and Diagnosis   The episode of disturbed behavior that finally resulted in a psychiatric consultation consisted of hostility, angry outbursts, irritability, psychomotor agitation (couldn't sit still), pressured speech (talked "a-mile-a-minute"), flight of ideas (wife could not follow what he was saying), grandiosity (gave unsolicited advice to his director and other performers), distractibility (attention shifted from interviewer to traffic outside the window to pictures and plants in the room), decreased need for sleep, and poor judgment (bought $75 worth of baseball cards). This clinical picture is called a manic episode. Although more commonly there is elated or expansive mood, sometimes, as in this case, the pervasive mood disturbance is one of irritability. Manic episodes always consist of a disturbance in mood accompanied by several of the associated symptoms described above (psychomotor agitation, decreased need for sleep, etc.).

The occurrence of a manic episode indicates the diagnosis of *bipolar disorder.* As the name "bipolar" suggests, there are usually two phases to the disorder: major depressive episodes and manic episodes, but the diagnosis is made even in the absence of a history of a depressive episode. This is because patients with bipolar disorder who have only had one or more manic episodes usually will eventually also have a depressive episode, and their response to treatment and positive family history for the disorder is no different from patients who have had both phases of the disorder. (In fact, this patient's father apparently also had bipolar disorder, and this helped confirm the consultant's diagnosis.)

Bipolar disorder is a form of affective disorder. All of the affective disorders involve a disturbance in mood, either of depression or, more rarely (as with bipolar disorder), elation.

Treatment   Unlike many forms of psychopathology, the manifestations of a manic episode are usually so dramatic and disruptive that they can hardly be ignored, and frequently in-patient hospitalization is required to protect the patient from acting impulsively in an extremely self-damaging manner, such as squandering a family fortune or ruining one's reputation by sexual promiscuity. Unfortunately, patients in a manic episode often fail to recognize that they are ill and therefore may not appreciate the need for treatment. This patient, because he was neither suicidal nor homicidal, could not be forced against his will to remain in the hospital. He did, however, agree to see a doctor as an outpatient. Recognizing that he might have the same illness that had disrupted his father's life, he agreed to take medication. The fact that his father's condition responded well to lithium treatment suggested that Mr. Jacobson himself would have a positive response.

The treatment of the manic phase of bipolar disorder begins with management of the acute episode. This is usually accomplished by means of antipsychotic medication to control the agitation and excitement quickly. Results can be seen within hours to a few days. In Mr. Jacobson's case, it was imperative to initiate treatment quickly, since he was still in the early phases of a manic episode when seen and had not yet done any irreparable harm to himself, his wife, or anyone else. Psychotherapeutic methods are not effective when a patient is so agitated and distractible that he or she cannot sit in a chair, let alone concentrate on a therapist's questions or comments. Lithium carbonate is usually given, once the danger of complete loss of control has passed, to normalize the mood disturbance. This process takes more time, usually a couple of weeks before the full effect is evident. Lithium is then continued for at least six months in order to ensure recovery from the manic episode, and it may be given, afterward, in smaller doses to prevent the recurrence of future manic and depressive episodes. The decision of whether to use lithium prophylactically, and for how long, depends on the frequency and severity of the episodes and the presence of any medical contraindications. Because excessive lithium can be extremely toxic, its use is always monitored by periodic tests that measure the concentration in the blood.

Etiology and Course   The etiology of bipolar disorder is still unknown, although there is considerable evidence that the vulnerability to the disorder has a strong genetic component. Bipolar disorder usually begins before age 30, and individuals not receiving prophylactic treatment with lithium are at great risk for repeated episodes of both depression and mania. Typically, and in contrast to schizophrenia, between episodes of the illness the individual returns to his or her usual level of functioning.

Although psychotherapy has not been shown to be effective in treating the symptoms of bipolar disorder, it may be useful in helping the individual to learn to live with an illness that may periodically disrupt his or her life.

CUCKOO CLOCKS

Terrence O'Reilly, a single 39-year-old transit authority clerk, was brought to the hospital in May, 1973, by the police after his increasingly hyperactive and bizarre behavior and nonstop talking alarmed his family. He loudly proclaimed that he was not in need of treatment, and threatened legal action against the hospital and police.

The family reported that a month prior to admission Mr. O'Reilly took a leave of absence from his civil service job, purchased a large number of cuckoo clocks and then an expensive car which he planned to use as a mobile showroom for his wares, anticipating that he would make a great deal of money. He proceeded to "tear around town" buying and selling the clocks and other merchandise, and when he was not out, he was continuously on the phone making "deals." He rarely slept and, uncharacteristically, spent every evening in neighborhood bars drinking heavily and, according to him, "wheeling and dealing." Two weeks before admission his mother died suddenly of a heart attack. He cried for two days, but then his mood began to soar again. At the time of admission he was $3000 in debt and had driven his family to exhaustion with his excessive activity and overtalkativeness. He said, however, that he felt "on top of the world."

Mr. O'Reilly first sought psychiatric treatment in 1960 at the age of 26 when he was attending college on the GI bill. He was feeling depressed and hopeless, unable to function at school, and afraid to ask girls for dates. He felt he was a "mama's boy" who would never amount to anything. Treated with outpatient psychotherapy for one year, he managed to finish college and obtain a job as an administrative assistant. Several years later, after losing a job, Mr. O'Reilly again became depressed and was in treatment (psychotherapy plus low doses of a tranquilizer) for over a year.

His third depression began about six months prior to this admission. He felt that his job was a dead end, felt incompetent and without energy or interest in things. He again began psychotherapy, and also received a minor tranquilizer and an antidepressant. His energy level increased, and he developed an interest in many new activities, culminating in the frantic overactivity that led to his hospitalization.

He was the oldest of five children, first generation Irish Americans living in a predominantly Irish community in a large eastern city. He was described as a very responsible "good" child who often took care of his younger siblings. He was much loved and respected by them. He did well in parochial school, although socially he was rather shy and self-conscious. After graduation from high school he worked in a supermarket for two years before being drafted. In the Army he was trained as a clerk, and was pleased to have a job that was both safe and relatively interesting. He made some good friends in the service and began to have his first love affairs. After receiving an honorable discharge, he took advantage of the GI bill to become the first college student in his family.

Between the episodes of illness described above he had functioned fairly well on his jobs. He had many friends in the neighborhood, but had only a few serious girl friends. His weekends were spent playing ball and drinking, often heavily, with his buddies in neighborhood bars. After his mother's death he continued to live with his elderly father, a retired postal worker.

His father was a "heavy drinker" who was often violent when drunk. One sister had been hospitalized several times for violent behavior associated with alcohol, and another sister was treated with electroconvulsive treatment for a postpartum depression. She is now well. The other two siblings have families of their own and have never been ill.

During his 1973 hospitalization the patient was treated with large doses of antipsychotic medication. He refused to take another drug, lithium, which was also prescribed, because he feared that it would be too easy for him to kill himself with lithium if he again became depressed. By three weeks his mood stabilized and he was released to return to work and continue psychotherapy as an outpatient.

The following year he again became overactive, overtalkative, and grandiose. He wrote letters to public officials telling them how to run the city and the state. He referred to himself as "the string puller" (implying that he was a puppeteer and his associates were all puppets). His provocative and intrusive behavior eventually cost him his job. Attempts by his father to restrain him led to his throwing furniture and clothing out of the window of his apartment, and he was brought to the emergency room by the police. During this hospitalization he was treated with phenothiazines, and after the acute symptoms were under control, he agreed to take lithium prophylactically. He was discharged to a day-hospital program after six weeks. In the program he was very successful—well liked by the other patients and helpful to the staff, and for the following year, he was treated by a psychiatric resident with whom he developed the most meaningful therapeutic relationship that he had ever had. When the resident completed his training and moved to another city, Mr. O'Reilly was transferred to a new therapist. He was never able to establish the same kind of therapeutic bond with the new therapist. He eventually dropped out of the day-hospital program, and his visits to the clinic became less frequent. He saw his therapist intermittently, but refused to continue taking the lithium because it made no sense to take it when he was no longer "crazy."

Over the next two years he remained on welfare, apparently demoralized and feeling that his life was going nowhere. He was unable to find a job. Full of doubts about himself, he was anxious during job interviews and unsure about how to explain the gaps in his work history. He now lived by himself in his old apartment, his father having moved to the suburban home of one of his sisters. He hung out with friends in the street, and often drank heavily with them and lamented that he could never find a woman with whom he really felt comfortable. Although he acknowledged feeling somewhat depressed and having trouble sleeping, he said he was "getting along."

His sister planned a large family party to celebrate his 45th birthday. When he did not arrive and could not be reached by phone, she asked the police to check his apartment. He was found dead. By his bed were an empty vial of sleeping pills and an almost empty pint of bourbon.

DISCUSSION

Psychopathology and Diagnosis   Like Mr. Jacobson in the previous case, Mr. O'Reilly was experiencing a manic episode when brought to the hospital in 1973. His mood was euphoric ("on top of the world"), a more common manifestation of manic mood than the irritable mood displayed by Mr. Jacobson. However, the same associated symptoms that comprise the manic syndrome were present: overtalkativeness, overactivity, decreased need for sleep, grandiosity, and poor judgment. His history is more typical for *bipolar disorder* than is Jacobson's in that he also had several episodes of depression.

Course and Treatment   Mr. O'Reilly, like most patients with bipolar disorder, recovered from his early episodes of both depression and mania and was able to return to work. Unlike most patients with this disorder, however, after a number of episodes, one of which caused him to lose his job, he never fully recovered and eventually succumbed to what appeared to be suicide, the most serious danger associated with depression. We do not know to what extent the failure to recover from his last episode was due to residual depressive symptoms, feelings of demoralization at being unable to find work, or an underlying personality disorder that made it difficult for him to push himself to obtain a job and satisfying heterosexual relations. In addition, we do not know what role his excessive drinking played in his tragic outcome. His case does illustrate the common problem of convincing patients to continue taking a prophylactic medicine when they no longer feel sick. Since lithium has a prophylactic action against both depressive and manic episodes, perhaps if he had continued to take lithium he would not have become so depressed that he took his life.

Mr. O'Reilly's case also illustrates a recurrent problem created by the use of trainees as therapists. Each year when psychology interns, social work students, and psychiatric residents complete their training, they leave behind a number of patients who have difficulty making the transition to a new therapist. If Mr. O'Reilly's relationship with his new therapist had been better, he might have been helped both with his demoralization and his resistence to medication, and he might have realized that suicide was not the only solution to his problems.

WEEPING WIDOW

Paula Stansky was a 57-year-old woman, widow and mother of four children, who was hospitalized on the psychiatry service of a large county hospital near her home because, according to her children, she was refusing to eat and take care of herself.

The patient lived in a small, five-room woodframe row house with her two younger, unmarried children, aged 18 and 22. She was described as a usually cheerful, friendly woman who took meticulous care of her home. She took great pride in having raised her children essentially by herself, with relatively limited resources, over the fourteen years since her husband had died in an accident at the coal mine where he had worked for over twenty years. About two months prior to her hospitalization, however, her younger children reported a change in their mother's usual disposition, for no apparent reason. She appeared more easily fatigued, not as cheerful, and lackadaisical about her housework. Over the course of the next few weeks, she stopped going to church and canceled her usual weekly bingo outing with neighborhood women. As the house became increasingly neglected and their mother began to spend more time sleeping or rocking in her favorite chair, apparently preoccupied, the younger children called their married brother and sister for advice.

Her 26-year-old son, who lived in a nearby town, became worried when his mother canceled the regular Sunday family dinner. He recalled a similar period about ten years previously, when he was a teenager, when his mother had gone to a hospital for about three weeks.

When her son, in response to the telephone call, arrived at her house, Ms. Stansky denied that anything was wrong. She claimed to be only tired, "possibly the flu." For the ensuing week, her children tried to "cheer her up," but with no success. After several days had gone by without her taking a bath, changing her clothes, or eating any food, her children put her in the car and drove her to the hospital emergency room where she was admitted.

On admission, Ms. Stansky was mostly mute, answering virtually no questions except correctly identifying the hospital and the day of the week. She cried periodically throughout the interview, but only shook her head back and forth when asked if she could tell the interviewer what she was feeling or thinking about. She was agitated, frequently wringing her hands, rolling her head toward the ceiling, and rocking in her chair. Her clothes were loosely fitting; her hair was in disarray. The history from her children indicated that during the past week she had been waking up at 3:00 A.M., unable to fall back to sleep. She also seemed to them to have lost considerable weight. Her weight on admission was 125 pounds, down from her usual weight of 140 to 150 pounds.

Records from Ms. Stansky's previous hospitalization described a similar episode, also without apparent precipitants, which had led to a suicide attempt by wrist-cutting. Ms. Stansky at that time was given a course of ten electroconvulsive therapy (ECT) treatments and was reported to have fully recovered when discharged from the hospital. The history taken from the family confirmed that until recently their mother had functioned well and had not received outpatient care, to the best of their knowledge.

The first-year psychiatric resident in charge of Ms. Stansky's case decided to start her on an antidepressant medication, even though she knew that Ms. Stansky had responded to ECT in the past. The resident felt that ECT was not a "humane" treatment and should be used, if at all, only as a last resort.

After one week of hospitalization, Ms. Stansky was receiving what should have been an effective dose of medication, but she showed little improvement. Therefore, starting on the tenth hospital day, the medication was gradually increased until a maximum daily dose was reached several days later. During daily psychotherapy sessions she continued to be unable to talk about how she felt or to describe what in her life was troubling her. On the seventeenth hospital day, after the resident had gone home, the on-call doctor received an emergency call from Ms. Stansky's ward. She was in considerable pain, pointing to and clutching at her lower abdomen and writhing on her bed. An observant nurse indicated that she had not voided urine for over 24 hours; the resident put in a urinary catheter and a large quantity of urine was passed, relieving the pain. All medications were discontinued.

On the following day the ward staff decided that the urinary retention was a side effect of the medication and that it was unwise to continue with it. The resident in charge of the case now decided that ECT was necessary, and two days later Ms. Stansky received her first ECT treatment. The patient was given medications to relax her muscles and put her to sleep just before the electric current was sent through electrodes placed on both sides of her head, in order to induce a seizure. Because of the use of the muscle relaxant, the only sign of the seizure was rhythmic contractions observable in the muscles of her feet.

For the next two weeks Ms. Stansky received treatments every other day. She was groggy for several hours after each treatment and could not recall the trips up to the treatment room or some of the events of that day. After three treatments she was talking to the staff and other patients, and after five treatments she was observed on several occasions to be laughing while watching television or visiting with her children. Ms. Stansky received a total of eight ECT treatments and was discharged home, back to her usual self, except for some slight problems with recent memory. A follow-up evaluation six months later indicated that she was functioning well in her roles as homemaker and mother, was socializing again with friends, and seemed to require no continuing care. Her memory loss, except for the mornings on which she had received the ECT treatments, had disappeared.

DISCUSSION

Psychopathology and Diagnosis   By the time Ms. Stansky was hospitalized, it was apparent that she was suffering from a major depressive episode. Although she did not complain of a depressed mood, she no longer was her usual cheerful self and had evidently lost interest in her usual activities. In fact, many patients with a clinically significant depression, particularly the elderly, do not actually describe sad feelings, but rather a loss of interest or pleasure. In addition, she had the characteristic associated features of the depressive syndrome: fatigue, sleep disturbance, loss of appetite, weight loss, psychomotor agitation, and diminution of speech.

Several features of her depression indicated that it was particularly severe. She demonstrated lack of reactivity, in that she did not seem to feel better in response to her children's efforts to "cheer her up." Also, she had considerable weight loss, marked psychomotor agitation, and early morning awakening. This form of severe depression is particularly responsive to somatic therapy, and in the past was referred to as an endogenous depression, since it often seemed to arise without any precipitating stress (*endogenous* = arising from within). Now this subtype of depression is called melancholia, a term resurrected from antiquity that does not have the etiologic implications of the term endogenous. Although this kind of depression often occurs without any apparent psychosocial precipitant, frequently it is precipitated by stressful life events.

Treatment   The severity of this patient's depression made her virtually inaccessible to attempts at psychotherapy. In considering somatic therapy for Ms. Stansky, the resident had two choices: antidepressant medication and ECT. Numerous well-designed studies have shown that both treatments are effective in relieving the symptoms of most patients with a moderate to severe depression. Although it is reasonable first to attempt to treat most severe depressions with antidepressant medication before trying ECT, in this case the resident neglected the fact that the patient had had a good response to ECT in the past. A past history of a good response to a particular somatic therapy usually bodes well for the use of that therapy for a similar current episode.

Ms. Stansky developed urinary retention, an uncommon but significant side effect of the antidepressant medication, which led to the resident's decision to give ECT. She received the usual number of ECT treatments (six to ten for depressed patients) and showed a characteristic prompt recovery. Her transitory memory deficits are also quite typical of ECT, although more recently it has been discovered that memory impairment is minimized by applying both electrodes to the nondominant hemisphere (usually the left side). The anesthesia and muscle relaxants were given to Ms. Stansky in order to avoid the possibility of fractures or dislocations during the seizures, serious problems when ECT was first used.

In spite of the improvements that have been made in ECT, it continues to be a controversial treatment. Most clinicians are convinced that the evidence shows that it is a safe and effective treatment if used for certain specific disorders, while acknowledging that in the past the treatment was often given to patients with other disorders not likely to benefit from it. On the other hand, objections have been raised to ECT on ethical grounds and on the grounds that memory loss may be a significant long-term complication in many more cases than is currently assumed by those who advocate its use.

Prognosis Major depression tends to be a recurrent episodic illness with recovery from each episode. In patients who have had several and frequent episodes, consideration is given to the use of prophylactic therapy, usually low-dose antidepressant medications.

Many clinicians would be uncomfortable with the notion that severe depressions can arise in the absence of some life stress. In this case they would undoubtedly make a methodical search to identify precipitating events or circumstances for Ms. Stansky's two depressive episodes. Should such a search prove fruitful, therapy would then be directed at helping Ms. Stansky find better ways of coping with the stresses.

LEARNING TO COPE

On her first visit to the clinic, Mary Griffith had a fragile air about her. Looking frightened, she sat with her coat on, her body perfectly still except for her hands twisting nervously on her lap and her quivering lower lip. Her eye contact was minimal, and her speech verged on a whisper.

Mary was 25 years old and had just begun her senior year in college. She had come seeking help for "depression" after she had seen a notice advertising a program for "coping with depression." Asked to recount how her life had been going recently, Mary began to weep. Sobbing, she said that for the last year or so she felt she was losing control of her life and that recent stresses (starting school again, friction with her boyfriend) had left her feeling worthless and frightened. Because of a gradual deterioration in her vision, she was now forced to wear glasses all day. "The glasses make me look terrible," she said, and "I don't look people in the eye much any more." Also, to her dismay, Mary had gained 20 pounds in the past year. She viewed herself as overweight and unattractive. At times she was convinced that with enough money to buy contact lenses and enough time to exercise she could cast off her depression; at other times she believed nothing would help. She also complained of difficulty falling asleep, loss of energy, and not feeling interested in anything anymore.

Mary saw her life deteriorating in other spheres, as well. She felt overwhelmed by schoolwork and, for the first time in her life, was on academic probation. Twice before in the past seven years feelings of inadequacy and pressure from part-time jobs (as a waitress, bartender, and salesclerk) had caused her to leave school. She felt certain that unless she could stop her current downward spiral she would do so again—this time permanently. She despaired of ever getting her degree.

In addition to her dissatisfaction with her appearance and her fears about her academic future, Mary complained of a lack of friends. Her social network consisted solely of her boyfriend, with whom she was living. Although there were times she experienced this relationship as almost unbearably frustrating, she felt helpless to change it and was pessimistic about its permanence.

At the end of the intake interview, Mary filled out a rating scale of depressive symptoms, and scored well within the "severe" range.

In her freshman year at college six years ago, she sought assistance at the counseling center for distress that resulted from the breakup of her first heterosexual relationship, the death of her cat, and a bothersome living situation. She felt she was wasting the counselor's time and did not return for a second session. Her distress led her to drop out of school. To help herself through the breakup she began dating again and also became very close to another woman, who soon became her roommate. A year later she experienced another, less serious episode of depression that she attributed to academic stress. Although these episodes were the worst periods of depression, she could not recall a time since high school when she did not feel somewhat depressed.

Mary was the fourth in a family of five daughters. Her mother, a fundamentalist Baptist, made sure that Mary attended church and church retreats, but forbade her to participate in ordinary afterschool activities with her classmates. Consequently, Mary had little opportunity to develop friendships and viewed herself as socially isolated throughout her adolescence.

In the judgment of her therapist, Mary's depression could best be approached with a treatment that emphasized learning new skills. Her current life was almost devoid of activities she enjoyed or positive interactions with others. Further, day-to-day disappointments were extremely debilitating to her self-esteem and sense of worth. Therefore, it was thought that Mary could benefit from increasing her pleasant activities and interactions, and from learning how to cope better with stressful situations.

The therapist employed a twelve-session treatment program that emphasizes these goals and has been found to be effective in treating depression. In the first five sessions, the therapist works with the client on decreasing both the frequency and aversiveness of unpleasant events. In the next five sessions, the therapeutic aim is to increase the client's participation in (and comfort with) potentially enjoyable activities. The final two meetings are devoted to designing a plan for maintaining treatment gains and for preventing future episodes of depression. During treatment, the mastery of new skills is continually stressed. The skills considered most important for Mary's treatment include relaxation (to help her sleep better), cognitive control (to decrease her recurrent self-criticial thoughts), assertion (to help with interpersonal difficulties), and time management (to cope with feelings of being "overwhelmed"). The therapist discussed these recommendations with Mary, and they agreed to work together.

Prior to beginning treatment, Mary filled out two questionnaires to help her identify the particular pleasant and unpleasant activities and interactions that might be most related to her mood. She was provided a list of those activities and instructed to keep track of her mood and activities every day. In this way she could monitor her own progress throughout treatment as well as learn what particular activities actually did affect her feelings of depression. Her scores on these questionnaires indicated that while Mary had not experienced any recent major life events, she was experiencing an above-average number of unpleasant events in day-to-day matters.

During the first five sessions, Mary learned to reduce the aversiveness of unpleasant events that occurred day to day. She began practicing progressive muscle relaxation and maintained a relaxation log, a daily record that helped her follow her success in controlling her tension. Later she learned to combine relaxation with covert (mental) rehearsal of how she wanted to behave in situations she found stressful. After two weeks of practicing relaxation, Mary's insomnia, which had bothered her intermittently since childhood, had almost vanished. She was no longer keeping herself awake at night with worrisome thoughts.

The next five sessions were devoted to increasing pleasant activities. For Mary, this was approached by teaching her better ways to manage her time. As a science major, Mary spent many hours writing lab reports and studying for exams. She also worked at a part-time job. In first discussing with the therapist her low number of enjoyable activities, Mary complained that she lacked the hours even to finish her work, let alone amuse herself. The therapist, convinced that Mary could make time for pleasant activities with efficient planning, assigned the book, *How to Get Control of Your Time and Your Life* by Alan Lakein (see *References)*. She was also asked to fill out a detailed schedule of her activities for each day of the week. Making such a daily plan helped Mary to curtail or even eliminate many "unnecessary" activities that interfered with schoolwork, such as watching television. She soon began being able to finish her assignments more quickly, and as a result not only worried less about her grades but also had time for more rewarding endeavors.

In considering pleasant activities to include in her schedule, Mary decided that three mornings each week, before leaving for class, she would exercise. The therapist, doubting that early morning exercise could be truly pleasant for Mary, encouraged her to choose a more pleasant activity, but she persisted. Indeed, Mary succeeded with her plan (she made her morning shower contingent on 15 minutes of exercise), and she did enjoy it. She also consulted a nutritionist about a weight-loss program. Thus, by increasing pleasant activities she also took two important steps toward improving her health and appearance.

During this phase, therapy also focused on interpersonal skills, especially assertion. Mary had often expressed her wish to be more comfortable asking questions in class. She and the therapist agreed that role playing would be helpful. Rational-emotive techniques (see Case 19, "Two's Company, Three's a Crowd") for disputing self-defeating attitudes that kept her from asking questions were also used. Soon she was able to convince herself that asking questions in class was not a sign of stupidity (as she had thought), but of curiosity.

In her last two sessions, Mary reviewed her accomplishments and identified aspects of treatment that had helped her most in controlling her depression. Relaxation, she decided, was the most powerful skill she had learned. Scheduling her time had also been beneficial; she was now aware of the importance of balancing her obligations at school with enjoyable activities. Another improvement that Mary did not mention but that the therapist noted was that she was no longer so self-critical. Indeed, many of her statements now projected self-confidence.

At the last therapy session, Mary again completed the depression symptom inventory. Her posttreatment score was significantly lower than the pretherapy score, corroborating the therapist's impression that Mary was markedly improved.

Mary returned to the clinic for a follow-up interview one month after ending therapy. School was going well, she said. She was especially enjoying a foreign language course and was even making plans to visit that country. Since her last session, Mary had also begun to think seriously and optimistically about the future, although still unsure about the work she would like to do upon graduation. She no longer felt limited to staying within her present, often unsatisfying, field. In regard to her boyfriend, Mary spoke admiringly of him and confided that just the night before they had discussed marriage. Apparently, her gains in therapy had spurred improvements in their relationship. Mary's social life apart from her boyfriend was still fairly limited, but she had begun walking home every day with a woman she had met in class, and she looked forward to their conversations. As one of Mary's complaints at the beginning of therapy had been a lack of friends, especially women, this new relationship was an encouraging development.

Mary's behavior during the final interview conveyed a new self-assurance. She spoke in a more audible, more assertive voice and maintained long periods of appropriate eye contact. Although she had not lost weight, she was more attentive to and pleased with her appearance; she also looked more attractive. Even while discussing difficult problems experienced in the past, Mary was able to avoid making self-deprecating remarks. Instead, she focused on how she had coped with those experiences and on what they had taught her. Her score on the depression symptom list at follow-up indicated that she was maintaining the improvement she had shown at termination.

Mary's success in controlling her depression illustrates the value of a skills-based approach to therapy. Mary mastered skills by doing many assignments. As she acquired the skills to increase pleasant activities and to cope with day-to-day irritations, Mary was able to make improvements in diverse areas of her life. Monitoring her progress enabled her to discover the relationship between her depression and the degree to which she had engaged in pleasant activities. More than ever before, she felt confident in her ability to create a satisfying future for herself.

DISCUSSION

Psychopathology and Diagnosis Many of Mary's symptoms have been experienced by most people at some time in their lives: feelings of depression and pessimism about the future, insomnia, low self-esteem, loss of energy, and a general feeling of being overwhelmed. It is the combination of these symptoms, their persistence over time, and their interference with Mary's functioning, both academically and socially, that indicates the presence of a mental disorder. In Mary's case there is apparently a chronic, mild depression that is called *dysthymic disorder* (from Greek *dys,* bad or difficult, and *thymia,* mood). In addition, there have been some more severe episodes involving a greater number of depressive symptoms (full depressive syndrome), called major depression.

Individuals with dysthymic disorder frequently, as in Mary's case, have superimposed episodes of major depression. It is at those times that they are likely to seek treatment. Both dysthymic disorder and major depression are common disorders in the population, and are among the most frequent diagnoses of psychiatric outpatients. But many people with these disorders are never seen by mental health professionals, and are treated in the offices of nonpsychiatric physicians.

Treatment   There is no consensus in the mental health field as to the most effective treatment for mild depression. Antidepressant drugs and/or a variety of psychological treatments are used. The treatment approach in Mary's case involved a variety of behavioral and educational techniques; it did not involve exploration of unconscious conflicts or focus on the way in which the patient's problems were reexperienced in the relationship with the therapist (see Case 10, "Long-Suffering"). The treatment approach used in Mary's case is one of a number of new, short-term psychotherapeutic programs developed in recent years. These new treatments have several features in common. They tend to be brief and often time-limited (i.e., an agreement is made at the beginning of treatment about how many sessions there will be). They all focus on current problems and relationships rather than early childhood experiences. They often include standardized assessment procedures so that the effect of therapy over time can be measured with some objectivity. Since there is some evidence that all of these treatments are effective, a focus of current research is to compare treatments with each other, with and without drugs.

Mary is certainly a lot better than she was at the beginning of treatment; in fact, she is not only recovered from the current episode, but she seems to be better than she has been in many years. Although one could hypothesize that the treatment has nothing to do with her recovery from a major depression, since that illness tends to be episodic and self-limiting, it is harder to understand the improvement in her chronic mild depression without acknowledging the role of the treatment.

Mary and Dr. Rosenthal (see Case 16, "My Best Friend") both had dysthymic disorder, yet their treatments, both apparently effective, were very different. Mary's treatment was a highly structured program that took only twelve weeks, whereas Dr. Rosenthal's treatment was individually tailored and is still in progress after three years. Although it may seem that Dr. Rosenthal's treatment has brought about more fundamental changes because it involved an exploration of the origins of his difficulties, we do not have evidence as to the relative long-term efficacy of these two kinds of treatment. Until such evidence is available, the choice of treatment will be based on the personal treatment orientation of therapists and the cost in time and money to the patient.

Prognosis   It is impossible to predict how long Mary's improvement will last. Because of her history of several previous depressive episodes, she is at risk for a recurrence. However, even assuming that this happens, any sustained improvement in her chronic mild depression would make the treatment worthwhile.

DEATH OF A FAMILY

Diane Markos, a 38-year-old single female, was referred for cognitive therapy by a therapist who had been treating her for nearly five years for "mild depression." Her condition had recently become much worse. Within a period of three months her depression had intensified to the point that she had lost 15 pounds, she felt tired all the time, she had withdrawn herself from nearly all her usual social activities, and she openly acknowledged thoughts of overdosing on pills. Psychotherapy and treatment with antidepressant medication had produced no improvement.

This change occurred shortly after the breakup of a relationship she had been having with a man for approximately two years. Further discussion with the patient revealed that there had never actually been a commitment of marriage, but she had clung to this hope from early in the relationship. She now saw herself as fat (she was actually about 10 pounds overweight), unattractive, and doomed to be a spinster.

The patient lived alone and worked full-time as a pediatric nurse while pursuing a master's degree in nursing part-time. Although she had never had a wide circle of friends, the past two years had seen her social contacts become even more limited. Other than the few evenings that she spent with her boyfriend, she had gradually managed to work herself into a life of all work and no play, and she was intensely lonely.

The patient was a straight A student, but she had had numerous interpersonal difficulties with fellow students and instructors. She perceived the students as unfriendly and the instructors as uncooperative and unconcerned with the students. She was currently having a particularly difficult time with one professor with whom she was angry for his unavailability to her outside of class.

Her relations with coworkers were similarly troubled. Although she had a reputation as a good staff nurse, she had never been able to hold supervisory positions for any length of time without interpersonal conflicts. Disagreements with underlings and supervisors would engender feelings of rejection and anger in her. On one occasion this had led to her being removed from a supervisory post, and on another she had resigned herself.

The patient's early family history provided some clues to the sources of her current difficulties. She was the eldest of three children and had a sister four years younger and a brother eight years younger than herself. Her younger sister had many health problems early in life, and the patient felt that this caused her parents to shower much more attention onto her sister while they were growing up. Also, she was frequently expected to play the role of caretaker for her younger siblings, and she felt that her parents' love was contingent on her playing the role of "mother's little helper." She felt that her sister and brother had been allowed to lead a much more carefree childhood.

In her later life the sister outgrew her health problems and became very attractive and popular. The patient did not see herself as similarly blessed, and related feeling awkward and unattractive throughout most of her adolescence and young adulthood. In the course of her previous therapy the patient became aware of the jealousy she felt toward her sister, as well as the previously unacknowledged guilt she experienced from it. In fact, her sister's marriage seemed to have been the impetus behind her initial entry into therapy.

In short, the patient saw her past and present as an unhappy life of servitude, rejection, and failure. And she could envision no other scenario for her future. She felt quite hopeless, and was therefore considered to be a serious suicidal risk by her new therapist. For this reason, the first issue dealt with in therapy was her hopelessness. By the end of the first session she had agreed that it was only sensible to adopt a "wait and see" attitude, and her immediate suicidal intent diminished significantly.

As homework she was asked to start keeping a record of *any* satisfactions or pleasures she was deriving from life. Examination of these records provided the material for the early interventions in her treatment. Activities which she already enjoyed (going to the movies, watching soap operas, preparing a favorite dessert, jogging) were increased in frequency and things which she thought she might enjoy were given as homework assignments (joining an exercise class, going to a ballet, enrolling in a poetry workshop).

She initially resisted interrupting the treadmill of all-work-no-play on which she had put herself, but finally accepted as reasonable the idea that she could "pamper" herself while she was feeling so depressed.

As her mood began to improve, attempts were made to understand more clearly the patient's perceptual world. It became apparent that the breakup of her romance had several levels of meaning for her. At one level it represented the loss of what had been an enjoyable relationship. At another level she framed this loss within the context of her advancing age and the diminishing prospect of ever having a family of her own. At yet another level, it represented to her a basic rejection as a desirable woman. What was particularly devastating about the breakup was that she had created an elaborate mental image of life as a married woman. She was going to have two children (preferably a boy first, then a girl) and live in the suburbs. She had even picked out names for the children! It was as if a real family had been destroyed and she was grieving over the deaths of her never-born children.

She was asked to write down her thoughts during stressful situations, and these served as major topics of discussion in later therapy sessions. By the end of ten sessions it was clear that the patient was distorting her perception of reality in several consistent ways. Her thinking often tended to be dichotomous. When she finally did get a B from her professor, she concluded that she had failed miserably. There was no recognition of any middle ground between total academic success and total academic failure. Moreover, she tended to magnify the importance of events like this as if they were an indictment of her as a total human being.

In social situations she often assumed that her emotions were transparent to others. She thought that it would be obvious to anyone how anxious she was and desperate for friendship. Because she thought this, she frequently avoided social situations or became so anxious in them that her idea became a self-fulfilling prophecy.

The therapy actively challenged the logical basis for many of these ideas, and gradually the patient was able to incorporate this reality testing into her own thinking. The therapist asked her to write down her most depressing thoughts and then examine their validity herself. Initially he coached her to ask certain key questions about the thoughts, such as:

"What is the evidence for this?"

"Am I seeing things only in a black or white fashion?"

"Am I taking things out of context?"

"What kind of distortion in my thinking could this be?"

"What's the most useful thing to do?"

Many of her distortions seemed to stem from underlying attitudes that recurred with such regularity that she and the therapist were able to group them under general themes, such as: "If I care for others, they should/must care for me," or "If something good happens to me, I'll have to pay for it later with pain," or "People either love me or hate me." Once these themes became clear to the patient, she was able to see the arbitrary and frequently illogical basis of much of her depressed thinking.

However, there remained in many of her perceptions two streams of thought, one objective and logical and one idiosyncratic, the result of well-entrenched perceptual habits. Rather than try to contradict these more intractable assumptions, the therapist encouraged her to test them out actively in reality. He asked her to make predictions about real-life events based on these assumptions. A number of such experiments were conducted. For example, she predicted that in any social situation she would be seen as overweight and unattractive and that no man would want to be seen with her in public. The experiment consisted of her agreeing to go to a singles' bar for at least an hour on ten separate occasions. Contrary to her prediction, she was asked to dance on six separate occasions by four different men. Also, being propositioned on two separate occasions effectively demolished the notion that no man would find her desirable.

Besides her distorted thinking, there were some realistic aspects to her situation that had to be addressed in treatment. It was a reality that she could no longer have children without some risk, and it was quite likely that she would never have a child of her own. For these kinds of issues the therapist asked her to rethink her philosophical evaluation of the issue and essentially ask herself, "Is this so terrible?" With this approach she gradually reframed her single status. While it precluded many satisfactions, it also facilitated others, such as freedom of travel, economic indulgence, and flexibility of life style.

There still remained a group of problems that were real and required active problem solving. At work, for example, she had been denied an increase in salary when she finally did obtain her degree. A careful appraisal of the situation suggested that she really had been treated unfairly.

For a problem like this, asking herself "What's the most productive thing to do?" proved particularly useful. The therapist worked with her to examine the options available to her (e.g., quitting, appealing to a higher authority, etc.). She was eventually able to work out an appropriate plan involving the formal appeal process where she worked. Eventually she struck a compromise with her superiors—getting a raise, but also taking on added responsibilities.

At the end of twenty-two sessions she no longer felt significantly depressed, she felt more energetic, and there was no evidence of any suicidal ideation. She was continuing to lose weight, but now as the result of planned dieting. Her job situation was also improved and she seemed to be handling her new responsibilities well. Most importantly, she demonstrated an awareness of her own perceptual process that made continued improvement likely. In effect she had become her own therapist—she knew a lot about how her mind worked, and she was able to use this to think and act more effectively.

DISCUSSION

Psychopathology and Diagnosis   Diane Markos, like Mary in the previous case (Case 24, "Learning to Cope"), suffered from chronic mild depression—dysthymic disorder—and recently also developed a major depression. The only diagnostic difference is that Mary's *major depression* is recurrent, while Diane has had only a single episode. Also significant is the contrast in the degree to which the episode seems to be precipitated by a major life event. Diane's episode occurred after she lost what might realistically be viewed as her last chance to get married and have a family, goals that had been a central focus in her life. This kind of depression is often referred to as "reactive," indicating it is in response to a specific environmental stress. Mary's episodes apparently followed minor stresses, such as the breakup of a freshman romance and death of a cat, and starting school again with its academic pressure.

Treatment   Diane received cognitive therapy after five years of traditional psychotherapy and a more recent course of antidepressant drugs, both of which were ineffective. Although her cognitive therapist felt that she was suicidal, he apparently thought this was a long-term risk and not an imminent danger that would have necessitated hospitalization for her own protection. It was particularly important that she became somewhat less hopeless by the end of the first session, since hopelessness is highly correlated with suicidal attempts.

The initial focus of cognitive treatment was to ask her to suspend judgment about the hopelessness of her condition until she had the opportunity to see whether a novel therapeutic approach might make a change in her life. The therapist used the behavioral strategy of encouraging her to engage in activities that gave her pleasure, the major focus in the previous case, but relied even more heavily on cognitive techniques. These involved encouraging her to challenge her customary way of viewing herself and her environment, for example, her tendency to think in terms of total failure or total success, and to exaggerate the personal significance of trivial events. Most importantly, because of the realistic limits imposed by her age on her particular goals, he helped her to reassess the possibility of being contented without necessarily being married or having children. Although there was no fixed time limit on her treatment, after twenty-two sessions she was no longer depressed, and revised her way of thinking about her life, and was therefore more hopeful about her future.

The cases of Diane and Mary illustrate how cognitive-behavioral treatments for depression can be applied in very different ways. In Mary's case, the therapist assumed the content of her thinking was essentially accurate, but she had an inadequate amount of social reinforcement in her life. Therefore, new skills were taught to improve her social and personal effectiveness. In Diane's case, the therapist not only questioned the accuracy of the content of her thinking, but he also questioned how she was processing her everyday experiences; he believed that her thinking was distorted. Although Diane's therapy involved some training in social skills, this assumed a much less crucial role than in Mary's therapy. Finally, some of Diane's concrete problems could not be solved (e.g., having a family), and the only way of dealing with them was to philosophically reevaluate their importance to her happiness. Overall, Diane's treatment consisted of more vigorous modification of what is called "cognitive structure," that is, the content (thoughts, images, and assumptions) of one's thinking and the processes of one's thinking (overgeneralization, all-or-none thinking, etc.). Through questioning and behavioral assignments, the therapist attempted to change some of the assumptions Diane had about her life and the way she perceived it.

Both therapies focused on goals of increased activities, increased socializing, and the eradication of maladaptive thinking. The goals of treatment were thus quite similar, even though the methods were quite distinct.

Prognosis Dysthymic disorder without treatment tends to be chronic. It appears as if cognitive therapy has been successful in interrupting Diane's habitual depressive pattern of viewing herself and relating to the world. Although any individual who has had a major depression is at risk for a future episode, Diane has only had one episode, and this was precipitated by a major stress. If cognitive therapy enables her to deal more effectively with future stressful events, then her long-term prognosis is good.

STORMY WEATHER

Dr. Dubray, a 35-year-old college professor, was referred to a mood clinic by a social worker who was treating his wife for marital problems. The referral note indicated that both Ms. Dubray and the therapist suspected that the inconsistencies in Dr. Dubray's treatment of his wife, including repeated episodes of infidelity, were indicative of an emotional disorder. Dr. Dubray was described as a generally loving and caring spouse who would periodically drink to excess, become verbally abusive toward his wife, and seek "one-night stands" in a neighborhood bar. Similar behavior had led to three previous divorces, and Dr. Dubray now appeared willing to seek professional help to avert a fourth one. He had shown poor compliance with past psychotherapeutic efforts, during which his diagnoses had spanned a range of personality disorders such as passive-aggressive, narcissistic, and antisocial.

Dr. Dubray had grown up in a small southern town. His father was a lawyer who was given to alcoholic excesses. It was his mother who kept the family together. He described his childhood years as "rocky," oscillating with the tempestuous relationship of his parents. He was quieter and more introspective than his siblings and other peers. His mother regarded him as a "child prodigy" and believed that he would "outshine everybody," proving to the world that "an alcoholic's son could shake off his father's liabilities" and become a prominent member of society.

To his mother's frustration, Dr. Dubray's high school and college years were quite uneven, both academically and interpersonally. His grades would typically alternate between As and Fs, to the utter despair of his teachers, who thought he was "brilliant but lazy and apathetic." It took him ten years to obtain a Ph.D. in contemporary literature. He had no difficulty charming the most desired women on campus, but they would "dump" him after a few months, having found his periodic outbursts of anger and verbal abusiveness unbearable. (This was essentially what had also happened in his first three marriages, none of which had lasted more than one year.) He is a charismatic teacher, but again quite uneven; he often comes to class with alcohol on his breath.

His current marriage had lasted three years; Ms. Dubray also had serious problems with alcohol and, because of her marked dependency needs, had elected to stay with him. The marriage had been childless by mutual consent because of the couple's fear that a child might inherit their "nervous proclivities."

When examined, Dr. Dubray denied subjective mood swings per se. He described what he called a fluctuation in his energy level from "a nadir to a zenith." The "nadirs" lasted five to six days, during which he felt mentally clouded, physically slowed down, and wanted to stay in bed for 15 to 16 hours. During the "zeniths" of his energy, which usually lasted two to three days but occasionally extended to a week, he felt "physically fit," with sharpened mental activity, increased self-confidence, and a decreased need for sleep. He elaborated: "I sleep less, but my sleep is of better quality. I just feel perfect—with a lot of energy. I can't wait for the next day. There's nothing I cannot do. I have lots of goals. My work habits are high, and I generally succeed."

However, during some of these times he felt so "wired up" that he had to drink alcohol or smoke marijuana to "bring myself down." It was during these periods that he became irritable, lost his temper, and sought the company of "loose women." He claimed that he "had these affairs for no reason at all" and would feel quite guilty a few days later. He had great difficulty understanding why his energy level fluctuated such that sometimes he would "pace like a panther until I could no longer work or think—then I would become paralyzed, as if my will and spirit were paralyzed; I could move, but without zest or life."

At such times he would resort to the use of stimulant drugs like dexedrine, but eventually he switched into restlessness again. Dr. Dubray also described "even days," irregularly interspersed with the "low" and "high" periods, during which he had a sense of "serenity and peace" but dreaded the onslaught of the other periods. These periods of extreme moods seemed to come "out of the blue, like the weather," and seemed unrelated to external circumstances. It was this very unpredictability of his swings from one state to another, he said, that robbed him of self-confidence, made him feel like "a nervous wreck and a failure," contemplating suicide "as a way out." He elaborated: "As if I have no ego control, things happen to me controlled by some capricious chemical imbalance within me; Doctor, I am sick, but sometimes I think I am a sinner."

Family history revealed that the patient's mother suffered from periodic depressions in the fall and the winter, but had never been treated; she viewed emotional illness as equivalent to moral failure or sinfulness. Her younger brother was a diagnosed manic-depressive, had refused to take lithium carbonate regularly, and had shot himself "accidentally" while hunting alone. One of the patient's sisters had suffered from recurrent severe depressions and was now stabilized on lithium.

In view of the disastrous effects of his mood swings on his personal, marital, and professional life, it was decided to give Dr. Dubray a trial of lithium carbonate after appropriate medical workup. Dr. Dubray's intelligence and the generally unpleasant nature of both the "down" and the "up" phases of his illness assured proper compliance with this treatment when the nature of the illness and expected outcome with lithium salts were explained to him. After twelve months of lithium treatment he now sleeps an average of 7 to 8 hours per night, stimulant and alcohol use have ceased, although he occasionally smokes a "joint," and the promiscuous behavior has disappeared. Energy oscillations do occur, but at a more manageable level, without progressing to "paralysis" or to "restless wiring up." He is now being seen every other month for serum lithium level determinations and receives supportive individual psychotherapy. His stabilization has had a salutary effect on his wife, in that she has accepted treatment for her alcohol problem. When marital problems arise, they see the social worker together.

DISCUSSION

Psychopathology and Diagnosis Dr. Dubray's life is in turmoil because of his unpredictable behavior. He has angry outbursts toward his wife, is impulsively unfaithful to her, and sometimes abuses alcohol and marijuana. His ability to maintain stable relationships with women is seriously impaired—resulting in three previous divorces. His academic and professional performance has always been uneven. This long-standing pattern of pervasive difficulty relating to others and functioning effectively certainly suggests a personality disorder, which, in fact, was the diagnosis made by his previous therapists.

A closer look at the pattern of his difficulties reveals a clustering of symptoms during two distinct phases of a repeating cycle. During the periods that he describes as his "nadir," he has symptoms that are characteristic of the depressive syndrome: he has difficulty concentrating, less energy, psychomotor retardation, and he oversleeps. He sometimes treats himself with amphetamines at such times. During his "zeniths" he has symptoms that are characteristic of the manic syndrome: he is full of energy, needs less sleep, is more active and full of ideas. During these periods he is likely to abuse alcohol and marijuana, lose his temper, and be sexually promiscuous. Even though he does not describe his mood swings as changes from depression to euphoria, it seems pretty clear that during his zeniths he is feeling very good and that during his nadirs he is dysphoric.

Does Dr. Dubray have bipolar disorder (previously called manic-depressive illness)? He states that his "low" periods generally only last five or six days and his "high" periods only two or three days. Both the short duration (less than two weeks for the depressive episodes, and one week for the manic episodes) and the relatively mild nature of the symptoms do not reach the threshold for full-fledged bipolar disorder. These mild, short-lived "highs" are referred to as hypomanic episodes. A pattern of frequent and recurrent periods of hypomania and depression is diagnosed as *cyclothymic disorder*. This is classified with other affective disorders, even though the repetitive interpersonal and occupational difficulties caused by the mood swings may suggest an underlying personality disorder. (Therefore, the additional diagnosis of a personality disorder would not be given in this case.)

When Dr. Dubray drinks to excess, he is abusive toward his wife. It is noted that he often comes to class with alcohol on his breath. This certainly suggests a diagnosis of alcohol abuse, even though it appears that he drinks to excess only when he is in one of his "highs." His alcohol abuse is symptomatic of his mood disorder, whereas in his wife's case, alcohol abuse is apparently the primary emotional disorder.

Course and Family History Cyclothymic disorder is considered to be part of a spectrum that includes bipolar disorder. This is both because patients with cyclothymic disorder often later develop full manic and depressive episodes, and because patients with cyclothymic disorder frequently have family members with clear bipolar disorder. In Dr. Dubray's case, his mother and sister had recurrent depressions, and his brother was diagnosed as manic-depressive.

Treatment Dr. Dubray, like many patients with mood disorders, has attempted to "treat" himself by taking stimulants when he was depressed and alcohol and marijuana when he was high. Stimulants are not effective in treating depression and expose the individual to the dangers of drug dependence and toxic reactions. The loss of inhibition caused by the hypomania is only exacerbated by the use of alcohol, which in Dr. Dubray's case led to his uncharacteristic and aggressive sexual behavior. Because his previous therapists did not recognize his underlying mood disorder, he had never been tried on lithium carbonate. After one year on this treatment he seems to be doing much better. It is hoped that this, combined with his wife's treatment for her problems with alcohol, and their continuing marital therapy, will give this couple the chance for a reasonably satisfactory life.

SCHIZOPHRENIC DISORDERS

STATUE

Todd Phillips, a 16-year-old high school student, was referred to a psychiatric hospital by his family physician. His family had been very upset by his increasingly strange behavior over the preceding eight months. They had consulted their family physician, who treated him with small doses of antipsychotic medication, without any improvement.

Although Todd has had many problems since he was a small child, there was a distinct change about eight months ago. He began spending more and more time in his room and seemed uninterested in doing many of his usual activities. His grades dropped. He started stuttering. He used to weigh about 215 pounds, but began to eat less, and lost 35 pounds. For no known reason, he started drinking large quantities of water.

More recently, there was a change for the worse. A few months ago he began taking Tai Chi lessons and often stood for long periods in karatelike positions, oblivious to what was going on around him. He stopped doing his homework. He took an inordinately long time to get dressed, eat his meals, or bathe. Before getting dressed in the morning he would go through an elaborate ritual of arranging his clothes on the bed before putting them on. When his parents asked him a question, he repeated the question over and over and did not seem to hear or understand what was said.

At school he received demerits for the first time for being late to class. His family began to lose patience with him when he eventually refused to go to school. When his father tried to get him out of bed in the morning, he lay motionless, sometimes having wet the bed during the night. It was at this point that his parents, in desperation, consulted their family physician.

When first seen in the hospital, Todd was a disheveled looking, somewhat obese adolescent, standing motionless in the center of the room with his head flexed forward and his hands at his sides. He appeared perplexed, but was correctly oriented to time and place. He was able to do simple calculations, and his recent and remote memory were intact. He answered questions slowly and in a peculiar manner. An example of his speech follows:

Q: Why did you come to the hospital?
A: Why did I come? Why did I come to the hospital? I came to the hospital because of crazy things with my hands. Sometimes my hands jump up like that . . . wait a minute . . . I guess it's happening . . . Well, yes, see it's been happening (making robotlike gestures with his hands).
Q: What thoughts go through your head?
A: What thoughts go through my head? What thoughts go through my head? Well, I think about things . . . like . . . yes, well . . . I think thoughts . . . I have thoughts. I think thoughts.
Q: What thoughts?
A: What thoughts? What kinds of thoughts? I think thoughts.
Q: Do you hear voices?
A: Do I hear voices? I hear voices. People talk. Do I hear voices? No . . . people talk. I hear voices. I hear voices when people talk.
Q: Are you sick?
A: Am I sick? No I'm not sick . . . these fidgeting habits, these fidgeting habits. I have habits. I have fidgeting habits.

Throughout the examination he made repetitive chewing and biting motions. Occasionally, when questioned, he would smile enigmatically. He seemed unresponsive to much of what was going on around him. His infrequent movements were slow and jerky, and he often assumed the karatelike postures that his parents described, in which he would remain frozen. If the examiner placed the patient's hands in an awkward position the patient remained frozen in that position for several minutes.

Physical and neurological examinations, and laboratory tests were within normal limits. On admission the Wechsler Adult Intelligence Scale verbal IQ was 101 (performance test not administered). The psychologist noted that his responses were slow.

Todd is the oldest of four sons. His father is a bricklayer and his mother a secretary. The family has always lived in the same suburb of a midwestern city. There is a large extended family on his mother's side. The only evidence of serious mental illness in the family is that the mother's oldest brother was confined to a state mental hospital for the ten years before his death at age 53 in 1950. All that she remembers is that he left home at 18, had little contact with the family, and drifted around the country from job to job until he apparently had a "nervous breakdown" in his twenties.

Todd's mother reports that when she was pregnant with him she had persistent bleeding and stayed in bed for two months in order to avoid a spontaneous abortion. She also took large doses of vitamin C and vitamin K. She was in labor for two days, and when it was determined that the baby was in a breech position, he was delivered by caesarean section. There was some question as to whether the umbilical cord had been wrapped around his neck. However, he was considered to be a normal, healthy infant. His mother claimed that he began to say his first words at four months, and by six months was already putting words together. Toilet training was not forced, and he was completely trained by age 3. His mother taught him to read, and she states that he was able to read at $2^1/_2$. Although he was noted to have poor motor coordination, he walked at eleven months.

Todd was first taken to a child psychiatrist at the age of 2 when he refused solid food and insisted on drinking from a bottle after his brother was born.

He never enjoyed school, although he did fairly well in first and second grades, and even won some spelling contests. At 8 he was seen by a psychiatrist who diagnosed him as "hyperactive" and placed him on Ritalin, which he took for three years. The psychiatrist felt that he may have suffered some brain damage from oxygen deprivation because of the cord wrapped around his neck at birth. However, psychological testing at that time indicated that he had a "high IQ" and an "outstanding vocabulary." In fifth grade he was considered to have a learning disability in mathematics and was put in a special class. He had difficulty coping with large classes, and was sent for a time to a private school with smaller classes.

His parents know little of his sexual behavior or knowledge, but assume that he learned about these matters from "the outside." He was interested in girls during his early teens, but no girls returned his interest. During his preteen years he had a recircumcision. This has always been of great concern to him. There is no history of delinquent behavior or use of drugs.

He has generally been very inhibited and passive, which has been a handicap in school and in making friends. He has always been scapegoated, teased, and ridiculed by his peers. From time to time, with his parents' encouragement, he played baseball, but he was never very good. However, he said that he wanted to be a ballplayer or a disk jockey when he grew up. Until recently, he enjoyed watching TV, listening to records, and reading about sports and science fiction.

DISCUSSION

Psychopathology and Diagnosis The most striking feature of this case is the patient's bizarre behavior. The posturing and strange gestures, the uncommunicative speech, and urinating on himself in bed are all clearly out of the range of usual behavior and are not understandable in the context in which they occur. Such behavior suggests the presence of a psychotic disorder, that is, one in which the individual at some point in the illness is grossly out of touch with reality.

The posturing and gesturing are examples of catatonic behavior. His passively remaining in postures into which he is placed is another type of catatonic behavior that is called waxy flexibility.

Although the patient seems to answer questions, there is little information conveyed to the listener by what he says. This is referred to as poverty of content of speech.

Other significant aspects of this case are that the disturbed behavior has lasted a considerable period of time (eight months) and represents a significant deterioration from a previous level of functioning. This change is apparent even though he never functioned at a very high level.

The combination of catatonic motor behavior, uncommunicative speech, and deterioration from a previous level of functioning and the persistence of the disturbance for a considerable period of time suggest a diagnosis of *schizophrenia, catatonic type*. However, severe disturbances in mood (mania or depression) as well as certain organic etiologies (e.g., amphetamines or a hallucinogen) may cause similar symptoms. The only suggestion of an organic factor in this case is Todd's excessive drinking of water. Although a concomitant physical illness to account for this symptom should, of course, be ruled out, there is no known physical illness that could explain all of Todd's symptoms. The absence of a mood disturbance or of a known organic factor in this case further confirms the diagnosis of schizophrenia.

This case illustrates many common features of schizophrenia. Typically, as in this case, there is a gradual increase in psychopathology prior to the development of the overt psychotic symptoms. This often takes the form of social withdrawal, apathy, impairment in role functioning, and eccentricities of behavior and communication. An example of eccentric behavior in this case was a compulsive dressing ritual and his drinking of large quantities of water.

Although catatonic symptoms used to characterize the most commonly seen subtype of the illness, in the last 30 or 40 years in Europe and North America it has become quite rare. The reasons for this change are not known.

Course The onset of schizophrenia occurs typically during adolescence or early adult life, and usually there is no clear environmental precipitant. Often, as in this case, the premorbid personality of individuals who later develop schizophrenia is introverted. Relationships with peers are often inadequate, and the child may be scapegoated by peers. Commonly there is a history of a variety of childhood problems that may be diagnosed, as in Todd's case, as learning disabilities and hyperactivity.

Etiology In the developmental history pre- and perinatal complications are not particularly common among individuals who later develop schizophrenia, but do occur more frequently than in the general population. This suggests that in a subset of individuals with schizophrenia, perinatal brain damage may play an etiologic role. Certain aspects of Todd's reported developmental history are enigmatic. It is hard to believe that his intellectual development was as precocious as his mother claims. This may reflect more about her need to deny the fact that she had a disturbed child than about his actual development.

Although most individuals with schizophrenia do not have a family history of schizophrenia, schizophrenia is more common in their first-degree relatives than in the general population. This suggests the role of a genetic vulnerability to the illness. There is little information about the illness of Todd's uncle; what is known (inadequate work history, isolation from family, and chronic hospitalization) is suggestive of schizophrenia.

Treatment The psychotic symptoms that necessitated hospitalization will most likely subside in a short period of time in response to antipsychotic medication. (This will be in much larger doses than those given by his family physician.) Unlike his unfortunate uncle, Todd will probably be able to leave the hospital within a few weeks or months because of the effectiveness of the medication in controlling the psychotic symptoms. However, it is unlikely that Todd will then be back to his premorbid level of functioning. More likely, he will be left with many of the same symptoms that heralded the development of his illness, such as social withdrawal, apathy, and academic difficulties. Schizophrenia is always characterized by these three phases of illness: a prodromal phase in which there are symptoms such as social isolation and odd behavior, an active phase during which there are overt psychotic symptoms, and a residual phase characterized by symptoms such as those seen during the prodromal phase. Over the course of years, then, there are typically repeated episodes of the active phase, separated by residual symptoms.

Todd will most likely be treated in an outpatient clinic where the treatment will involve psychotherapeutic management to help him cope with the continuing effects of his illness. So that family members may be helpful to him, they may also be included in his treatment.

A decision will have to be made as to how long Todd should remain on antipsychotic medication. It is known that maintenance antipsychotic medication does decrease the likelihood of another episode of psychotic symptoms that would seriously disrupt his life. However, this medication can cause side effects that are unpleasant but reversible, such as stiffness or tremor, or more serious side effects that are irreversible, such as chronic involuntary movements of the muscles of the face and limbs, called tardive dyskinesia. The chewing and biting motions that were noted at his intake examination may actually be symptoms of tardive dyskinesia, since he had previously been on small doses of antipsychotic medication.

Prognosis The long-term prognosis for Todd is poor. With currently available treatment there may well be recurrences of the psychotic symptoms (which probably will take a different form), and between such episodes increasing residual social and occupational impairment.

"TELEKINISES"

Glenn Davis is a 22-year-old commercial artist who lives with his parents and a younger brother in a large metropolitan area. He did well in public elementary and high school, and, according to him, had no significant psychological problems until the events which he describes in a document that he gave to one of his psychiatrists. It is presented here, unedited (including spelling errors), with only the identifying information changed.

I have been an artist since my childhood, being gifted with the ability to draw. I graduated The School of Art in June 1977, having won the prestigious J. award for excellence in Photography.

In 1978 after completing my first year in the R. College, I began working freelance; Photography and Illustration. In the summer of 1978 I began to get a great interest in Fashion Illustration, as I wanted to utilize it to better my Photographic ideas and goal as a Fashion Photographer. In September of 1978, I enrolled in evening classes at B. School of Design, to further my drawing talent and ability. The first two classes went rather smoothly and I increased my drawing capability greatly, but by the third class an occurance began. I was sitting in class thinking to myself what I was going to draw next, when suddenly in an instant someone accross the room said fairly loud what I had just thought. I was completely amazed and could not understand it. Then it happened again and again, and that was the last time I went to that class.

I have analized a possible explanation for the occurance, it may not be correct but it is of my own belief and possibly a very real one. I was not depressed in any manner at the time, I had just won a weekend trip to the V. Resort, had met several very beautiful women and I was very happy. But in that classroom there were these two people who always sat next to each other, a woman and a man, and I could tell that they were extremely jealous of my talent. Now I believe when a person has a good job set for himself, his life is going the way he wants it to, certain people develope added sensory powers. These two individuals may have possessed some ability of Telekinises and by their sheer jealousy, they both first communicated silently to themselves and with both of their powers combined, snapped something in my brain, possibly using too great a polarity to tap my imagination or just to throw a hatred wave, which in turn opened up or activated a channel or series of certain cells within my brain.

In the days and weeks following I noticed it happen again and again, this time with people of all natures, on the street, in stores, etc., being able to read my thoughts and commenting their criticism and at many times laughing at them. Having these catalysts and this somehow formed anity present began to drive me mad, it affected my work and my life began to disolve because of this severe abnormality that suddenly exploded into my life.

Then suddenly I began to hear voices, the first ones were of those two people in that classroom. I remembered them at the end of that four hour class saying things that had no meaning to me at that time, laughing at times and looking directly at me. Then in the weeks to come everything that they said actually happened, the disorientations caused by them and the situations to be transfered because of what they somehow did. I would be working on an illustration and suddenly thought of a unique belt design and I heard in the back of my mind in my inner ear a replay of what they said, the exact discription of the belt. When I heard that I changed the design and then I again recalled them saying, "He caught us, now he is changing the design." It took about 4-8 weeks to totally exhaust all that they had said in the last two hours of that class. The damage was done.

I then began to hear other, all different sounding voices, people whom had read my thoughts, the voice patterns at that time. In the weeks to follow going into 1979 all calibers of voices began to emerge from my inner hearing, (it has now steadied to at least five main all different sounding voices, at high velocity peaks when I am alone the various voice patterns, with telepathy possibly added range up to 50 and more). As the voices continued I found I could not travel anywhere, in the subways, etc., thinking silently to myself because all my silent thoughts were somehow being picked up and read, (I feel I am a very intelligent young man, always scored highly in school and I could tell that this occurance was positively going on, because I tested it on numerous occasions many times over). Then the incoming telepathic mind to mind communications began in the early to mid of 1979. I would go into stores, The Subway, on the street, or any public place and people would be able to talk directly into my mind and hearing, insulting and saying anything they felt about me, reading my inner thoughts and saying them back at me with their criticism. I would be infront of someone, he would look directly at me and speak into my head, which I would hear his voice and if I told him to go screw himself I would be able to tell by his movements and facial expression that he heard me.

In the mid to end of 1979 I tried to continue my Photography and Illustration work, but the voices made it impossible as they would shatter my concentration and neccessary refind thinking and intelligence I needed to complete my work. I tried extremely hard and continued loging my ideas and have never stopped despite what these people, voices have been telling me. Since then I have been praying to the Good Lord a great deal and he has helped me ease the pain of what I am going through.

In 1980 after two years of this I tried Holostic Healing a great deal but I could not break the barrier of it. I could no longer do much personal work at home, so I worked at various jobs throughout 1980 hoping by going out every day, my brain would get strong enough to be able to stop it. I worked with a Computer Firm, a Photographic Color Lab and a Messenger Service, holding all these jobs but the attaganistic voices and severe telepathy continued and became so intollarable that I was forced to quit each one.

By 1981 I was unemployed, unable to work because of this massive destruction. Then the pains began, severe nerve impulses and spasms on all parts of my body, my leg muscles and nerves would jerk continuously for hours, my eye nerves, my arms, chest. The voices and telepathy accelerated to astranomical levels, nonstop for every waking moment. I would be for weeks in a zombie like state, trying to draw anything just to relieve the pain. At some points I would break free and go out to see a movie and I remember twice it paralized both my legs with excrucianating pain for over thirty minutes at both instances. Soon following a pain began in the back of my head and is still continuing.

Then hallucinagenic like facial images began, continuing hour upon hour accompaning the voices along with Telesthesia like transmissions, causing deeper attaganism to insanity, vomital levels. This brain formed disease or whatever it is, is slowly killing me. I must dwelve my mind into all forms of morbid disgust or spacing fantasy when I go out, otherwise they would tear me to pieces, knowing my name, my birthdate to all the names of all the women I have loved on this earth and step by step discription of all the beautiful love we shared together. The combination of the inner voices, facial images, the pains and telepathy, the voices speaking the lowest disgust imaginable, try nothing but to tear me apart and are trying to cause me a painful extremely agonising death.

Since the beginning of this year I have been keeping a carefull log of all that I have been going through, this is the last entry which I have made.

Friday November 20th, 1981.

The insanity I was going through at my home became intollarable to a highest severe state, I just had to go out to try to ease the massive pain. I took the subway to a park, rested for a few moments then the telepathy began again, from the moment I had contact with people. I tried to find a quiet place but the telepathic voices would not stop. The pain in my head continued, nerve endings in my legs, arms, chest, face, spasmatating constantly. I held my head, yelling for it to stop but it did not, I collapsed onto the pavement. I decided there was nothing I could do but to try to make it back home. I walked through the streets, every person I past was spitting their dirt into my head, all types of voice patterns from each nationality, pulling things from my head, twisting them around, others just atta-ganising as if they were amused by what they were perceiving and knowledgingly doing.

My vision began to blurr, tears forming in my eyes. The pain in my head grew greater, nerve pains and spasms getting more painfull as if stinging pain was actually being thrown onto my body by the people I was passing, my face, neck, chest, body. Suddenly one of them looked at me with such jelousy and hatred, smirking, and as he past me I felt an highly severe pain near my heart on my chest area, as if he threw the pain directly at me. At that point I held onto a building edge tightly (I was at the corner), turned to my left and vomited profousously, over and over again, my stomach excerting extreme pain. Then a motorist saw me, got out of his car (he seen that I was very neatly dressed and could not understand what had happened), and helped me to my feet. He asked me if I wanted to be driven to a hospital, I asked if he could just drive me to my home which he did. When I got home I vomited again, the voices and pains continuing. I made it to my bedroom and fell unconsciouly onto my bed. I awoke the following evening with the voices, facial images and nerve pains continuing.

(I have kept myself from commiting suicide, by my constant thought of my Good Brothers and "Rocky", with the words, "That a good fighter never goes down".)

In the process of trying to find help, Mr. Davis admitted himself to the inpatient psychiatric unit of a city hospital, where he stayed for one week. The antipsychotic medication he was given made him too drowsy and uncomfortable, so he checked out and discontinued the medication. He then saw a neurologist and requested brain x-rays, believing there was some organic damage to his brain. The neurologist sent him to the emergency room of a university hospital, and it was there that he finally got help. After trying several different antipsychotic medications, he and his doctor settled on one that eliminated "90 percent" of the voices and unpleasant sensations, but did not make him drowsy. He continued to see his doctor as an outpatient, and while he was not immediately able to return to work, he was busy preparing a new portfolio.

DISCUSSION

Psychopathology and Diagnosis   Because all of the information that is available in this case comes from the patient himself, we do not know if, as he claims, he was entirely well until he started having the strange experiences that he describes so vividly. The appearance of psychotic symptoms out of the blue, without any preceding disturbance in functioning, is so unusual that we wonder whether there were indeed prior changes that Mr. Davis did not note.

He describes a number of experiences, both cognitive (certain beliefs) and per-ceptual (hearing voices), that are so far outside the range of usual human experience as to be obviously pathological. He has a number of bizarre delusions: he experiences his thoughts as being communicated to strangers through a process that he calls "Telekinises," he believes that there are people who have the power to "snap" something in his brain, perhaps by sending out a "hatred wave." He begins to have auditory hallucinations: he hears many voices criticizing him and echoing his own thoughts. Next he experiences somatic hallucinations: he feels "nerve impulses" and pain in all parts of his body. In an attempt to explain all of these strange experiences, he concludes that there must be some people who are trying to hurt him. Thus his delusions are not only bizarre, they are persecutory.

In Mr. Davis's written account of his illness there is a peculiar use of language. In some instances he seems to be making up his own words: " . . . this somehow formed *anity* present began to drive me mad . . . ," "others just *attaganising* as if they were amused . . . ." Made-up words or words used in an extremely idiosyncratic way are called neologisms. In other instances he puts words and phrases together in a strange way: "Then in the weeks to come everything that they said actually happened, the disorientations caused by them and the situations to be transfered because of what they somehow did." This unusual use of language that interferes with communication is sometimes referred to as thought disorder, and suggests disorganization of thinking. In its more extreme forms (see Case 31, "Never Say Die") this may make meaningful communication impossible.

Mr. Davis says that he was unable to concentrate and therefore unable to hold even a low-level job. His difficulty concentrating may have been not only because of the voices but because his thinking was disorganized.

Mr. Davis believes that he may have something "organically" wrong with his brain, but there is nothing in this case to suggest the real presence of a known organic factor. There is also nothing to suggest an affective disorder. Therefore, the combination of delusions, hallucinations, thought disorder, and marked deterioration in functioning, with a duration of three years, establishes the diagnosis of *schizophrenia*.

Since persecutory delusions are the most prominent symptom of Mr. Davis's illness, the subtype is paranoid. Contrasting this case with Case 32, "Framed," illustrates the difference between schizophrenia, paranoid type, and paranoia. In both disorders there are persecutory delusions, but in schizophrenia there are other psychotic symptoms in addition, such as hallucinations or formal thought disorder. In addition, in schizophrenia there is always marked deterioration in functioning, whereas in paranoia often social functioning remains intact.

Course   The paranoid subtype of schizophrenia tends to have its onset at a later age and a more favorable prognosis. Mr. Davis has responded to low doses of an antipsychotic medication, and it is hoped that he will not have a recurrence of his acute symptoms.

EVERYTHING BELONGS TO GOD

Harold Jameson is a single 28-year-old Black man who has been attending a day hospital in a community mental health center. Three days after his therapist left for vacation, he appeared in the emergency room of a local hospital complaining that he was confused, depressed, and fearful. He had been hearing voices and "seeing colors," and requested admission to the inpatient unit because he was afraid to go home.

The first indications of Mr. Jameson's illness occurred when he was 19. He had graduated from high school and was studying voice and working in a music store. He precipitously left the Catholic church, in which he had been raised, and became passionately involved with a fundamentalist Christian group. He spent all his free time at church, going on weekend retreats and entering into "consecrations" that involved fasting and abstaining from sex and alcohol. He soon began to feel that his employer was treating him like a slave, and quit his job. He claimed to be "the ambassador of Christ" and became preoccupied with what he felt was his special mission. On a visit to the World's Fair, he upset his mother by making bizarre gestures, standing and staring for long periods, and laughing and crying to himself. The next day he went to work at a new job but walked out after an hour. He was picked up by the police in Macy's, where he had shoplifted some clothing in a very obvious manner, claiming that he was not stealing because "everything belongs to God."

Admitted to the city hospital, he was agitated and unable to sleep; he heard the voice of God and saw the face of the Devil. He was transferred to a state hospital where he remained for three months, and was treated with antipsychotic medication.

After being discharged he resumed his voice lessons and found a part-time job as a custodian. He functioned relatively well for nine months, but then had a recurrence of the same symptoms and was rehospitalized.

During the intervening eight years, Mr. Jameson has been hospitalized seven times for periods ranging from two weeks to three months. Most of these episodes of illness have begun with increasing preoccupation with religion, followed by agitation, delusions, and hallucinations, until finally Mr. Jameson would begin talking in a manner that did not make sense, and he would be brought to the hospital by his family or associates. Mr. Jameson apparently had stopped taking his medication prior to several of these admissions, because he felt he was well and did not need it any longer.

During his last few hospitalizations there were other complicating factors. Mr. Jameson had begun to drink heavily and smoke marijuana, and this, combined with his history of illness, made it more difficult for him to get jobs. He spent some time in a vocational rehabilitation program, but for most of the past three years has been either in a day hospital or just "hanging out."

Two of his previous hospitalizations were apparently precipitated by specific events: his father's hospitalization for medical problems and his therapist's leaving. On admission both of these times he was depressed, not sleeping or eating, and had made suicide gestures by taking increased doses of his medication. He also heard voices telling him to kill himself. During these hospitalizations he received antidepressants as well as antipsychotic medication.

Mr. Jameson is the second son of a middle-class family living in Harlem. His father was a printer until severe arthritis made it impossible for him to work. Even when he was working, the father was a "binge drinker" who was frequently abusive and violent with his wife and children; during his eight years on disability his binges have merged into one another, and he is nearly always somewhat intoxicated and hostile. Ms. Jameson is an anxious, timid woman who works as a secretary for the Red Cross. She was at home with the children until the patient was 11. She then spent three years in and out of psychiatric hospitals for unknown reasons. (The children were placed in a Catholic home during this time.) Since the patient was 14 she has been working full-time at her current job. Mr. Jameson has a brother two years older who was the "bad boy" of the family. He is a heroin addict, and has been living away from home, on welfare, since he was 18.

Mr. Jameson describes his early years as "happy." According to the family, he walked and talked "at the normal times." He was pleasant and friendly, probably overly obedient, and clearly had an intense relationship with his mother, who counted on him to fulfill some of her own unrealized dreams. He was an average student, but because of his musical talent got a lot of recognition from peers and school personnel. He received a music scholarship on graduation from high school.

Mr. Jameson claims to have had close friends during his high school years, but became more isolated as he grew older. He had his only serious girl friend at 18, but she left him because he refused to continue a sexual relationship. (This was prior to his becoming involved with the fundamentalist church. Joining the church was part of his attempt to "purify" himself.)

When not acutely ill, Mr. Jameson is an engaging, alert, somewhat obsequious young man who speaks in an ornate and convoluted manner, using many multisyllabic words, and sometimes making up his own words. The following is a verbatim excerpt from an interview done when he was attending the day hospital:

Q: How do you spend your time?

A: I spend my days by, of course, perhaps shopping in the morning very quickly for what might be, or what is, rather, my lunch, and from that point I go to the clinic branch at approximately 9:00 and spend the day there in which I might be involved with musical programs, or devising basically any kind of musical forms that I can in order to participate with the O.T. program.

Q: Did you have a group of friends that you hung out with?

A: We found that most of our time was consumed being involved with studies or tasks that might be assigned or what have you. But after school most of the coagulations would begin as far as basically about friendships and et cetera.

Mr. Jameson was hospitalized and begun on prolixin—a long-acting, injectable antipsychotic drug, and within two weeks the delusions and hallucinations had disappeared and he was no longer anxious. He returned to the day hospital and resumed treatment with his therapist who had returned from vacation. In the next five years Mr. Jameson had no further hospitalizations. He stated that the medication made him feel good, and although he was not able to work, he had no recurrences of the delusions, hallucinations, and disorganization that had occurred in the past. He lived with his mother (his father was now chronically hospitalized), and spent his days at the day hospital, where he organized a patients' chorus. Mr. Jameson's use of alcohol and marijuana tapered off, to the point that it no longer seemed to create problems for him. His inability to return to work or school was, in part, the result of his unwillingness to give up grandiose notions of what was an appropriate job for him. He claimed to be content with his life.

DISCUSSION

Psychopathology and Diagnosis   There can be little doubt about the diagnosis of schizophrenia in this case. Mr. Jameson has a history of delusions (e.g., he was the "ambassador of Christ") and hallucinations (e.g., he heard the voice of God and saw the face of the Devil), incoherent speech (talking in a manner that did not make sense), bizarre behavior (e.g., laughing and crying to himself in public), and deterioration in his functioning over a period of many years. This clinical picture is characteristic of the illness.

Schizophrenia is subclassified according to the most prominent symptoms of the current episode. Because of the lack of prominence of persecutory delusions (as in paranoid subtype), frequent incoherence and inappropriate or silly affect (as in disorganized subtype), and catatonic behavior (as in catatonic subtype), the most appropriate subtype is undifferentiated. The course of the illness is considered "chronic" because signs of the illness have been present for many years, and "with an acute exacerbation" as evidenced by the recurrence of psychotic symptoms ("hearing voices and 'seeing colors' ") that he described in the emergency room.

The only other diagnosis that should be considered for this case is major depression, recurrent, with psychotic features, since several of Mr. Jameson's episodes were characterized by depressed mood along with delusions and hallucinations. However, it does not appear that the full depressive syndrome (that is, a depressed mood accompanied by several other symptoms of depression such as loss of appetite, trouble sleeping, difficulty concentrating, and suicidal thoughts) was present during each episode. In addition, in between the acute episodes the patient was still unable to work and was somewhat socially isolated. These are classic signs of residual schizophrenia, and suggest that diagnosis rather than major depression, which tends to be episodic. Therefore, *schizophrenia* is the primary diagnosis, although there are also superimposed depressions.

The individual with schizophrenia is not immune to other psychological problems; in fact, depression and substance abuse are relatively common in individuals with the disorder. Two of Mr. Jameson's hospitalizations were primarily for symptoms of depression occurring after stressful life events—his father's hospitalization and his therapist's leaving. During these periods he had insomnia, poor appetite, and was suicidal. Severe depressions, such as this, occurring in a patient with chronic schizophrenia are different from major depressions occurring in individuals without a chronic psychotic disorder. For that reason, such depressions are diagnosed as atypical depressions. Mr. Jameson also apparently used alcohol and marijuana to excess, perhaps even to the extent of warranting the additional diagnoses of alcohol and cannabis abuse.

Course As is often the case, the first signs of Mr. Jameson's schizophrenic illness appeared during late adolescence. Since then there has been a typical course of recurrent acute psychotic episodes (referred to as acute exacerbations) with increasing functional impairment between each episode.

Treatment Mr. Jameson was treated with antipsychotic medication, both to control the acute psychotic episodes and to prevent further episodes. Even when patients are told the importance of continuing to take their medication, they often stop after the acute episode subsides. In Mr. Jameson's case the reason that he often stopped taking his medication is not clear. Some patients do so because they find the side effects very unpleasant. Others may stop because they do not like to think of themselves as ill and requiring medication. In some cases patients may stop taking the medicine as their thinking becomes disorganized with the onset of another exacerbation. Eventually Mr. Jameson was given antipsychotic medication in a long-acting injectable form that only needs to be given every two weeks. This was probably done because of a concern that, on his own, he would again discontinue taking his daily medication. This seems to have been a wise decision, since there have not been any exacerbations requiring hospitalization since that time.

For the last five years, Mr. Jameson's life has revolved around the day hospital. Although it is true that he has not been able to work, marry, and have a family, and certainly has not fulfilled his early promise as a singer, his life is probably considerably better than it would have been if he had lived twenty or thirty years ago. With the help of antipsychotic medication, psychotherapeutic management, and the structure provided by the day hospital he has been spared a life that in the past might have been spent on the back ward of a state hospital.

Prognosis The prognosis for Mr. Jameson is certainly not good. It is unlikely that he will ever function very much better than he does currently—barring some breakthrough in the treatment of chronic schizophrenia. A particularly difficult time for him will be when his mother dies and he no longer has a home. Whether he will be able to manage his own household remains to be seen.

ANOTHER DIMENSION

Police took Rick Wheeler off an airplane at International Airport "probably because I was on another dimension" and brought him to the hospital three days after his discharge from a nearby state hospital. He is a neatly groomed 26-year-old man with wide-staring eyes, friendly and cheerful, but without seeming to be in much emotional contact with his interviewer. He knows who and where he is, and knows the date if asked correctly:

Q: What is the date?
A: Well, I think we're back to ground zero.
Q: What is the date in conventional time?
A: January 15, 1981. [Correct]

On admission he stated that he is Jesus Christ, that he can move mountains, that the Devil wants to kill him and his food contains ground-up corpses, and that he had been born from his father's sexual organs. His speech is quite difficult to follow. For example, he plans to leave this city "because things happen here I don't approve of. I approve of other things but I don't approve of the other things. And believe me it's worse for them in the end."

Q: For whom?
A: Them.
Q: Who is "them"?
A: Them. You know we can both walk out of here together.

He admitted to hearing voices continually, but would not discuss their messages. Occasionally he saw solid objects as transparent.

Physical examination and laboratory studies were all normal.

His family reported that Rick was developing normally until be began abusing drugs in adolescence, but he himself says his problems began about third grade, and that he never seriously abused any drugs besides alcohol. First and second grades went well and he easily learned to read, but thereafter deteriorated: "I could comprehend but I couldn't store . . . it's like looking at something but being unable to take it in." He had a D average until he left high school, halfway through his junior year. He then attended vocational rehabilitation classes, where he showed some talent for auto mechanics but couldn't focus his attention long enough to really master anything. He has never held a full-time job. His social adjustment was always poor, from early elementary school, and he showed no interest in girls until, at 19, he married a woman he had met while both were patients in a state hospital. He has no idea where she and their daughter are, and he has had no further interest in women.

He was first hospitalized at age 16, and there have been about 20 hospitalizations since, all with symptoms similar to his present ones, although his condition is gradually getting worse. For several years he has been supported on federal disability. Typically he is released from the hospital about the first of the month, in time to get his monthly check, which he spends in about a week's time, largely on liquor. He is then arrested for drunkenness and destruction of property and sent to jail, or he is picked up because of bizarre behavior and sent to a mental hospital, where his mental status gradually improves in time for him to be discharged about the first of the next month. (Numerous attempts to commit him involuntarily for longer periods of time have failed, as after a few weeks of treatment he appears reasonably competent in court.) He has been declared incompetent to receive his own checks. Various relatives have handled his money, but are now afraid to do so. For example, he recently set his grandmother's house on fire in retaliation for her withholding some of his money from him (which she was in fact not doing). He has been arrested several times for carrying concealed firearms.

Rick is the eldest of five children, his siblings all without a history of mental disorder. His paternal grandmother was a heavy abuser of stimulants, and a paternal uncle spent three years in a mental hospital, with unknown symptoms.

He is convinced there is nothing wrong with his mind, and no reason for him to be in the hospital. Indeed, in the hospital he is in even greater danger than usual, he believes, and therefore regularly demands his release.

In the present hospitalization Rick was treated for five weeks with two different antipsychotic medications, but showed no improvement. Since he could not earn a living and could not manage his own disability payments, and since everyone else was afraid to manage his money for him, a guardianship was requested for him in the hope of being able to give him longer term treatment than he would voluntarily accept. (In some states, a guardian is a legally appointed person who is able to make decisions on behalf of a patient who is judged to be incompetent.) At this time he still believed he had supernatural powers and special connections with the governments of the world; he still refused most food because it was being "influenced" and contained ground corpses; he still felt his bodily organs were being rearranged; and he still threatened bodily harm to anyone who didn't cooperate with him, including a staff member who would not give him $34 for a $4 money order made out to "God in Heaven." He was still difficult to follow: "I did something for a whole something, let's put it that way. It's very important to them but it didn't affect this." He was certain, however, that he could evade the guardianship and regain his freedom—"if I don't talk supernatural I can pass a psychiatric exam"—and indeed his conversation about his very complex legal and financial affairs was quite lucid and rational. As he had predicted, the court dismissed the application for guardianship and Rick was discharged from the hospital. Arrangements were made for him to live in a protected boarding house, where he remained for four days after his discharge and then disappeared.

DISCUSSION

Psychopathology and Diagnosis   Rick Wheeler's long history of delusions (e.g., he was born from his father's sexual organs), hallucinations (he hears voices continually), and disorganized speech clearly establishes a diagnosis of *chronic schizophrenia*. Because of the mixture of different kinds of psychotic symptoms, the subtype is undifferentiated.

In many respects Rick's illness is similar to Harold Jameson's (Case 29, "Everything Belongs to God"). Both were first hospitalized in late adolescence and had many subsequent hospitalizations associated with bizarre behavior and flagrant delusions. Both also had problems with alcohol abuse. Rick's illness differs from Harold Jameson's in that the psychotic symptoms seem to be always present, even when he is discharged as somewhat improved. Another difference is that Rick's speech is almost always disorganized, and despite the fact that he seems to speak in whole sentences, very little information is actually communicated. This is called poverty of content of speech, and is generally a poor prognostic sign. This patient also demonstrates emotional responses that are inappropriate to the content of his delusions. He is cheerful and friendly to the interviewer while he claims that "the Devil wants to kill me and my food contains ground-up corpses."

Treatment   Rick is, unfortunately, in that small group of individuals with schizophrenia who do not seem to respond to antipsychotic medication. His condition poses a terrible dilemma for his family and for the community. His behavior is sometimes violent and antisocial; this leads to his arrest and confinement in jail. However, it is then obvious that he is mentally ill and in need of treatment. He is not brought to trial because he is not competent to stand trial. Once he is sent to a mental hospital, it is impossible to hold him involuntarily for more than a few weeks because he improves enough to appear reasonably competent and no longer dangerous. He is released and the cycle begins again.

Before our society became concerned with the civil liberties of mental patients, large numbers of patients remained involuntarily hospitalized for years, even when many of them could have lived in the community. The laws that now guarantee the rights of these patients to remain in the community unless they are an imminent danger to themselves or others creates a "Catch-22" for patients such as Rick Wheeler. He cannot be kept in jail because he is "crazy." He cannot be kept in a hospital because he does not stay "crazy" enough.

NEVER SAY DIE

Robert is a young man of 23 who appeared for his second admission to a psychiatric hospital at the urging of his parents because of, in his own words, "the social pressure to perform." His voice tone was expressionless, without feeling, and he grimaced as he spoke. He answered questions in a peculiar and illogical way. He said that concentrating on the questions was like "looking into a bright sun." When asked, "How have you been feeling?" he answered, "I'm as sure as you can help me as I have ice cubes in my ears." When asked to telephone his family, he refused because "insects come out of the little holes."

On admission, physical and neurological exams were within normal limits. His full-scale IQ on the Wechsler Adult Intelligence Scale was 98, but he had considerable difficulty on comprehension questions due to his very special and illogical speech. On the ward he was withdrawn and slept 15 hours a day, but never felt that he had enough rest. He heard "voices," but seemed less interested in them than in the "numbness" of his eyebrows, which he attributed to a bee sting some months ago.

During his hospitalization Robert became preoccupied with his misdeeds as an adolescent. Repeatedly, he requested to be sent to jail for various reasons, not the least of which was that little work would be expected of him there. He felt pressure from his parents to work, but he had very little motivation to do so and had no career plans.

A major concern of his was his physical health. He was preoccupied with his diet, fasting for long periods and drinking no liquids that were certain colors. He described himself as a "urine reservoir," and received "messages" directing his diet and his personal hygiene from the ward television set. He believed that soap commercials, for example, were warning him against using excessive amounts of colored soap.

Robert is a middle child of four children. His father is an attorney and his mother a nurse. Robert was born while his father was completing law school. The other siblings include brothers six and eight years older than Robert, both of whom have completed college and married, and a brother four years his junior. His younger brother was reported to have had academic difficulties and involvement with street drugs. Medical and family history are unremarkable except for an aunt who had alcoholism.

His mother reports that her pregnancy with Robert was normal and his delivery uncomplicated. He achieved all developmental milestones at the appropriate times. His mother described Robert as a child as "a darling and popular kid" with many playmates. At age 5 he sustained a head injury with loss of consciousness for approximately 7 hours, but there were no apparent consequences of this injury, and subsequent electroencephalograms and neurological exams have been normal. In elementary school Robert did quite well and received good grades. In junior high, however, both he and his parents noted a marked decline in his academic performance. In addition, he was observed to be somewhat withdrawn socially and "quieter."

In high school much conflict developed between Robert and his parents, chiefly around his deteriorating schoolwork and intermittent use of marijuana and alcohol. During this period there were other behavioral problems as well. Robert was involved in several car accidents and in a series of petty robberies in which he was a passive participant. At the point of graduation from high school his grade average was sharply lower than his earlier performance. Despite this, Robert entered technical school upon graduation, but dropped out six months later, again with a poor performance record. For the next year he supported himself with odd jobs.

At age 18 his behavior changed dramatically. He made an abrupt change in his eating habits, refusing any liquid that contained certain colors. He was said to be "depressed," and expressed ideas that were incomprehensible to those around him. He was hospitalized for the first time and treated with a course of electroconvulsive therapy and antidepressants. He was followed for one year after hospitalization on medication, but with little symptomatic relief. Eventually, Robert discontinued his medication and began to drift between home and elsewhere around the country, living out of a suitcase and working at odd jobs. While visiting his parents he mentioned hearing the voices of men and women, but dismissed these as having been present "ever since he was born." His functioning varied little for the five years prior to his second hospital admission.

Upon this second admission, Robert was considered a candidate for an aftercare study supported by the National Institute of Mental Health, designed to explore factors that either precipitate or avoid relapse, and that enhance or impair personal and social adjustment among patients with schizophrenia. The program seeks to apply treatments that logically follow from the theory that in schizophrenia there is a psychophysiological deficit that is triggered or exacerbated by certain environmental stimuli. Medication helps in regulating internal states, and psychosocial treatments are designed to help gain control over adverse external stimuli. Robert and his family voluntarily agreed to participate in the program from the two years following hospital discharge. The patient and his family then entered a study in which patients were randomly assigned to one of four treatment groups, each of which included supportive psychotherapy and medication management, either alone or in combination with social skills therapy, family therapy, or both. Robert and his family were assigned to the treatment group that received all three therapies.

Evidence of persistent psychosis, the absence of social skills needed to establish and sustain even modest interpersonal relations, and a family overwhelmed with an illness beyond their understanding and management made Robert an ideal candidate for the program—and a clinical challenge. Here was a patient with a clear deteriorating course; the prognosis painted with the broad brush of hopelessness and despair.

Robert's three clinicians met weekly to share information and revise goals and strategies that strove to enhance patient and family adjustment to everyday life stress or crisis events. The principal goal of the team was the resolution of his psychosis and the prevention of a relapse.

Robert met biweekly with his nurse clinician in order to identify the goals of treatment clearly as he progressed through the aftercare program. The nurse clinician continued to observe and assess the clinical course of the illness and both the wanted and the undesirable effects of the antipsychotic medication. These systematic data became a source of information to the team in modifying the nature and timing of treatment strategies.

A large component of supportive psychotherapy includes educating the patient about schizophrenia, his antipsychotic medication, and its side effects. The nurse clinician assisted Robert in integrating suggestions for improving his coping style needed to deal effectively with the pressures of family, social, and vocational life.

After months of difficulty, an optimal dose of medication was achieved that provided relief from his confused thinking and altered perceptions with minimal side effects. Knowledge of Robert's small steps in mastering the environment and awareness of his family's increased skills in managing were important sources of information needed to adjust medication appropriately. Since few expectations for performance are made in the first year post discharge, time to "heal" was encouraged. One effect was a gradual return of a more normal mood and affect without antidepressant medication.

Robert participated in a social skills training program for two years following his hospitalization. The major goals of this therapy were to teach him specific social skills needed to decrease family conflict, as well as conversational skills necessary for positive social interactions with family and others. A basic tenet of this therapy is that the responsibility for changing behavior is the patient's, and there is an expectation that his behavior can, with help, be controlled. The pace of this therapy, by design, was quite slow and based upon empirical data regarding his difficulties in processing new information, his vulnerability to overstimulation, and his poor premorbid social functioning. Using behavioral and family assessments, several behavioral targets for social skills training were identified, including decreasing the length of his statements and irrelevant remarks, increasing the modulation of his voice tone, and decreasing his facial grimaces. Robert also demonstrated several types of deficits in social perception, namely, in the ability to identify and interpret the feelings and intentions of others. In addition, this assessment identified key interactional problems in his family amenable to social skills training.

Using the techniques of instruction, modeling, role playing, and feedback, the social skills therapist coached Robert to make more effective and simple responses and to interpret the social cues of his family members more accurately. Robert also completed homework assignments in which he practiced various types of responses to specific family members. Problem situations involving strangers, friends, and employers became the focus of social skills training in the second year of the program. Robert made gradual, sustained progress, especially in expressing his feelings in a clear, concise way and in initiating appropriate conversations with his family and others.

Shortly after Robert was hospitalized his family entered the treatment program. The goals were to increase the stability of the family environment by increasing the family's knowledge of schizophrenia and their self-confidence and ability to react positively to Robert. By educating the family members in appropriate management techniques for coping with Robert's symptomatology, the treatment team helped them to decrease the pressures placed on him and thus diminish the possibility of overstimulation from aspects of family life that could lead to relapse. Structuring the family environment decreased the anxiety of all family members and allowed Robert and his family to move at a slow, nonthreatening pace toward individuation and emancipation.

These goals were accomplished through a four-phase family treatment program. Phase I involved connecting with the family and giving them a chance to discuss their feelings about Robert and his illness. This was particularly helpful for Robert's younger brother, who felt angry and helpless because his brother was making life at home miserable with his bizarre rituals and rules of living. Giving the family a chance to ventilate without Robert being there helped reduce their stress and made them more receptive to practical suggestions on how to cope with him.

Phase II was a day-long workshop for the family (also attended by members of four or five other families with similar problems) that provided information about schizophrenia and psychotropic medication, and gave concrete suggestions for management. In addition, the workshop had the added benefit of promoting a process of de-isolation, since Robert's family met a number of other people who were in a similar situation.

The effect of the workshop was immediate. During the next family session Robert's father was able to express an understanding of his son's lethargy and lack of motivation. His mother, who to this point had been extremely overinvolved and accepting of her son's behavior even when he was abusive toward her, was able to begin to see that she needed to set some limits with him.

Phase III was a reinforcement of the management themes discussed in the workshop. Rules of living were discussed, and appropriate expectations for Robert were established. Many of the issues raised at the beginning of treatment were discussed and worked out in a low-key, benign manner. For example, one of Robert's rules was that everyone, including guests, had to take off their shoes before entering the house. For a period of time the family went along with this so as not to upset Robert, but his siblings were becoming increasingly distressed because Robert made their friends observe this rule also. During one session, it was decided that this rule was unreasonable, and after some discussion, Robert agreed not to get upset about other people disregarding it. "Insight" into why he developed this rule was ignored and the discussion focused only on what to do about it.

As Robert's clinical state stabilized, gradual pressure was placed on him to reassume some responsibility around the house in the form of chores. Each step was decided as a family, and they were helped to understand that recovery was a slow process with numerous ups and downs.

Phase IV was a maintenance phase as Robert began to resume his normal role in the family and assume added responsibilities. After eighteen months of post-hospital treatment, he entered vocational training for welding. During this time progress was very slow and gradual, but there were no relapses or rehospitalizations. Robert became more active physically and demonstrated a sincere interest in social and vocational activities. In social situations, he responded more spontaneously and appropriately to others and spoke with greater affective expression. In addition, the vocational counselors reported considerable gains in his ability to sustain goal-directed, self-motivated activities for longer periods of time. Although competitive employment is not possible at this time, progress is definitely being made toward this goal. Importantly, the family viewed themselves as a primary and positive resource for Robert, and able to help in the management of his illness.

DISCUSSION

Psychopathology and Diagnosis Robert's most obvious symptom when admitted to the hospital was his peculiar manner of speaking. Most of what he said made no sense because the connections between ideas was either missing or entirely unclear. What did he mean when he said, "I'm as sure as you can help me as I have ice cubes in my ears," or when he said that concentrating on their questions was like "looking into a bright sun"? While a poet may purposely speak in metaphors, Robert clearly was unable to speak in a way that others could understand. When speech is so disorganized that it makes no sense, it is described as incoherent. Incoherent speech is an extreme form of what is sometimes referred to more generally as thought disorder. Thought disorder includes various disturbances in the form of speech that interfere with its understandability, and is distinguished from disturbances in the content of speech, such as delusions.

The combination of incoherence, delusions (e.g., messages from the television set), hallucinations (hearing voices of men and women), and a long illness involving deterioration in functioning all suggest the diagnosis of *schizophrenia*. The absence of a known organic etiology and a persistent affective syndrome confirm the diagnosis. Because Robert's predominant symptoms when he was admitted were incoherence accompanied by blunted affect, the subtype would be disorganized. This subtype used to be called hebephrenic because often such patients act in a silly, childlike manner (from Greek *hebe*, child).

Treatment The unique feature of Robert's treatment is the combination of medication, supportive psychotherapy, social skills therapy, and family therapy. The medication treats the acute psychotic symptoms and, hopefully, works against relapses, but is of no value in treating the negative symptoms of his illness— the absence of appropriate affective responses and social judgment which has left his life in a shambles. For these problems Robert's treatment employs an educational model: Robert and his family are taught about his illness and how he needs to practice certain more adaptive behaviors, such as speaking more concisely and coherently and controlling his facial grimaces. Although considerable attention is given to teaching Robert how to deal with his family and other psychological stresses, no use is made of the psychodynamic model in which the patient is encouraged to explore childhood experiences or the current unconscious origins of his maladaptive behavior. Psychodynamic psychotherapy in the treatment of schizophrenia was quite popular in recent decades, but several more recent studies have cast doubt on its effectiveness.

Prognosis   Robert's illness is characterized by many features that generally predict a very poor outcome: early onset, blunted affect, and social isolation. The treatment that he is now getting probably gives him the best available chance to function independently in the community.

PARANOID DISORDERS

FRAMED

Pete Dunn was brought to the hospital by his brother, who took seriously Pete's threat to kill the people who were after him, and who he believed were trying to "frame" him as a homosexual.

He is a slender 22-year-old man. He was rather angry at being hospitalized—"there ain't no reason for me being here"—and primarily concerned with how to get out of the hospital, but he was appropriate and cooperative in interviews. He knew who and where he was, knew the date, and had no difficulty with his memory. He talked perfectly rationally and logically, and there was nothing unusual about his speech. Aside from his desire to leave the hospital, the main theme of his conversation was that there was a conspiracy to spread the rumor that he was a homosexual. He denied ever seeing visions or hearing voices. He did report overhearing people referring to him as a "punk," probably a misinterpretation of an actual conversation. He had no experience of his thoughts being broadcast, of thoughts being inserted into his mind, or other similar phenomena. He considered all his difficulties realistic, and was certain that he had no "mental problems."

In Pete's view, his difficulties began about two years before, when a coworker took a dislike to him and started the rumor that he was a homosexual. A year later, when Pete cursed at another fellow employee for insinuating he was a homosexual, he got fired; but the same man who had started all the trouble had conspired with the police, so that wherever Pete went—jail, a new job—he believed that people thought he was a homosexual. He lost another job after he cursed out another fellow employee for the same thing. He felt that on at least two occasions these people were threatening to attack him, so he began carrying a gun to defend himself, and he made plans to jump one of them.

According to the family, Pete's fears seemed quite plausible at first, but when they tried to verify his story, they could find no evidence of any such conspiracy. They said that in the past several months he more frequently accused people of being out to get him, calling him a "sissy," framing him, being out to kill him. First he began taking a knife with him everywhere, then he took to carrying an empty gun (and bullets in his pocket), which he actually pulled on a neighbor, who himself owned a gun but talked Pete out of a confrontation. He had lately been too frightened to go to work, so he had been staying home with his family. However, he had recently come to believe that both his mother and his brother were also involved in the conspiracy.

Pete has an older brother and three younger half-sisters. There is no family history of mental illness. His father died when he was a small child. He got along well with his family, but resented his stepfather. He did poorly in school, quit halfway through high school, then attended technical school for a year, learning the sheetmetal trade. Until shortly before his admission he had supported himself at a variety of unskilled and semiskilled jobs. His work has always been satisfactory, but he lost jobs recently because of his fear of other employees, or his uncontrollable anger at them because of the "conspiracy."

As far as can be determined, there is no history of homosexuality, and Pete said that his sexual dreams and fantasies all involved females. He was married about eight months prior to his hospital admission, to a woman he had known for two-and-a-half years. She was pregnant at the time. He described her as "everything anyone could ever want." He and his wife separated a few days after their marriage, when he lost his job, but he has remained emotionally close to her and their year-old son. He spends much of his time after work visiting them. He has no other friends.

Shortly after separating from his wife, he was convicted on two counts of drunken driving, and became involved in an alcoholism treatment program. Apparently there have been no other social effects of his drinking. According to him, his excessive drinking was limited to periods of emotional turmoil, and never exceeded a six-pack of beer in an evening, after which he would typically fall asleep; this was his drinking pattern during the period right before his admission to the hospital. He denied ever having used illicit drugs. His brother confirmed that, despite the drunken-driving charges, alcohol had not been a frequent or major source of difficulty.

Throughout his seventeen-day hospitalization his behavior and appearance seemed that of a perfectly normal, if rather shy, person. He slept and ate well, kept himself neat and clean, and obeyed hospital rules. He took part in activities in an emotionally uninvolved way, and otherwise mostly kept to himself, reading or watching television. He made no friends. He was always polite in daily interviews with his therapist; he never refused to answer any of her questions, but he never volunteered any information. He did not seem hostile, and he gave no impression of either liking or disliking the therapist.

During his hospitalization he was treated with fairly high doses of antipsychotic medication. After seventeen days of treatment he remained absolutely convinced of the conspiracy to frame him as a homosexual, but his conversation was no longer dominated by his need to take revenge on his persecutors, and he seemed somewhat calmer about the whole situation. There were no longer any legal grounds to keep him in the hospital against his will, and he insisted on leaving. He refused to continue medication or any kind of outpatient treatment after discharge, reiterating that there was "nothing wrong" with him and that the medication only made him sleepy. He had been in communication with his estranged wife, and when he assured her he would get a job, she agreed to have him live with her again. It seemed unlikely that he could keep a job, since he was still convinced of the conspiracy against him; but since he would not participate in any follow-up, it is not known what became of him.

DISCUSSION

Psychopathology and Diagnosis   Pete Dunn's primary symptom is his unwarranted conviction that there is a conspiracy directed at him to frame him as a homosexual and to kill him. His delusions are systematized in that they all revolve around the single theme of a conspiracy against him as a homosexual. The delusions do not have the bizarre, patently absurd quality of delusions often seen in schizophrenia (see Case 31, "Never Say Die"). His emotional reaction of anger and his taking steps to defend himself are understandable and appropriate given the content of his delusions, whereas in schizophrenia the emotional reaction is often inappropriate to the content of the delusion (see Case 30, "Another Dimension"). The persistence of persecutory delusions in the absence of other psychotic symptoms, such as prominent hallucinations or disorganization of speech, indicates a paranoid disorder. When the persecutory delusions persist for more than six months, this is called *paranoia*.

Etiology and Prevalence   Although there was no apparent psychosocial stressor that precipitated Mr. Dunn's illness, paranoid disorders often are precipitated by a major stressor, such as immigration. Paranoid disorders are not nearly as common as schizophrenia, particularly in treatment settings, perhaps because many individuals with the disorder may go through life without seeking treatment.

Course   Although Mr. Dunn first became ill with symptoms of paranoia when he was 20, more commonly the illness begins in middle or late adult life. Usually the course is chronic, but there may be little interference with daily social and occupational functioning. For example, a patient with paranoia may believe that he has been wronged by the government and may spend years in fruitless correspondence with various government agencies, yet continue to live harmoniously with his family and hold a steady job. This is unfortunately not true of Mr. Dunn, since his delusion involves his coworkers and associates wherever he happens to be. On the other hand, in response to the persecutory delusions the individual may become violent and dangerous to others.

Treatment and Prognosis   As with schizophrenia, the psychotic symptoms are treated with antipsychotic drugs which frequently are effective. In Mr. Dunn's case the drugs were helpful in lessening his preoccupation with his persecutory delusions, which enabled him to leave the hospital, although he continued to believe that there was a conspiracy against him. It is likely that without further treatment he will again become preoccupied with his delusions and may again need to be hospitalized.

PSYCHOTIC DISORDERS NOT ELSEWHERE CLASSIFIED

CAMPUS EXILE

Cynthia Adams is a 19-year-old female college freshman who suddenly began to feel strange after leaving her parents' home for the first time and beginning school. She felt "spaced out," "in a fog," and as if she were looking at herself in a movie. She couldn't sleep at night and took to pacing restlessly about the dormitory lobby. She soon became convinced that people were looking at her strangely, laughing behind her back, and communicating with one another about her strange appearance. Cynthia couldn't concentrate on reading, even a newspaper, and eventually stopped attending classes. She talked to no one and felt like an exile.

These symptoms lasted several weeks. The patient then called home and asked if she might return home and drop out of school for the semester. Her parents, who had expected great things of her, underestimated the difficulty she was having and refused. The patient now developed the notion that she was the victim of a plot. The content of these thoughts quickly became more elaborate. At first she believed that she had been poisoned with LSD by a jealous girl living in a nearby dormitory room. Before long she believed that her teachers were part of the plot against her and that they noticed that she looked crazy. She was also being persecuted by the Black Panthers because her views on race were not advanced enough. Cynthia then began to hear voices which sounded like those of her sister and mother. They called her a "dumb slut" and "jerk-off queen" and accused her of a variety of sexual misdeeds with the college football team. The patient felt agitated and desperate. She couldn't get the thoughts and voices out of her head and couldn't stand living with them. She took fifty aspirins and finally went to the hospital emergency room.

This was Cynthia's first psychiatric episode. Previously she had been a highly successful student, quite popular and socially active. She had never used illicit drugs other than occasionally marijuana. The only indication that she might have trouble leaving home to go to college was her unusually strong attachment to her family and reluctance to attend summer camp as a child or to be separated from them for other reasons. The family history was negative for psychiatric disorder, except for one maternal uncle who was diagnosed as schizophrenic and once spent four months in a mental hospital.

Cynthia came to the emergency room with hallucinations and delusions. Her affect was agitated and dysphoric but not depressed. She was acutely depersonalized and seemed to be vague, distant, and confused. She spoke in an overly abstract and metaphorical language that lacked clear content, and her associations were often difficult to follow. She was well oriented and had no cognitive deficits.

Cynthia was admitted to the hospital and placed on gradually increasing doses of haloperidol, an antipsychotic agent. She showed a very rapid and complete response. Within several days she was less agitated and sleeping well; within one week her voices had disappeared; within two weeks she was without delusions. Within three weeks she was discharged. On a follow-up visit one week later she had no symptoms and appeared to be very much herself again. She was embarrassed by the whole episode, regarded it as a kind of nightmare, and found herself gradually forgetting what had happened. She had decided to return home and drop out of the school for the semester, and her parents had agreed.

DISCUSSION

Psychopathology and Diagnosis Cynthia's illness began abruptly, and within a few weeks she was experiencing a variety of psychotic symptoms. She had persecutory delusions (she was the victim of a plot, she was being poisoned with LSD, she was persecuted by the Black Panthers), auditory hallucinations (calling her "dumb slut" and "jerk-off queen" and accusing her of sexual misdeeds), and disorganized thinking ("her associations were . . . difficult to follow"). In addition, she described depersonalization (looking at herself as though she were in a movie) and had psychomotor agitation (restlessly pacing about the dorm).

Until the last few years, this clinical picture would have been called acute schizophrenia because of the sudden onset of delusions, hallucinations, and disorganized thinking. However, many studies have shown that when such symptoms develop relatively suddenly in a person without previous signs of psychopathology, and are of brief duration, with complete recovery, the illness is fundamentally different from schizophrenia. Patients with this kind of illness do not have an increased prevalence of schizophrenia among their relatives, as do patients whose schizophrenia has a more chronic and often deteriorating course. Disorders with symptoms similar to the active phase of schizophrenia, but which are of greater than two weeks' but less than six months' duration, are called schizophreniform ("like schizophrenia"). This would be the diagnosis of Cynthia's illness, and may well be the diagnosis that would now be given to her uncle.

Etiology and Course Schizophreniform disorder frequently follows a psychosocial stressor, such as living away from home for the first time. Obviously the stressor itself does not cause the disorder, and individuals who develop the disorder in response to stress must have some underlying psychological and/or biological vulnerability. (Most beginning college students obviously do not respond so catastrophically to the stress of being away from home for the first time.) In most cases there are no recurrences, and the individual continues to function as well as before the illness. In a small number of cases, however, the illness takes a more malignant turn in that there are recurrences and a deteriorating course, which indicates that the illness has evolved into schizophrenia.

The diagnosis of schizophreniform disorder is sometimes made in the early months of a psychotic episode when the outcome is as yet unknown. If recovery occurs within the six-month period, the diagnosis of schizophreniform disorder is confirmed; if the psychotic symptoms persist, or there are residual symptoms such as social withdrawal, blunted affect, or odd speech, the diagnosis would have to be changed to schizophrenia.

A psychotic episode in a young person is frequently caused by drugs or an affective disorder. In Cynthia's case, there is evidence of neither.

Treatment   Cynthia received the appropriate treatment for an acute psychotic episode. She was hospitalized because she was dangerous to herself and needed supervision. Antipsychotic medication was given to alleviate her symptoms rapidly. Although the symptoms would very likely have remitted in the course of a few months, Cynthia was probably spared weeks of misery by the use of the medication. She will very likely remain on the medication for only a few weeks following her hospitalization, unlike patients with schizophrenia, who generally continue to take medication because of its prophylactic action against exacerbation of the illness.

Although some mental health professionals believe that exploratory psychotherapy is helpful during the acute illness, most would disagree. They would recommend exploratory psychotherapy following recovery in order to help the patient cope better with future stressors.

After she recovered, Cynthia reported that she gradually forgot much of what had happened. This common phenomenon, sometimes known as "sealing over," enables the patient to avoid the potentially devastating effect on self-esteem of the reality of having been "crazy." However, this self-protective process may interfere with the patient's ability to be introspective during psychotherapy following recovery.

THE HITCH

Carl, a 38-year-old bookkeeper, entered the hospital on a court order for the determination of competency to stand trial. He was arrested shortly after he had assaulted a hitchhiker to whom he had given a ride approximately 2 hours before.

Carl had left southern California to travel to Wyoming where he was going to visit his brother. After having driven the first day he stopped, had several beers, and then stayed in a motel that night. The next morning he resumed his travel and picked up two hitchhikers on the freeway just before noon. He became increasingly suspicious of the hitchhiker sitting in the passenger side of the front seat. He described the events as follows:

> This guy kept looking at me and smiling. On one occasion he asked me what I did for recreation. I became convinced that he was homosexual and was planning on propositioning me. It seemed like he was always reaching in his pocket and touching something. I thought maybe it was a gun. I looked in the rearview mirror but the other hitchhiker seemed unconcerned and was either asleep or dozing.
>
> Then the guy in the front seat asked me if he could put a cassette tape in my car stereo. After he turned it on, he let his hand touch my leg. All this time he was playing with something in his coat pocket with his other hand.
>
> I became convinced that the two guys were together and they were going to hurt me. About this time, I noticed there was something metal in the guy's hand. I thought it was a gun or a pocket knife. I asked him what he had and he quickly took his hand out of his pocket and said, "nothing." About this time I looked in the rearview mirror and I thought the guy in the back was getting some rope out of his knapsack.

I told the guys I had to stop the car for a minute, and so I pulled off the freeway and went around to the passenger side of the car, jerked the door open, and grabbed the guy's right hand. I slugged him and he fell down. Then I told the guy in the back that if he got out I would let him have it too. About that time, the guy that I had hit started getting up, and so I kicked him in the stomach. Then I felt in his coat pocket, but there was nothing there. I ordered the other hitchhiker out and looked through his knapsack, but there was no rope there either. About that time a highway patrolman came up and I told him that these guys were going to molest me or hurt me. But the other two guys convinced the patrolman that that wasn't true. And so I was arrested and charged with aggravated assault.

Carl is the oldest child in the family, with two brothers and three half-sisters. His father died in a car accident when Carl was 2, and his mother has remarried twice since then. Carl quit school when he was in the seventh grade, and by the time he was 15 years of age he was supporting himself. He first tried construction work, then worked as a salesman, and finally took evening classes and gained skills in book-keeping. He initially worked for a company, but after a few years found that he could make more money by "doing freelance work" for a number of accountants on a part-time basis.

He used illicit drugs, primarily marijuana, on only three different occasions, but said that he much preferred alcohol. He saw himself as an alcoholic: "not one that has to drink every morning, but a person who is very dependent on alcohol none-theless." He was hospitalized for alcoholism about a year ago after several weekend binges, but felt that the treatment was of only limited benefit. After having been discharged he became involved in Alcoholics Anonymous and successfully disconti n-ued drinking for about nine months. Shortly before the assault and battery incident he had started drinking again, this time restricting himself to beer.

When he was 20 he was arrested after he and his girl friend went to a party where all the other guests were gay. All of the party guests were arrested, presumably because neighbors had reported that a "drug party" was in progress, but the others were allowed to leave jail the next day by posting bail and pleading guilty to a charge of disturbing the peace. Carl did not have any money, so he was sentenced to three days in jail. During this three-day period of time he was beaten up and sexually assaulted by three other inmates.

Immediately following this assault Carl slashed his wrists and spent the next two weeks on a psychiatric ward. He said his intention in slashing his wrists was to get out of jail and go someplace where he would not be subjected to brutality.

He first married when he was 20 years of age. This marriage lasted but two years. He described his marriage as the "blind leading the blind," and both he and his wife were happy to terminate the marriage. He married again when he was 32 and describes his present marriage as being very happy, a marriage as he had dreamed of having all his life. He and his wife have a 3-year-old child. His wife currently works as a secretary. According to her, he was a consistently good husband and father, and in recent years he had advanced in his work and increased his income.

Shortly after Carl's incarceration for assaulting the hitchhiker, it was decided to move him from one side of the jail to the other because of heating problems. When the sheriff told Carl he was going to have to be moved, Carl became convinced that he was to be executed momentarily. He reportedly started screaming, yelling, and saying his blood would be splattered on the cell walls. A local psychiatrist saw Carl that evening and described him as being agitated, frightened, and trembling.

Both on the ward and during the interview, Carl talked in a circumstantial manner. It was difficult for him to relate material in a direct and straightforward way. He would spend a considerable length of time just to make a minor point. It was impossible for him to sort out the important from the irrelevant.

While on the ward, he frequently wrote in a journal. When asked about it, he said that he was trying to keep a diary of the daily events of his hospital life. However, when he finally allowed an examiner to read the material, it turned out to be filled with suspicion, mistrust, concerns about the motives of other patients and staff, and frequent mention of his fear of somone hurting or killing him. The entries were written in a disconnected manner.

Some of Carl's friends and relatives described similar problems in his ability to communicate. For the past five or six years they had had difficulty conversing with him because of his continual talking around the subject. In addition, they mentioned that he had become more withdrawn and did not seem to be "the person they used to know." One friend of his also mentioned an event in which he was driving on the freeway, when it seemed to him as though automobiles and people were hung from strings and were smashing into each other. When asked about this, he minimized the incident. He did say, however, that this happened when he had not been drinking.

Carl scored in the above-average range of intelligence on the Wechsler Adult Intelligence Scale, achieving a verbal IQ of 111, a performance IQ of 114, and a full-scale IQ of 113. There were no gaps in his memory, and while on the ward his judgment and orientation were intact. He took several perceptual motor tests, doing them in a careful and meticulous manner; quantitatively, he received zero errors on these tests. An electroencephalogram and neurological examination were both negative. It was concluded that there was no evidence of organic cerebral dysfunction.

Psychotropic medication was offered him, but he was very reluctant to take any because of an adverse reaction he had had to a similar medication when he was in the hospital for his alcoholism. Nevertheless, after a few days he agreed to take medication on a trial basis, and after ten days, both he and the staff were surprised at how much more lucid, clear-minded, and friendly he became. In addition, he quit writing in his journal. His personal grooming had always been immaculate.

After spending six weeks in the hospital, Carl improved significantly and was sent back to court as being competent to stand trial with the recommendation that he stay on his medication. The court was informed that in the three examiners' opinions, Carl had a viable defense of insanity. In order not to have to stand trial he elected to plead guilty to a reduced charge of assault, which is a misdemeanor, as opposed to the original felony charge of aggravated assault. He was placed on probation with the requirement that he continue to receive psychiatric care, and he was allowed to return to his home in California.

Carl corresponded several times with one of the examiners, writing that he was taking the medication, was feeling much better than he had for several years, was more effective at his work, and his friends and relatives had commented that he was warmer and friendlier and more like his old self.

DISCUSSION

Psychopathology and Diagnosis   Carl was seen by the prison psychiatrist after he became agitated and overtly psychotic in his cell, believing that he was to be executed. However, in retrospect it is clear that Carl had been ill for several years. His friends had noticed a change—he was more withdrawn and difficult to understand. The incident in which it seemed to him as though "automobiles and people were hung from strings and were smashing into each other" probably represented a period of derealization, in which the perception of one's surroundings is altered so that a sense of the ordinary reality of the external world is lost. If there actually were cars on the road and he mistakenly saw them smashing into each other, this was probably an illusion, an altered perception of an actual sensory stimulus, and not a hallucination, a sensory perception in the absence of an external stimulus.

Carl's description of how he experienced the incident with the hitchhikers reveals that he became inordinately suspicious soon after picking them up. He first had ideas of reference in which he suspected that events had a particular personal meaning, although they really had no connection to him (he thought that the hitchhiker might be reaching into his pocket for a gun). Then he had delusions of reference in which he was convinced that the metal object that he saw in the hitchhiker's hand was a gun and that the hitchhiker in the back seat was getting some rope out of his knapsack. In jail he developed the persecutory delusion that he was about to be executed, and his speech and writing became more disorganized and difficult to follow. This probably represented loosening of associations, or thought disorder, in which ideas shift from one subject to another that is completely unrelated, without the speaker showing any awareness that the topics are unconnected. There is also evidence that he demonstrated circumstantiality—speech that is indirect and delayed in reaching the point because of unnecessary details and parenthetic remarks. (Loosening of associations always indicates serious psychopathology, whereas circumstantiality may be observed in individuals who are not ill. The reader is likely to have observed circumstantiality even among some friends and professors.)

The persecutory delusions, delusions of reference, perceptual distortions, and loosening of associations suggest a diagnosis of schizophrenia. However, Carl's wife confirms that despite his being ill for several years there has been no deterioration in his occupational functioning. This feature makes a diagnosis of schizophrenia very unlikely, since schizophrenia always involves deterioration in several important areas of functioning.

The prominent persecutory delusions with emotional responses appropriate to the content of the delusions suggest a paranoid disorder. However, marked loosening of associations is incompatible with a paranoid disorder. Therefore, the appropriate diagnosis is *atypical psychosis*, which indicates a psychotic disorder, but one in which there are unusual features that preclude a more specific psychotic diagnosis, such as schizophrenia or a paranoid disorder.

Carl himself offers the additional diagnosis of alcoholism because of his "dependence" on alcohol and his hospitalization after several episodes of binge drinking.

Etiology   When Carl was 20 he was sexually assaulted in jail. This undoubtedly was a traumatic experience. Whether or not it contributed to the later development of his psychotic disorder, it must certainly have influenced the content, that is, that he was going to be homosexually assaulted by the hitchhiker.

Course and Treatment   In contrast to Case 30, "Another Dimension," Carl's case represents a felicitous interaction between the criminal justice system and the mental health system. Clearly it would be absurd to punish Carl by sentencing him to jail for his irrational assault of the hitchhiker. His transfer from a jail to a hospital enabled him to receive a treatment (antipsychotic medication) that was effective in eliminating his psychotic symptoms and enabling him to return to a productive life in society.

Prognosis   Because of Carl's good social and work history, the brief duration of the overt psychotic symptoms, his good response to medication, and his willingness to keep taking it, the prognosis is good.

FACTITIOUS DISORDERS

LITTLE JOEY

Joey is a divorced, unemployed 39-year-old sheet metal worker who came to a Miami hospital of his own accord for surgical treatment of a self-inflicted stab wound to his abdomen with evisceration of the bowel. After surgery he was transferred to the psychiatric unit seven weeks ago, because he stated that, if released, he would "finish the job." He has had about twenty prior psychiatric hospitalizations.

He is a small, sharp-faced, multitattooed man of malnourished appearance, looking his stated age. His face and eyes are always very sad in repose, and remain sad even when he is laughing and in good spirits. He is well groomed and well dressed when feeling good, otherwise unshaven, unkempt, and wearing a messy hospital gown. While sometimes adopting a wheedling tone, he generally appears frank and dignified in conversation and has a warm, shrewd sense of humor.

During the past year Joey has been living alone on welfare, lonely and sad, but enjoying working as a volunteer in a Chicago hospital. He has had occasional casual girl friends, and occasionally he would enjoy going to the horse races. During this period he frequently cut his abdomen, at least three times seriously enough to require hospital admission.

About two weeks prior to the present hospitalization Joey began to feel "wanderlust" for no apparent reason. He went to the Greyhound station and gave the bus station ticket agent nearly all his money and asked for a ticket to "anywhere." He hoped for a pleasant climate and assumed he would find a job. (He also had in mind that he might go to the hospital, and would be more warmly treated in a new hospital than in the Chicago hospitals, most of which are quite familiar with him.) On his arrival in Miami it was raining, he knew no one and nothing about the city, and the bleakness of his situation was so oppressive that after several days he returned to the bus station, slashed his abdomen, and took himself to the hospital. He does not think he intended to die, although he would not have minded dying.

Joey was first hospitalized at 8 "because my mother couldn't handle me." His behavior included lying, frequent fights, cruelty to animals (once he threw a cat out of a window), and playing hooky so often he was rarely in school. He cannot recall why he did these things. After 30 days observation he was sent to a residential institution for orphans and incorrigible children, where he remained until he was about 14, earning mediocre grades in school. He then went to technical school where he studied automotive mechanics for one and a half years; he enjoyed mechanics, but hated the boredom and routine and left school. He traveled around from city to city, picking up odd jobs for a few days or weeks, doing his work, peacefully coexisting with employees and coworkers, then moving on because he couldn't bear to be in the same place for too long a time. "I've got the wanderlust. I can't explain it. I've been roaming around since I was a little kid." He was in occasional legal trouble (bicycle theft, minor burglaries), but never spent more than a few days in jail. In his early twenties, with no previous drug history, he was persuaded by an acquaintance to mainline heroin, and soon had a $75-a-day habit, which he supported by more serious crimes. These included grand theft and armed robbery (although he emphasizes, "I never hurt anybody"), and his longest jail term was 30 months. After several years' addiction, in response to frighteningly more rigorous laws, he painfully quit heroin "cold turkey." (Records from another hospital cite a history of successful methadone treatment, but he firmly denies ever having taken methadone.) He has used no illicit drugs since, and he reverted to less frequent, less serious lawbreaking.

About seven years ago he was in jail awaiting sentence for burglary, and a cellmate told him that judges were impressed by the emotional straits of prisoners who mutilated themselves, but that such superficialities as wrist-slashing had little impact. The cellmate therefore, at the patient's request, cut the patient's abdomen open for him with a razor blade. Surgery was performed, and criminal charges were dropped. Thereafter, finding his life so lonely that he would often go days without talking to anyone, he cut his abdomen about once every six weeks, often superficially so that only bandaging was required, but sometimes so deeply that the bowel was exposed. He had major reparative surgery at least seven times. He found that this was an effective means of gaining attention ("You're in the hospital, you push a button, the nurses will come and talk to you"), and also that cutting his abdomen relieved "nervous tension." In addition, he states that he often seriously wants to die to escape his loneliness and his impulses to cut himself. He had several psychiatric hospitalizations during this period, and states that every one of his psychiatric hospitalizations ended with his elopement or departure against medical advice. He was treated with various antipsychotic medications, but says their only effect was to make him sleepy.

About four years ago he first heard "a voice" telling him to hurt himself. On the day the hallucination began he had lost $400, all he had, at the racetrack. The voice was male, but not his own; it was garbled and difficult to understand, but definitely did not come from within his head, sounding exactly like another person speaking to him. (In one interview, pressed for greater detail: "So did the voice say, 'Cut your stomach, Joey'?" he replied, "It didn't use my name, just 'Cut your stomach.' " In a subsequent interview the next day he reported, "It never said 'Cut your stomach,' just 'hurt yourself.' ") He had met other patients with auditory hallucinations ("But theirs were worse than mine. They were sick."), but nevertheless, "The first time I heard it, it drove me up a wall, I didn't know what to make of it, it scared me." Sometimes he gained admission to psychiatric hospitals complaining of the voice commanding suicide, but without any actual gesture. This hallucination (but never any others) persisted intermittently, but has not been heard in the last seven months.

About four years ago, also, he developed the conviction that his abdomen-cutting served to lessen the pain of the "poor old people being mugged on the South Side of Chicago." He cannot explain the mechanism of this help, vehemently denies that it is a sacrifice through God, and asserts that if someone told it to him, he'd think they were crazy—but it really happens. He also occasionally wishes "I could get rid of these damn stupid reasons I've got . . . I'm cutting my stomach for these poor old people on the South Side, and they don't even know it."

He now states that ever since he can remember he has been quite sad and lonely, the only exception being when he has been in a close relationship with a woman. Generally he has a poor appetite, sleeps fitfully, has little interest in or energy for anything, is bored, and spends many daytime hours huddled in bed remembering past good times. His memory is good (according to him), but concentration is poor. He finds his life so lonely that he often sits in railroad and bus stations, or buys cups of coffee, just to be near people and feel himself part of their conversations. He hates being alone, but calls himself a "loner" and feels trapped by long-term relationships.

When he has a girl friend he is in good spirits, feels no urge to cut himself, is not tense, starts thinking hopefully about the future, sleeps well, is full of pep, and gains weight (estimating that his appetite about doubles).

Joey's father died before he was born and his mother remarried during his infancy. He reports his mother as "warm and loving." He respected his stepfather but detested the routine nature of his 9-to-5 job and determined his own life would not be so boring.

He was in the Army (records from another hospital say Air Force, but he denies this) about fourteen months at age 18, but was discharged as "unadaptable" after many AWOL incidents. ("I didn't like taking orders.")

He first had sex with his first serious girl friend in his late teens, a relationship that lasted about a year. In his early twenties there was a nine-month homosexual liaison with an older man who lived with him and supported him; this involved a strong mutual fondness. The patient denies any other homosexual relationships.

About age 30 he married a nurse, and was very happy with her until their first child arrived. ("Then she started paying more attention to the baby than to me.") Divorced after five years and two children, he does not know where his wife and children are. Records from another hospital indicate another wife. The patient at first denies this, shaking his head over the other hospital's inefficiency; then he admits having "lived common-law" with a woman; then he admits to having two children with her. He says he doesn't know why he didn't mention this earlier—it didn't seem relevant.

He has had many girl friends of several weeks duration, typically meeting someone who is herself very lonely and precariously balanced, staying and traveling with her for a few weeks, then having the relationship dissolve in a friendly way.

During his two months in this hospital, Joey was extremely sensitive to others' feelings about him and was especially gratified by the attention he received from attractive female staff members, such as student nurses. He was courteous, gentlemanly, and "watched his language"; his appreciative remarks never approached the improper. He was very considerate of and helpful with the most disturbed patients and elderly or physically handicapped patients, and loved the praise he got for this. He had a passion for fairness: he did not quarrel with restriction of privileges when he agreed he had been in the wrong, but was infuriated at the least unexplained infringement of his rights, and would leap into the fray to help the underdog, even when the underdog was a violent patient being gently restrained by a large number of staff members.

He was intensely attached to his therapist, but occasionally, without explanation, grew very angry with her, "fired" her, and refused to speak to her, but returned in a few hours or days and "unfired" her. He demanded independence, but was manifestly relieved to be given limits and clearly arranged this. For example, he requested discharge almost daily, but only after saying that if discharged he would go "finish the job." While very friendly, he was not "sticky" with ward staff, and frequently himself ended his short interviews, having received enough attention for the day.

His mood improved somewhat during his first month in the hospital when he received an antidepressant, but he remained quite sad and unsociable and repeatedly reopened his wound. Medication was stopped for a week, and his mood worsened considerably. After being switched to a different antidepressant for two weeks, his mood markedly improved. He socialized with other patients, wore street clothes instead of a hospital gown, had more energy, gained 12 pounds, slept and ate well, and was remarkably cheerful at times. He had not lost the impulse to cut his abdomen, although he kept the impulse in check. After about a week of "feeling 99 percent better" and "better than I have in years," he began worrying that things were going too well and that at his present rate he would soon be discharged, and his impulse to cut his abdomen strengthened.

Numerous plans were made for living arrangements after discharge; Joey investigated and rejected all of them. He finally left the hospital without any predetermined plans.

A year later Joey returned to the hospital for a visit. Nobody recognized him at first because he was so emaciated, and his hair had turned a dusty gray and was closely cropped. His greeting was, "Doctor, I got cancer." In fact he had metastases throughout his body, had had radiation treatment and chemotherapy, and was expected to die within a few months. He had ready access to painkilling medication, but used it very sparingly. He had been so ill that doctors had urged him to stay in the hospital, but now he only wanted "to be out in the sunshine." The irony of the situation was not lost on him—"now I can stay in the hospital legit, I don't want to."

He was afraid of death, asked if this were normal, and seemed reassured to hear that it was. He openly and thoughtfully talked about the afterlife, and seemed comforted at the limited emotional contact he received.

With his familiar skill at manipulation, he inveigled various staff members to make social support arrangements for him on short notice, then rejected all these arrangements as not being up to snuff.

He returned twice more, each time with a deep suntan, evidently coming for the comfort of a familiar person to talk to and touch. During his last visit he called his mother in Chicago and made arrangements to return there to die. We do not know whether or not he followed through with this plan.

DISCUSSION

Psychopathology and Diagnosis Since age 8, Joey has had extensive contact with mental health facilities for a plethora of problems. These include antisocial behavior, drug addiction, depressed mood, social isolation, and perceptions and ideation that suggest hallucinations and delusions. The most striking aspect of this case, however, and the reason for his current hospitalization, is his deliberate self-infliction of serious abdominal stab wounds.

People who are severely depressed may seriously injure themselves in an unsuccessful suicide attempt, but Joey denies that he slashed his stomach in order to kill himself. Individuals who are grossly psychotic may injure themselves in response to a hallucinatory command or in the process of acting on a delusional belief. Joey does, at one point, claim that he hears a voice telling him to cut his stomach and also that his wounds somehow help to lessen the pain of the Chicago poor. However, it is not at all clear that Joey really heard such a voice or really believed that there was a relationship between his wounds and lessening the suffering of others. What is much more convincing is his report that he learned, while in jail, that he could expect better treatment as a mental patient than as a prisoner, and that serious self-inflicted wounds of a dramatic nature were the ticket to entry into the mental health system: only a crazy person would deliberately injure himself.

If an individual deliberately feigns or causes an illness or injury for some obvious environmental gain, this is called malingering. Malingering is an act, and not necessarily a symptom of a mental disorder. Examples include feigning physical illness in order to justify disability compensation or self-inflicting wounds to avoid military combat. In Joey's case, initially his goal in injuring himself was quite understandable, given the context of his life. He was in jail and realized that he would be better off in a hospital. As time went on, however, what he gained from such self-inflicted injuries became less obvious. What he seemed to gain most from these hospital stays was relief from his loneliness, clearly a need more psychological than environmental. The times that his self-mutilation was done deliberately to reduce his level of tension also reflects a psychological need rather than a need motivated by his environmental circumstances. Over time, then, Joey's self-mutilation becomes a way of life for him, providing him with a way to assume the role of "patient." His recurrent episodes of this symptom suggests a compulsive quality to his actions that, although deliberate and purposeful, cannot be controlled.

When a person feigns being ill for reasons not understandable in light of their environmental circumstances and apparently only to assume the patient role, this is called factitious disorder (factitious = non-genuine). The most common form of factitious disorder involves voluntarily producing physical symptoms. For example, the individual may take a medicine that interferes with the clotting of blood and causes internal bleeding, or an individual may complain of severe abdominal pain that convinces a surgeon to do exploratory surgery. When multiple hospitalizations result from such factitous complaints, this is called chronic factitious disorder with physical symptoms, commonly known as Münchausen's syndrome (after Baron Karl F. H. von

Münchausen, a German author of fabulous stories). More rarely, as in Joey's case, the individual with a factitious disorder feigns having a mental disorder. This itself is a mental disorder and called *chronic factitious disorder with psychological symptoms.* An unusual twist in Joey's case is that he always signs himself out of the hospital rather than remaining in the "patient" role as long as he can. This, combined with his history of antisocial behavior, raises the suspicion of at least an element of malingering. The concepts of malingering and factitious disorder represent two extremes of a continuum, with most cases lying midway, with mixtures of both conditions.

Once Joey's self-inflicted wounds are understood as his way of feigning mental illness, it is perhaps easier to understand his complaints of hearing voices and believing that his wounds helped the suffering poor. These symptoms also seem not genuine in that delusions and hallucinations do not usually occur in the absence of other signs of psychotic decompensation.

As is invariably the case, Joey's factitious disorder occurs as part of a more widespread disturbance in psychological functioning. Joey has a chronic mild depressive disorder (dysthymic disorder, see Case 24, "Learning to Cope"), as well as a life-long history of antisocial behavior that suggests antisocial personality disorder (see Case 14, "Gary Gilmore").

Course and Treatment   All of Joey's problems are chronic and resistant to treatment. His mood disturbance responded somewhat to antidepressants but, as is usually the case with patients with factitious disorder, he was unable to examine his maladaptive pattern of behavior in therapy. Although he did form an intense relationship to his therapist, he disappeared before she was able to be of any great help to him. When he finally returned, it was too late, since he was now dying of a genuine illness, cancer.

DISORDERS OF IMPULSE CONTROL NOT ELSEWHERE CLASSIFIED

VESUVIUS

Mr. and Ms. Milano were referred to a private psychiatrist by their family doctor. They were on the verge of separation because of Mr. Milano's explosive rages and the inability of the rest of the family to deal with them. In their initial interview with the psychiatrist, the Milanos described the events of the previous evening as typical of the kinds of problems they were having.

Returning home from work, Mr. Milano walked up the front driveway to be greeted by their Irish setter who jumped on him with muddy paws. Karen, his daughter, rushed out of the house, demanding the car keys, and drove off. Ms. Milano, who was cooking dinner, met him with a list of complaints: the garage had not finished work on her car, the serviceman did not show up to fix the washing machine, and the kids were driving her crazy. She insisted that Mr. Milano reprimand their 17-year-old son, John, for failing to do his chores. After an unsuccessful confrontation with John, who "gave me a lot of lip," Mr. Milano felt his face flushing, his heart pounding rapidly, and saw "sparks" before his eyes. Rage welled up within him, and he began cursing at the top of his voice, feeling out of control. He threw a dining room chair across the room and smashed the window. Storming back into the kitchen, he turned over the kitchen table, breaking all the dishes and glasses that were on it, and punched his fist through a sheetrock wall. He then headed upstairs, where he proceeded to break lamps and kick doors. He was aware of what was happening, but felt driven to continue. John and his mother sought refuge at a neighbor's house and did not return until two hours later, when they saw Mr. Milano stomp out of the house and disappear down the street.

Similar episodes had occurred over the preceding fifteen years, and had become more frequent over the past five years, as the children reached adolescence. The destruction of property at home was so severe and had become so frequent (several times a month) that it was causing financial difficulties for the family. Twice he had hit the wall so hard that he fractured his hand, and he had required stitches at the local emergency room on many occasions. Several times he had driven off recklessly in his car, but although he had had numerous accidents, he had never seriously hurt himself or anyone else. These explosions had usually taken place at home, and, in fact, in the past fifteen years he had only lost control of himself twice on the job.

Mr. Milano is a 51-year-old engineer in a middle-management position in a small air-conditioning company. His wife, 49, is a housewife and volunteer at a local hospital, but is now looking for employment. They have three children: Deborah, who is a senior in college and living in her own apartment; John, a high school senior who is doing poorly in school; and Karen, a sophomore in high school. They own their own home in a middle-class suburban community.

Over the past few years the family appeared to be coming apart. Deborah rarely came home for a visit because of her parents' fights. For the same reason, Karen had run away several times. John dealt with the family conflict by becoming an avid participant in the high school drug culture, and spending as much time away from home as possible. The couple had been estranged for years, and Ms. Milano admitted that her recent interest in finding a job was to become financially independent so that she could divorce her husband.

Mr. Milano was described by his family as an irritable and quick-tempered individual with a short fuse. He had resorted to clubs and sticks to administer physical punishment to his children, but he had never assaulted his wife. All members of the family said that they were afraid of Mr. Milano's rages, and he also admitted that he was afraid of his rage and was always remorseful after the fact.

His history revealed that the patient had been hyperactive at school and showed poor attention span and concentration. He was seen by a neurologist who considered the diagnosis of minimal brain dysfunction (attention deficit disorder), though no treatment was given. He had no history of problems with alcohol.

Mr. Milano was hospitalized for several days for a complete diagnostic workup. Except for a history of mild hypertension there was no suggestion of medical problems. Physical, including neurological, examination and laboratory studies, including a glucose tolerance test and an electroencephalogram, were all within normal limits. The patient was placed on two anticonvulsant medications, one of which, because of its rapid-acting and sedative effects, could be taken whenever he felt tension mounting.

At his first appointment two weeks after discharge, Mr. Milano reported another explosive episode following a sequence similar to that described above. However, there was a difference this time in that he only stood in the middle of the living room, cursing at the top of his voice for 5 or 10 minutes. There was no destruction of property. He was followed infrequently for the next two years; it was obvious that the attacks occurred with approximately the same frequency, but the severity was considerably attenuated. On one occasion he discontinued his medicine, but a month later he had a more severe explosive episode, so he voluntarily resumed taking his drugs.

Several years later he called to report that he and his wife had separated. In spite of his improvement, the marriage apparently could not be revived following the long history of family strife. The two older children had left home, and the younger daughter had moved in with her mother. Mr. Milano was living at home alone, no longer taking anticonvulsants, and except for transitory temper outbursts on the job, not having difficulties.

DISCUSSION

Psychopathology and Diagnosis Recurrent episodes of uncontrolled expressions of anger may be symptomatic of several mental disorders. Organic mental disorders, including drug intoxication and dementia, may lead to violent behavior because there is a disinhibition of the normal mechanisms that control aggression. In paranoid disorders or schizophrenia, violent outbursts may be in response to delusions or hallucinations. Aggressive behavior is a common symptom of antisocial personality disorder, but it is part of a general pattern of inability to conform to social norms.

Mr. Milano's problems seem to be limited to episodic loss of control of aggressive impulses leading to destructive behavior that is grossly out of proportion to any provocation. Between his episodes, although he is described as "an irritable and quick-tempered individual with a short fuse," he shows no evidence of generalized impulsivity or of any other significant psychopathology. This clinical picture is one form of a disorder of impulse control, called *intermittent explosive disorder.* Other impulse control disorders include pathological gambling, kleptomania (stealing objects that are not for immediate use or of monetary value), and pyromania (morbid fascination with setting fires).

Treatment Frequently, but not invariably, individuals with intermittent explosive disorder have abnormal electroencephalograms, and in some cases, epilepsy. Even in the absence of such evidence suggesting underlying brain dysfunction, anticonvulsants are often effective in suppressing or preventing entirely the episodes of loss of control. In this patient's case, the rage outbursts were suppressed while he was on the medication. Mr. Milano's case also illustrates the importance of psychological factors, even in a disorder that seems to respond to a biological therapy. The fact that the attacks stopped after Mr. Milano was no longer living with his family suggests that the stress of familial conflict had been a factor in triggering his outbursts.

ADJUSTMENT DISORDER

MR. NICE GUY

Billy Ainsworth was a 21-year-old senior in a southwestern University. He requested treatment at the university counseling center because of difficulties that he had been having since his girl friend, Jill, broke up with him three months previously. The relationship with Jill had been "a real love relationship." Nonetheless, they decided to date other people, and eventually she came to prefer another man.

Since the breakup Billy had lost interest in his schoolwork, was not able to concentrate on his studies, and as a result had accumulated several "incompletes." He also had trouble sleeping and was preoccupied with thoughts about Jill, for whom he still cared. When thinking about her he felt sad, but at other times he was able to enjoy himself with friends and to pursue his interests in sports and politics.

In addition, he complained of difficulties in making a career choice. It was the fall of his senior year, and he had not yet decided whether he would go to graduate school, and if so, whether it would be law school or business school.

Born in a southern state, the second son of a working-class family, Billy described a family relationship that was harmonious but not close. His father was hardworking and "loyal to his family." The only argument he remembered ever having with his father concerned his decision to grow a beard—to which his father strongly objected. His mother was "outgoing" and "always got into my business," but he denied that he was complaining about her. He had positive feelings toward both parents, whom he felt were basically loving and supportive. Billy's 32-year-old brother was a highly successful lawyer to whom Billy was not particularly close.

During his high school and college years Billy was active in athletics and student affairs; he enjoyed other people's company and was well liked by his peers. As a junior in college he was elected president of a liberal student political group. He worked part-time as a busboy in the campus coffee shop to help support himself. He had been getting good grades in all of his courses until his current difficulties. He had dated several other girls before his relationship with Jill, but had "never been in love before."

He was seen twice a week in time-limited psychodynamically oriented psychotherapy. The therapist, a psychiatrist, explained at the outset that the therapy would last for three months; the patient was, in fact, seen for 25 sessions.

From the beginning, the patient and therapist had a good working relationship. The patient appeared animated and capable of relating comfortably to the therapist as a potential helper. In particular, he answered questions eagerly and worked diligently in exploring his feelings and experiences. Even when discussion of a topic was painful, he was able to stay focused on it. He was not overawed by the therapist's position or status; he was open, trusting, and appreciative of the therapist's interest. Perhaps most striking was his ability to maintain his positive feelings toward the therapist even when the therapist was blunt in his confrontation. In short, the therapist and patient clearly liked each other, and the work proceeded in an atmosphere of collaboration and mutual respect.

In keeping with the psychodynamic approach, the psychiatrist encouraged Billy to take the initiative in introducing topics and to let his mind wander. The therapist, however, assumed an active role in identifying themes and interpreting maladaptive patterns of behavior. For example, he soon drew attention to Billy's competitiveness with his brother. He also pointed out that Billy never got angry at any of the comments that the therapist made. However, he went on to interpret Billy's procrastination in completing academic assignments and recurrent lateness for therapy interviews as "passive-aggressive maneuvers," that is, indirect expressions of anger. The following exchange took place on the subject of Billy's perpetual lateness for appointments:

Therapist: Let's talk about what goes on between you and me. You come in late, but you are so infernally nice about it that I can't talk about being irritated . . . You keep me off in a corner; we are never able to break through the niceness. . . . Being late may be a way of expressing something against me. . . , but your niceness prevents it from being discussed openly. . . . It might be better if you came in on time and didn't act so nice to me.

Patient (taken aback, somewhat sheepishly): I can't quite get a grasp on my niceness. It seems too embedded. . . .

Billy's avoidance of negative feelings was viewed by the therapist as a defense against his wishes to be more competitive. This theme was discussed also in relation to his difficulties in completing assignments, making up his mind about graduate school, and accepting the finality of his breakup with Jill.

Eventually Billy came to see his procrastination as "balking." He was able to use this increased self-awareness to change his behavior, even though he continued to have doubts as to how successfully he could compete in his professional life or in his pursuit of romantic relationships.

During the final session the therapist complimented Billy on having taken a hard look at what was happening to him and getting him into trouble. He reasserted that, although Billy's problems had certainly not been fully resolved, he had increased his options. He was able to apply to law school, finish his "incompletes," and graduate on time. He was also more active in meeting and dating women, and felt more content with who he was and what he was doing. As Billy was leaving, the therapist suggested that Billy drop him a line now and then to let him know how he was. Nine months later Billy wrote that he was achieving "respectable grades" in law school, was living with three housemates with whom he got along well, and was feeling "pretty good" about himself.

DISCUSSION

Psychopathology and Diagnosis   Billy sought treatment because of his reaction to the breakup of his first love affair. He reacted with sadness, preoccupation with thoughts about his girl friend, difficulty concentrating on his schoolwork, and insomnia. While it is expected that the stress of losing a lover will cause distress in anyone, in Billy's case the distress was so severe that he was unable to function as a student—he accumulated several "incompletes" and was in danger of not graduating. Therefore, Billy's reaction would be considered outside the range of normality and more than just "love sickness."

Billy's symptoms—sadness, poor concentration, and insomnia—raise the question of a major depression. However, the depressed mood does not appear to be sustained and pervasive ("he was able to enjoy himself with friends and to pursue his interests in sports and politics"), and he did not have the full affective syndrome (no symptoms of psychomotor disturbance, poor appetite, weight loss, suicidal ideation, and guilt). Therefore, the appropriate diagnosis would be *adjustment disorder with depressed mood.* This diagnosis indicates that the disturbance is in excess of a normal and expected reaction to the stressor, but is so mild that it does not meet the criteria for a more specific disorder (such as major depression). Implicit in the diagnosis of adjustment disorder is the expectation that the disturbance will eventually remit after the stressor ceases or, if the stressor persists, once a new level of adaptation is achieved. In Billy's case, this would mean that one would expect, even without treatment, that he would eventually get over his distress at losing Jill.

During the course of Billy's therapy it became apparent that he also had long-standing personality traits that were interfering with his optimal functioning, that is, procrastination and avoidance of direct expression of anger. In fact, it would appear that the therapy focused primarily on these difficulties rather than on the symptoms of the adjustment disorder. From what we know about Billy, his personality difficulties never seriously interfered with his functioning or caused him significant distress. Therefore, these personality difficulties are best thought of as traits, rather than as symptoms of a personality disorder (compare with Case 13, "Uptight," and Case 10, "Long-Suffering").

Treatment   Billy was treated with psychodynamically oriented psychotherapy. This kind of psychotherapy makes use of some of the techniques of psychoanalysis, such as encouraging the patient to take the initiative in talking about whatever comes to his mind, and interpreting to the patient the way in which his psychopathology expresses itself in the relationship to the therapist. It differs from psychoanalysis in that it focuses primarily on current behavior and does not make use of any extensive analysis of dreams.

A comparison of this kind of treatment with the treatment given to Case 24, "Learning to Cope," shows how psychodynamically oriented psychotherapy differs from more behaviorally oriented treatments. In most behaviorally oriented treatments the problem to be worked on is rather explicitly defined and agreed upon at the very beginning of therapy, even though it may be reevaluated at a later point. In Billy's therapy, the initial complaint—distress at the breakup of his relationship with Jill—was only the entry ticket in a treatment that then dealt with Billy's more pervasive problems which emerged as the therapy progressed.

All psychotherapies, to be effective, require a good working relationship between the patient and the therapist. In Billy's case it is clear that the positive relationship between Billy and his therapist was a major factor in enabling Billy to make use of the therapist's interpretations and suggestions, even when they involved direct confrontation. In addition, Billy was a particularly good candidate for psychodynamically oriented psychotherapy because of his capacity and willingness to introspect about his feelings and experiences and to apply what he had learned toward modifying his everyday behavior.

Prognosis Billy has never had serious psychopathology, and we would predict that he is likely to continue to do reasonably well. Hopefully, Billy will continue to use the increased self-awareness that resulted from his therapy to deal more effectively with life problems that he will undoubtedly face in the future.

V CODES FOR CONDITIONS NOT ATTRIBUTABLE TO A MENTAL DISORDER THAT ARE A FOCUS OF ATTENTION OR TREATMENT

BORN AGAIN

Jo Ann Kapeta is a 35-year-old divorced woman referred by the Multiple Sclerosis Society to a psychiatric clinic in her neighborhood where there was a therapy group specifically for patients with multiple sclerosis.

Three years ago, when she was pregnant with her second child, she complained to her gynecologist of numbness and lack of control of her hands. He attributed these symptoms to poor circulation. These and other symptoms of incoordination and muscular weakness, particularly affecting her hands, persisted, however, and a year prior to this evaluation were eventually diagnosed as multiple sclerosis. As she came to understand the chronic and incapacitating nature of her illness, she reacted with anxiety, anger, and waves of depression. Her anxiety was primarily about how she could continue to take care of her two children, and how long she could continue working as a key punch supervisor. She was angry that there seemed to be nothing that she could do to stop the progression of the illness, and that although she "looked normal," there were simple tasks that she could not do, such as writing her name or changing a diaper. Feelings of hopelessness would overwhelm her from time to time, especially at night, and many nights she cried herself to sleep.

Two months after the diagnosis was made she was hospitalized for further tests. One day, with a bad headache after having had a spinal tap, she cried "hysterically" while attending Mass in the hospital chapel. This was the beginning of a search for a more satisfying religious experience that soon led her to become a "born again Christian." Her involvement with this new religion has made it possible for her to accept her illness, and she finds comfort both in reading the Bible and associating with fellow church members. At the same time she withdrew from former acquaintances with whom she used to go dancing and drinking.

She has continued to work as a key punch supervisor and to take care of her 13- and $2^1/_2$-year-old daughters, without financial or housekeeping help. She denies any sustained period of depression or anxiety other than during the three weeks that she was taking a steroid drug, a few months prior to the evaluation. During that time she felt that "the depression took over," and she was depressed all of the time, cried uncontrollably, and had difficulty sleeping.

DISCUSSION

Psychopathology and Diagnosis Because Ms. Kapeta requests help from a psychiatric clinic and is experiencing anxiety and depression, a clinician may consider making a diagnosis of an anxiety disorder, an affective disorder, or perhaps adjustment disorder. However, implicit in the notion of a mental disorder is the inference of a psychological dysfunction, that is, that something is not working the way it ought to.

What is not working in Ms. Kapeta's case? Her response of anxiety and depression to the knowledge that she has a progressively crippling and potentially life-threatening illness seems no less appropriate than terror in the face of a charging lion! Therefore we cannot infer any dysfunction of the normal mechanisms that produce appropriate feelings of anxiety and depression. Her anxiety and depression are not so severe that they interfere with her ability to carry out her normal responsibilities. In fact, she is coping far better than many individuals do even in the absence of such a severe stressor. Therefore, we cannot infer a dysfunction in her coping mechanisms, or what in psychoanalytic terms would be called her ego. We thus conclude that she does not have a mental disorder, and according to DSM-III, her difficulties would be classified only as a *"life circumstance problem."*

Under what circumstances would Ms. Kapeta be thought to have a mental disorder? If, for example, her depressed mood were persistent and part of a full depressive syndrome (see Case 23, "Weeping Widow"), a diagnosis of major depression would be made. (In fact, during the three weeks that she was taking a steroid drug she says that "the depression took over" and she was depressed all of the time. Drugs of this kind can interfere with the normal regulation of mood and produce a full depressive syndrome. This is called an organic affective syndrome. Thus, technically speaking, she did have a mental disorder for that three-week period.) Clinicians often see individuals who in response to major stresses present a clinical picture that is somewhere between Ms. Kapeta's "normal" reaction and a clearly pathological reaction. Since there is no sharply demarcated boundary between normality and pathology, the decision in such cases will be somewhat arbitrary and will be influenced by practical matters, such as the need to justify third-party reimbursement.

Treatment Ms. Kapeta was referred to the psychiatric clinic so that she could join a group composed of patients with multiple sclerosis. It is hoped that by participating in this group, she will learn new ways of coping with her illness and will gain emotional support from the other members who share her plight. This case illustrates that mental health professionals can often be useful to individuals who have life problems that are not considered to be symptoms of mental disorder.

DISORDERS USUALLY FIRST EVIDENT IN INFANCY, CHILDHOOD, OR ADOLESCENCE

SECOND SHADOW

David Whitmore, age 4, was brought to the Learning Disabilities Center of a teaching hospital by his worried parents. They were concerned because David could not run and jump like his 3-year-old cousin, and still talked like a baby. He would cling to his mother and not let her out of his sight, was afraid of new situations, and had frequent temper tantrums. His parents had finally become dissatisfied with their pediatrician's reassurances that he would "grow out of it."

David was evaluated by a multidisciplinary team consisting of a pediatrician, a psychologist, a speech and hearing specialist, and a child psychiatrist. The goal of the team was to define David's problems and arrive at a diagnosis.

David was a small, slim boy with blond, curly hair and delicate features. He hid behind his mother when approached by the pediatrician. During his examination the pediatrician noted that David was mildly hypotonic; that is, when picked up he felt less like an eager, strong child than like a sack of potatoes. His mother had previously noted, as did the pediatrician, that David moved very slowly and seemed to be very cautious in the way he placed each foot down on the floor. It was the way he walked, in fact, that most concerned Ms. Whitmore. Although his mother had not mentioned it, the pediatrician immediately observed that David was drooling from the corner of his mouth.

David was the second child born to his 36-year-old mother. Ms. Whitmore had been pregnant three other times, only to have each pregnancy end in the fourth month with a spontaneous abortion. During the pregnancy with David she had experienced a number of difficulties, including high blood pressure in the last trimester and repeated vomiting throughout the pregnancy. In the last month before delivery she had bleeding from the vagina, and her gynecologist ordered her to remain in bed for the remainder of the pregnancy. Although the delivery was smooth, David was born with the umbilical cord wrapped around his neck and required resuscitation with oxygen. He was considered to be premature by weight, weighing only $4^1/_2$ pounds at delivery, though not by date, since the pregnancy had gone full term.

His mother was not able to breast feed him, because his suck was very weak. She found him to be "flabby," suggesting low motor tone, from the beginning, which had been substantiated by the pediatrician. On the other hand, he seemed to have a marvelous disposition as an infant. He attained a regular eating schedule rapidly and seemed to be unperturbed by noises going on around him. As time went on, however, it became clear that his developmental motor milestones were delayed. He did not sit up until eight months (expected about five months), walk until nineteen months (expected before eighteen months), or utter his first word until age 3 (expected about one year). Toilet training had not been accomplished at the time of the interview at the age of 4 years, one month (expected about three years). On further questioning, the pediatrician discovered that there had been a history of language problems in other relatives in the family: two of the mother's brothers and one of the father's sisters had had delayed speech development.

The psychologist evaluated David next. The boy would only come into the room with his mother, and it was hard to pry him away from her for the testing. Throughout the test he whined, wiggled, and squirmed. He often said "No" and turned away when asked to do a task, such as assemble a block design. He seemed extremely shy. On the Stanford-Binet Intelligence Test he attained a mental age of 2.0 years, giving him an IQ of 55, which indicated retardation in speech and abstract thinking. His concentration was disrupted by the slightest distracting stimuli. Barely audible footsteps in the hall would cause him to stop what he was doing and look toward the door. During most of the testing he maintained only fleeting eye contact. His Vineland Social Maturity Index (derived from a questionnaire for parents to determine which daily living tasks the child has mastered, such as dressing, feeding self, using telephone, etc.) was only 2.6 years. David was therefore functioning in the mild mentally retarded range in intellectual and social areas.

During another visit David was seen by the speech and hearing specialist. From the beginning the specialist noted that David was anxious and refused to separate from his mother when he came in from the waiting room. By using parallel play techniques (in which the specialist played with toys in David's presence to provide a model) the speech specialist was able to get him to interact, and David was able to follow simple directions from her. On the other hand, he did not respond to strictly verbal commands; for example, when asked, "give me the doll," he ignored the request until the specialist held out her hand for the doll. His vocabulary was limited to 25 words, and his longest sentences were three words. The specialist also noted that he drooled, and slurred and mispronounced words so that it was very hard to understand him (e.g., "Me dwop wyon" for "I dropped the lion"). Gross motor function was noted to be at the 2-year level, while fine motor function was at the 2.5-year level. For example, David could not duplicate a circle with a pencil.

The next specialist to interview David and his mother was the child psychiatrist. The psychiatrist learned that Ms. Whitmore had become aware that there was something very wrong with David by the time he was 3 years old. As a result, she had let him continue to sleep in his crib until age $3\frac{1}{2}$, knowing that his cousin was able to go into a youth bed without side rails at age eighteen months. Ms. Whitmore also began to notice that David had emotional problems. He was currently very jealous and would scream if his brother referred to their mother as "my mommy." Like a 2-year-old, he screamed frequently to get attention and often cried. His mother referred to David as her "second shadow," because he refused to separate from her and never wanted to be away from her. She felt that he was becoming more and more spoiled and un-cooperative, and she did not know how to cope with these issues.

The psychiatrist made another appointment to see David alone. At that interview David screamed loud and long when his mother left the room and refused to sit down. As a result, his older brother Anthony came into the room. The screaming stopped, but it still took 5 minutes before David became relaxed enough to play. Even with the dolls, the blocks, and the toy house in front of him, David could not stay absorbed in play for any length of time, showing multiple anxiety-related play interruptions. Whenever the psychiatrist came into David's view, the boy stopped playing and ran behind his brother. When his mother was called into the room, David immediately relaxed and started to play with her and she played comfortably with him. He cooperated with her by handing her toys when she reached out her hand. He built a seven-block tower spontaneously and then had the toy polar bear knock it down.

Language production during the interview was scanty. The only intelligible word produced was "baby," although many jargon sounds were muttered during the rough-and-tumble play involving toy lions knocking one another down. At one point, he tried to put a small ball in a toy bear's mouth and said "yum-yum."

Because of his limited vocabulary, his clinging attachment to his mother, and his visible anxiety, David was referred for a prolonged evaluation in the Observational Nursery at the Learning Disabilities Center. Working with a therapist, the mother and child played together twice a week in this environment for several sessions over one month. During the early sessions David learned to tolerate his mother walking to the other side of the room, and by the fifth session he allowed her to leave the play area entirely. It became clear that, in response to David's special needs, both parents had become overprotective and had denied many of David's problems, particularly in language. The nursery personnel were able to help David's parents view the boy's deficiencies more realistically, and saw them through a period in which they felt guilty about David's disabilities.

Later, the diagnostic team met together to discuss the evaluation and plan the treatment. Their recommendations included a special class in the public school system for language-impaired children. David was also referred for a long course of speech therapy in order to strengthen the skills he did have. Further appointments were made with a social worker for the parents to work out their own guilt feelings about David's handicaps. Follow-up visits were scheduled on a yearly basis for routine reevaluations of David, after the special classes and speech therapy, in order to track his level of functioning and plan for any special needs he might develop in the future.

Within a period of about six months it was clear that David's visits to the Learning Disabilities Center had proven helpful. David was no longer anxious as he walked into the building, could play by himself or with other children, in a limited way, in the playroom, and could separate readily from his mother to accompany the speech therapist to her office. There was more reciprocal give-and-take play with the speech therapist, some increase in eye contact, and a decided increase in the use of language. David's functional level came up to the $3^1/_2$-year level by the time he was 5. His parents, who had been mildly depressed for the first three months after the initial interview, seemed to be much more accepting and less overprotective of David. His mother was firm, yet supportive with David in helping him separate from her. She also responded differently to his screaming and temper tamtrums. When these occurred, she had learned to walk away and ignore them. This frequently aborted the tantrum on the spot.

DISCUSSION

Psychopathology and Diagnosis   Initially, Ms. Whitmore did not fully recognize the extent of David's problems, but she did notice that his physical development lagged far behind that of other little boys his age. She was also aware that he was excessively attached to her, and that it was extremely difficult for him to separate from her. Although she did not think of it as a problem, she recalled that David had been remarkably placid and undemanding as an infant. During the evaluation period, other physical and psychological abnormalities were noted by the various clinicians: muscle flaccidity ("sack of potatoes") and drooling, subnormal IQ on a standardized test (55 on the Stanford-Binet Intelligence Test), problems with articulation, extremely limited vocabulary and sentence structure, temper tantrums, and negativistic behavior.

The combination of subnormal intelligence and functional impairment indicates the presence of mental retardation. David's IQ of 55 places him in the mildly mentally retarded range. His problems with articulation and language expression are developmental disabilities that go along with the other motor manifestations of his mental retardation. The clinging behavior David exhibited is more typical of a 2-year-old, and suggests a developmental lag in his emotional development as well, a common associated symptom of mental retardation.

Mental retardation is classified with other disorders that usually first begin in infancy, childhood, or adolescence. Although many of these disorders do not persist into adult life, mental retardation and several others do.

Etiology   David's mother's three previous spontaneous abortions and the complications during her pregnancy with David (high blood pressure, bleeding in the final months, and vomiting throughout) increased the possibility that David would have difficulties after birth. In addition, the birth itself was traumatic, with evidence of asphyxia (the cord was wrapped around the baby's neck and he required oxygen for resuscitation). Insufficient respiration at birth can lead to damage in various parts of the brain. David's flaccid muscle tone and poor sucking response shortly after birth suggest that some damage had actually occurred, either in utero or during the difficult delivery. Delayed milestones (the ages at which a child sits, stands, walks, talks, and is toilet trained) and incoordination are also evidence of abnormal central nervous system development. The excessive drooling suggests some disturbance in the part of the brain that controls and coordinates the mouth. This same area of the brain coordinates the tongue and speech, thus accounting for his problems with articulation.

David did not show any observable physical abnormalities, such as those found in Down's syndrome (mongolism—an inherited chromosomal abnormality that causes mental retardation and characteristic physical abnormalities). Like many other children with mental retardation, David is normal in appearance, but abnormal in behavior. It is this contradiction between the appearance of a normal child and an invisible handicap that leads parents to deny that they have a mentally retarded child. This denial further exacerbates the child's problem, because he may not be given the special attention and training that he needs. Parents who tend to overprotect such children from the rest of the world make them more dependent than need be on others for their survival.

Treatment and Prognosis   The diagnosis of mental retardation generally comes as a shock to most parents, almost like telling them their child has cancer. Yet the outlook is not as bleak as they may at first think. David's parents were very depressed after their first parent conference. With the help of the treatment team, David's parents became more hopeful as David's level of separation anxiety diminished. In addition, after only six months of language therapy, David's language skills increased from a 2-year-old level to that of a $3^1/_2$-year-old child. With special schooling and continued support from his parents, David will probably be able to function at home while growing up. Since he functions in the range termed educable mentally retarded, he can attend special schools. David can grow up at home, and can probably go on to live an independent life, working at a low-skill job, since he is not physically stigmatized the way some children with mental retardation are. Because of the early identification that led to special help for David and his family, he now has a better chance to become a functioning member of the community.

MIGHTY MOUSE

Larry is a 10-year-old boy who was referred for treatment since he was on the verge of being thrown out of school because of hyperactivity, destructiveness, stealing, and short attention span. These problems had become increasingly frequent at home and in school for the past four years. Larry's mother described him as an extremely active toddler, who was "always climbing." He frequently got up early in the morning and messed up his room before anybody else was awake. In nursery school at age 4 he was far more active than the other children in class, and he seemed to have great difficulty getting along with his peers. By first grade, in the public school, although he was reading on grade level, he obviously had difficulty sticking to academic tasks and had a lot of trouble getting along with other children. Because of his poor academic functioning, his small size, and the fact that he was the youngest one in his class (because he was born in December), his parents insisted that he repeat the first grade.

In second grade the teacher reported that he had extremely poor handwriting, poor coordination, and poor oral expression, and that he was "hyperactive." He rarely completed his assignments in class, was unable to work by himself, and became very disruptive when in an unsupervised classroom situation. His handwriting was very sloppy, and his notebooks were illegible. He called out frequently in class and interrupted and intruded into other children's activities and work, so that they complained about his constant talking and chatter. He could not wait his turn in games or in group situations. When asked to wait, he occasionally got into fights with other children. He had no friends, since the other children considered him irritating and obnoxious.

At home he was constantly touching things and knocking them off tables. By the time he was 8 he had destroyed three TV sets. After destroying or breaking something he would deny that he had been touching it, even though the adults in the room could see him breaking the object. He would take things from his brother and sister and store them under his bed, which was the source of much bickering among the siblings.

Because of all of these problems he was placed in a class for learning disabled children in third grade. This class was slightly smaller than the regular classes, and the teacher was experienced in working with difficult children. The teacher structured the classroom situation so as to reduce irrelevant stimuli and repeated instructions frequently to prevent Larry from deviating from the task. His behavior in the classroom improved, but he was still impossible to handle in other settings, such as in the lunchroom, at the playground, and at home on weekends. At the time of the referral he was unable to complete classroom assignments and was failing arithmetic.

Larry is the third child in a middle-class family. His 42-year-old father is a stockbroker and his mother, age 37, is a housewife. Larry has a 15-year-old brother and a 13-year-old sister, who apparently have never had any of Larry's problems.

According to his parents, the pregnancy was normal, but Larry was born in a breech delivery (feet first), and both the mother and child had a "difficult time." There were, however, no signs of birth complications such as anoxia (reduced oxygen to the brain), cyanosis (bluish coloring to the skin due to reduced oxygen in the blood), or jaundice (yellow pigmentation of skin and mucous membranes due to the presence of substances ordinarily removed from the body by the liver and kidney) at birth, and Larry ate and slept well, with no colic (acute abdominal pain sometimes associated with eating during infancy). He walked late, at 24 months, and did not talk clearly in sentences until he was $3^1/_2$. He was toilet trained by $3^1/_2$, and there was no soiling or bedwetting after that.

As part of the evaluation done by the child psychiatry clinic, he was tested with a Wechsler Intelligence Scale for Children, Revised (a standard individual IQ test used with children). He earned a full-scale score of 87, with a verbal scale score of 90 and a performance scale score of 80. His subtest scores showed a great deal of scatter. His Wide Range Achievement Test (another standard IQ test) scores were in the normal range.

Larry was a small, restless boy who talked rapidly with a lisp. During a physical examination the psychiatrist noted that Larry had minor anomalies (physical deviations from normal usually related to congenital or hereditary defects): a high arched palate, low-set ears, and a wide space between the first and second toes on his left foot. He talked constantly, jumping from subject to subject, and made incessant demands upon the physician to play different games with him. He would start one game, play it for a minute and a half, and then look around the room until something caught his eye. He was quite distractible—when someone knocked on the door he got up out of his seat and seemed to forget entirely about the game he was playing. While his parents were being interviewed, he went around the room, pulling things off the shelf, leaning across the physician's desk to grab something on top of the desk, and fooling with the light switch on the wall. His constant motion made it difficult to conduct an interview either with him or with his parents. Interestingly, his mother had a similar speech pattern, with rapid jumping from topic to topic.

A decision was made to initiate a trial of psychomotor stimulant medication, with an early morning dose and one at noon. His parents confirmed that within 45 minutes of taking the medicine he generally became quiet and attentive and was able to play games or engage in other activities to completion—something he could rarely do before. Improvement was immediately noted by his teachers.

After six months of continuous medication the former symptoms of hyperactivity and disorganization seemed to reappear despite the medication. For this reason, Larry was switched to a longer acting stimulant, taken each morning. He had an immediate response, similar to his initial response to the previous medication. The duration of medication effect extended well into the afternoon.

When last seen, two years later, Larry had continued to take the longer acting medication and to have a good response. Although his academic school work remained poor, he was no longer a behavioral problem and was able to complete assignments.

DISCUSSION

Psychopathology and Diagnosis As children grow up, they develop an increasing capacity to focus attention and delay acting on impulses. In addition, older children, unless engaged in a specific activity such as a sport or a game, are normally less active than younger children. One would expect a 10-year-old to be able to sit quietly for a considerably longer period of time than a 3-year-old. When there is hyperactivity, impulsivity, and inattention that would be "normal" only in a younger child, attention deficit disorder is diagnosed.

Larry has always been a particularly active child, but since he entered nursery school he has had problems with hyperactivity, impulsivity, and short attention span. Signs of hyperactivity included knocking things off tables and running around the doctor's office. Impulsivity was apparent in his inability to await his turn in games and calling out frequently in class. Because of his short attention span, he was unable to complete assignments and was easily distracted. He thus showed all the features of *attention deficit disorder with hyperactivity*.

There is little difficulty in making this diagnosis in Larry's case, since his behavior is so extreme and so different from that of his siblings and classmates. "Normal" children may exhibit many of these same deviant behaviors if they are in a chaotic home or school environment, but in such cases the child's reaction would be regarded as understandable in relation to the disturbed environment and would not represent a mental disorder in the child.

Associated Features Signs of attention deficit disorder are usually recognized by the beleaguered parents by the time the child is 3. However, it is usually not until the child enters school and is unable to meet the demands of the environment for sustained attention and self-control that he or she comes to the attention of mental health professionals. In the United States it is estimated that attention deficit disorder may occur in 3 percent of prepubertal children, and it is ten times more common in boys than in girls. Children with the disorder almost invariably have trouble achieving in school, and may therefore lose interest in school and develop a variety of additional problems such as truancy and other antisocial behaviors. Often the child with attention deficit disorder also has a specific developmental disorder, such as a reading disorder (see Case 46, "Not Stupid"). About 5 percent of the cases are also associated with a diagnosable neurological disorder.

Etiology The etiology of attention deficit disorder is unknown, although many assume that there is an underlying abnormality of the central nervous system. It is for this reason that in the past this condition was often referred to as minimal brain dysfunction. Evidence for this view is that many of the children with this disorder exhibit "soft neurologic signs": abnormalities such as poor hand-eye coordination, which suggest a neurologic disorder, but do not indicate the location of the disturbance within the brain. (Larry was noted to have extremely poor handwriting.) In addition, there are often a complicated birth history (Larry was born in breech position), minor physical anomalies (Larry had a high arched palate, low-set ears, and a wide space between the first and second toes of his left foot), and delayed developmental milestones (Larry was late walking and talking). Despite these hints of an organic etiology, no specific biologic abnormality has been demonstrated for this condition.

Treatment A common form of treatment is the use of stimulant medication, which in prepubertal children has the paradoxical effect of inhibiting hyperactivity and impulsivity. In addition, it seems to help the child sustain attention. Unfortunately, as demonstrated in Larry's case, tolerance to the medication may develop, and another stimulant must be tried. Most children with the disorder respond rapidly and dramatically to the treatment. Nevertheless, the treatment is controversial. Many arguments against drug treatment are made: it may be used indiscriminately to control children who are disruptive in school but do not have the disorder; it directs attention away from improving the school or family environment; and the long-term effects of giving drugs to children are unknown. Alternative treatments have primarily employed behavioral principles of reinforcing desired behavior in the school and at home (as was initially tried with Larry). The relative efficacy of behavioral modification and stimulant medication for the treatment of this disorder is controversial.

Prognosis At 12 Larry no longer had behavior problems, but his school performance had not improved. This combination of improved behavior but unchanged academic achievement is common following drug treatment. In some cases, behavioral treatment can have a beneficial effect on school achievement.

In most cases of attention deficit disorder the symptoms, particularly the motoric hyperactivity, disappear in adolescence. Less commonly, some or all of the symptoms persist into adulthood. One hopes that Larry will be among the more fortunate.

CON ARTIST

Carl Mason is a physically attractive, husky 12-year-old boy with brown hair, blue eyes, and a very pleasant smile. He was referred for inpatient psychiatric evaluation by his local community mental health center, where he had been seen at the request of the court. He had "stolen" the car of the couple in charge of the foster home where he had been sent to live for thirty days. After one evaluation session, both the community mental health center and his natural mother agreed that an inpatient evaluation and brief treatment were essential if he were to return to live with his natural parents. His mother felt unable to control him and described him as a "real con artist," stating, "He isn't dumb. He manipulates me and George (his stepfather)." She also stated, "He gets tired and bored with people, places, and things and jumps from one thing to another."

At the time of referral Carl was in the seventh grade in the public school. Although he is of normal intelligence (full-scale IQ of 100 on the Wechsler Intelligence Scale for Children, Revised), his school performance, with the exception of mathematics, was only at the fifth-grade level. His school report indicated that his classroom behavior with peers and with teachers was very poor. Teachers complained of his lack of respect for authority and rated him as extremely disturbed. Although teachers described his willingness to speak out in class and enter discussions as one of his strengths, they also indicated that he spoke without regard for whether peers or teachers were speaking at the same time.

Carl's father was a heavy drinker and frequently abused his wife and children and threatened violence in the home. (For example, on one occasion it is reported that his father wired the home with dynamite and threatened to detonate it.) Among the violent events that Carl witnessed was the attempted rape of his mother by his father. Carl, then 5 years old, and his two older brothers tried to protect their mother. It was Carl, however, the youngest, who is reported to have stabbed his father in the leg. After this event Carl's father left the home and the parents were permanently separated.

Carl's mother says that Carl was very close to her over the next few years and was distressed by frequent separations from her due to her repeated hospitalizations for a variety of medical conditions. These included a fracture sustained in a motorcycle accident, leg surgery, and diabetes.

Although Carl had been successfully toilet trained, reportedly by the age of ten months, he became enuretic (involuntary voiding of urine) and encopretic (passage of feces into places not appropriate for that purpose) at the age of 4. These problems have persisted, and are more frequent during periods of stress. At age 5 Carl entered kindergarten with no apparent difficulties. However, by the second grade, when he was 7 years old, teachers began to complain of disobedience, enuresis, encopresis, and fighting at school. He was referred at that time for psychiatric evaluation, and a recommendation was made that he be placed in a class for socially and emotionally disturbed children. However, his mother rejected this recommendation, claiming that Carl had no difficulties at home. She insisted that the teacher was hostile and that Carl saw the school impinging on his right to make his own decisions. It is important to note that while his mother stated there was no difficulty with Carl at home during this time, she also reported at the same time that she had had to stop his encopresis by smearing feces on his face. Carl's mother removed him from the public school and enrolled him in a parochial school. However, after one term he was asked to leave the parochial school because of behavior problems similar to those he had had in the public schools.

Shortly after Carl's father left the home, George, his current stepfather, moved in. Although he and Carl's mother did not get married for two-and-a-half years, George was consistently present in the house. When Carl was 8 years old, his mother married George. Shortly after the marriage, Carl was again referred for psychiatric evaluation and was placed on medication for his enuresis. Carl's eighth year was especially difficult, due in part to the hospitalization of his mother on yet another occasion. His behavior became increasingly unmanageable at home, and he was sent to live with his natural father for one month. At the end of that time he was "thrown out" and returned to live with his mother and stepfather. At age 9 Carl was hospitalized to determine if there were physical causes for his enuresis and encopresis, but all investigations were negative.

There were no further reports of contact with mental health services between the ages of 9 and 11. The family reported, in retrospect, that he had continued to have great difficulty in school and to "embarrass" his stepfather, who was a policeman, by getting into trouble in the community. There were no legal charges during this time, however, since fellow officers would merely return him to his stepfather, and the family would try to deal with this alone. However, at age 11 Carl's mother and stepfather contacted a children and youth services agency, stating they could no longer manage Carl or his older brother in their home because they were constantly skipping school, lying, and stealing. The agency initially placed the two boys in the same foster home with an expected thirty-day stay. This stay continued up until this hospitalization, partially due to another physical illness and hospitalization of their mother.

In foster care Carl was reportedly unhappy and made several attempts to run away. One one occasion he disappeared while on a shopping trip with his foster mother. When he was found several hours later, the security guard who returned him said that he had told a woman in the parking lot that his foster mother had abandoned him and he had no way to get home. He could give no reason for having made up this story. Also during this period Carl broke into a trailer and stole approximately $100. He left fingerprints which were easily identified. It is reported that he went to a pizza parlor after stealing the money, bought pizza for his friends, and gave the money to them. While in the foster home, Carl had several other contacts with mental health clinics and juvenile courts. He ran away from home on several occasions, broke into houses, stole money, and set fires. At school he had an extensive history of oppositional behavior and truancy. These problems culminated in his theft of his foster parents' car, precipitating the referral to the community mental health center.

When interviewed, Carl acknowledged occasional difficulty sleeping and complained of aches and pains in his chest, abdomen, and neck (with no organic evidence of injury or disease). He was often sad and had little positive to say about himself. He reported smoking half a pack of cigarettes daily for several years and occasionally getting drunk on alcohol.

Carl was admitted to a short-term psychiatric inpatient facility for children ages 6 to 12 years. Despite his belligerence and hostility toward authority, he was often quite cooperative and socially adept with both adults and peers. He claimed to have several good friends in his foster parents' neighborhood and often helped younger children on the inpatient unit, for example, helping them get dressed. This picture is consistent with the description of him given by his foster parents. Carl indicated that he did not feel he belonged in the hospital, had no intentions of talking about past behavior, expressed no remorse for anything he had done, and was critical of the numerous rules and procedures necessary in the hospital. By the end of the first day Carl had stolen some silverware from the cafeteria and stored it in his duffelbag.

Despite this, during the first three days in the hospital Carl demonstrated that he could easily join in games with peers, was able to learn the rules of the unit quickly, and that he could be an extremely pleasant young man. Nevertheless, by the end of the third day he had been involved in pushing incidents with other children, swore excessively at times for no apparent reason, and had demonstrated questionable judgment in putting children on his shoulders and running around the unit, risking injury both to himself and to the child on his shoulders. In this limited period of time he demonstrated to the staff his ability to be both socially adept as well as, at other times, cunning, aggressive, and hostile.

Because of the protracted history of Carl's aggressive behavior and the inability of his parents to manage him, a multifaceted treatment approach was undertaken, involving individual therapy, a ward management program during hospitalization, and parent management training. The individual cognitive therapy was provided to help

Carl with severe aggressiveness and poor relationships with peers and authority figures (parents, teachers, others).

Cognitive therapy for conduct problems helps children learn how to approach and resolve interpersonal situations in which they might ordinarily act impulsively or aggressively. Carl received eighteen sessions of individual treatment in which he learned and rehearsed problem-solving steps that could be applied to everyday situations. In this approach children are trained, whenever they confront a potentially difficult situation, to ask themselves the following five questions: (1) How should I behave in this situation? (2) What possible ways could I act? (3) What will happen to me if I act in each of these different ways? (4) Which way will I act? (5) (After acting) How well did I do what I was supposed to do? Carl practiced the application of these problem-solving skills on the unit during his hospitalization and at home on occasional weekends he spent with his parents.

The ward management program was also designed to assist Carl in gaining more consistent control over his behavior. With the nurse primarily responsible for his care he began to work on his impulsive behavior, his swearing and aggressive outbursts at staff and peers, and his compliance with ward rules. With successful management of these areas he was able to earn points for which he would be rewarded. The rewards he chose were predominantly those that allowed him special time alone with his nurse-therapist and visits home with his parents.

To prepare Carl's parents for his return home and to equip them to manage his behavior, they received six sessions of parent management training. Training focused on ways in which they could systematically provide rewarding consequences for Carl's appropriate behavior and mild punishment for inappropriate behavior. The punishments were predominantly those used in the hospital, which included loss of privileges for special events or having to spend time alone in his room until he could regain control.

Carl made progress both in his interaction on the unit and with his parents. On the unit he avoided fights by using the problem-solving approach he learned in therapy, and he was able to express himself without resorting to force. His use of the problem-solving skills was noted both on the unit and in the hospital classroom. On the unit he would ordinarily be easily provoked to a fight by being teased. If someone commented about what he was doing or teased him about his attire, his immediate reaction would be to hit them. When Carl applied the problem-solving steps, he could not be provoked as readily.

During the course of hospitalization Carl occasionally earned the opportunity to spend weekends with his family. At the beginning these visits were marked by many of the same problems that had preceded hospitalization. However, after several weeks of hospitalization the parents reported that Carl was much better at negotiating with them in situations that had ordinarily precipitated aggressiveness, noncompliance, and tantrums. Also, they felt more skilled in helping him manage his behavior better. As a result, when his parents asked him to do things around the house, he sometimes expressed anger, but he did the tasks and did not have a tantrum and strike out at others or throw things first. Similarly, when siblings "borrowed" things from his room, his typical response had been to hurt them and to destroy something of theirs. After treatment, he expressed his anger verbally (and intensely) and avoided physical destruction and aggression.

After approximately three months of hospitalization Carl was discharged to the care of his mother and stepfather. Arrangements were made to continue individual therapy with Carl and parent management training with his mother and stepfather. Carl was also placed in a special education classroom for socially and emotionally disturbed children. At discharge the parents felt that although Carl was much better, they had great concern about their ability to manage him at home. Indeed, they threatened him with the prospect of being sent to military school at the slightest sign of relapse. (Obviously, neither the spirit not the letter of parent management training had been totally adopted by the parents at the time of discharge.)

It is also clear that Carl's problems remain even as treatment continues. Within a few weeks after discharge Carl was suspended from school because of drinking whisky and giving it to his friends. Apart from this school episode, he was caught smoking cigarettes at home. Hence some of the behaviors that had gotten him into trouble prior to admission apparently have continued. Treatment is still underway, and follow-up evaluation is planned over the course of the next two years.

DISCUSSION

Psychopathology and Diagnosis   From an early age Carl's behavior has been persistently antisocial, that is, he has continually violated important social norms (lying, truancy, disobedience, running away from home) and the basic rights of others (stealing, fighting, setting fires, breaking into houses). This behavior has gotten him into trouble at home, at school, and in the community, and he seems to have no capacity to experience guilt or remorse. He has been punished by his parents, placed in a special class in school, brought into juvenile court, and finally admitted to a psychiatric hospital.

In Carl's case, the antisocial behavior is so pervasive and persistent that it clearly indicates psychopathology. However, antisocial behavior by itself is not always a symptom of a mental disorder. Children (or adults) may engage in antisocial behavior because they belong to a subgroup in which this behavior is expected, for example, an urban street gang or a terrorist organization. In such instances, although the antisocial behavior may even be persistent over time, it is localized to certain settings.

Antisocial behavior may also occur as a transient reaction to a stressful life situation; for example, a child may begin to fight, steal, and skip school after his parents' divorce. This would be considered adjustment disorder (see Case 37, "Mr. Nice Guy") with disturbance of conduct, and one would expect that the antisocial behavior would stop when the individual has adapted to the new situation.

When, as in Carl's case, the pattern of antisocial behavior is both persistent over time and pervades all areas of the individual's life, a diagnosis of conduct disorder is made. Conduct disorder is subdivided into either aggressive or nonaggressive, depending on whether or not the antisocial behavior involves physical violence against people or destruction of property. Examples of nonaggressive antisocial behavior would include lying, truancy, and shoplifting. Aggressive antisocial behavior includes mugging, assault, rape, and vandalism. Conduct disorder is also subclassified as socialized or undersocialized. The individual with the socialized type demonstrates significant attachments to peers, whereas the individual with the undersocialized type is usually a loner. These subtypes have important prognostic implications. The individual with the aggressive and undersocialized type is the most likely to have an antisocial personality disorder as an adult (see Case 14, "Gary Gilmore"), whereas children with the nonaggressive and socialized type are likely to "outgrow" the condition and achieve reasonable social and occupational adjustment as adults. The prognosis for Carl's subtype, aggressive and socialized, is generally intermediate.

Children with conduct disorder often also have other manifestations of psychopathology. Particularly common is attention deficit disorder, and in fact, Carl's mother describes him as "jumping from one thing to another," and his teachers indicate that he speaks out of turn in class (see Case 40, "Mighty Mouse"). In addition, Carl has had intermittent functional enuresis and functional encopresis, that is, enuresis and encopresis without any apparent organic cause.

Etiology   Several factors have been identified as being particularly common in the backgrounds of individuals who develop conduct disorder: parental alcoholism, child abuse, broken homes, and placement in foster care. Interestingly, all of these factors apply to Carl's background. From a psychoanalytic perspective, all of these factors involve a disruption in the child-parent relationship which is essential for the normal development of the superego (conscience). From a behavioral perspective, the family is the laboratory in which the child learns to model his behavior after his parents. Carl not only did not have a father throughout his development, but during the first five years of his life, when his father was present, he had the model of an aggressive male.

Treatment   Because of the absence of a treatment with demonstrated effectiveness and society's need to protect itself, most children with conduct disorder are circulated through the criminal justice system. Carl is fortunate in having found his way into the health care system, and specifically into an innovative treatment program. Standard forms of psychotherapy have not been shown to be effective with such children, whereas there is evidence that the social learning approach used in Carl's treatment has promise. The question of success or failure in Carl's case remains to be answered. In view of the chronicity of Carl's antisocial behavior, even a partially effective treatment may take a long time to produce significant changes and ultimately may not ensure long-term success in adapting to the world.

WHO AM I?

Mark Nielsen is a 21-year-old senior at a prestigious middle Atlantic college. He came to the counseling center in November of his senior year with complaints of insomnia and general feelings of tension. He was unclear about the source of the tension, although he stated that a relationship with a female classmate had recently ended. However, he tended to discount the importance of this because "we were really only casual friends." The insomnia had begun about two weeks previously, and he related this to worry about midterm exams. Otherwise, in the initial evaluation interview he was rather vague about emotional conflicts, but accepted the invitation to enter brief exploratory psychotherapy.

Mark was a handsome individual of medium height with the muscular build that suggested an athlete. In the initial interview he seemed edgy, but he spoke clearly and coherently. He was casually dressed in paint-stained dungarees, in a manner not uncharacteristic of his peers. He described his academic record as quite good for his first two years, but he had done less well during his junior year, which he attributed to "being upset" a good deal of the time in the last year. He was concerned that the drop from an A to a B-minus average would seriously limit his choices after graduation. Although he said he was "compulsive" at times about his work, there was no evidence of rituals, phobias, ideas of reference, or delusions. Concentration, memory, and orientation were intact.

Mark came from a family that put great emphasis on achievement. He was the oldest child with a younger brother, 19, and a younger sister, 17. Mark's father came from a rather poor farm family, but he had been in military service during the Korean war and had used the GI bill in the postwar period to further his education. He was now a successful family physician. Mark described his father as "anal," by which he meant meticulous with a strong sense of duty. Mark's mother was a frustrated artist, who had devoted her time to household duties and who became disorganized under any kind of pressure. Her family background was upper middle class, and initially there apparently had been some opposition to her marriage to Mark's father on the basis of it being socially inappropriate. Mark's brother was described as easygoing and "not a very good student." His sister was described as intense and intelligent, but socially rather awkward. There was no history of emotional illness in the family. Mark reported no particular difficulties that he remembered during childhood and adolescence, and no attempt was made to obtain information from the parents.

Mark was initiallly rather bland in therapy, maintaining the facade that "nothing is really wrong; I just need to be able to sleep." By the third interview, however, he began to describe conflicts that it soon became clear troubled him deeply.

Mark had started his college career with the plan of majoring in a social science, probably sociology. In his sophomore year he decided to go to medical school, but because he had taken none of the premed requirements, it was necessary to take them in his junior and senior years. This meant that during his senior year he had a particularly difficult academic schedule with a heavy emphasis on science. In his junior year he had taken a studio art course "for kicks" and found it far more enjoyable than his other courses. This led him to wonder if he had chosen the wrong career. He had mentioned the possibility of not applying to medical school at home, and this remark precipitated one of the few arguments that he had ever had with his father, who described artists as "bums" and went on to state that he had no intention of supporting Mark while he lounged around "in some scruffy loft."

Interspersed with expressing his concerns about his career choice, Mark hesitantly began to discuss his worries about his sexual identity. His earlier sexual history was unremarkable. He had begun masturbation when he was 13, and although he had felt somewhat guilty about it, he had read sufficiently so that he was somewhat reassured that it was a normal phase of development, and denied that this was "a problem." He had dated periodically (often as part of a group) during high school and on several occasions engaged in some sexual play short of intercourse, which he found pleasurable, but he had had no "heavy" romances. When he got to college he had two brief relationships that led to sexual intercourse, but he did not feel that either relationship had much emotional significance for him.

During his sophomore summer he had shared an apartment in New York with a male friend while taking a summer school science course. He found, somewhat to his surprise, that he became quite attached to him, and after some drinks one night they had sex. They both enjoyed it, and the relationship continued for the rest of the summer. Mark's apartment mate was quite clear that "he was straight" and dismissed the sex as "the next best thing while he was away from his girl friend." Mark, however, was confused by the events and began "to wonder whether I was really gay." Back at college during his junior year he went to a gay bar on a couple of occasions and was picked up by older men, but felt "disgusted" with the sex. He resolved to pursue women more actively and did succeed in developing a relationship that was sexually enjoyable, but the lack of emotional involvement when compared to his experience with his roommate during the summer confused him even further.

During college Mark's circle of friends varied rather widely. He had a relatively good singing voice that enabled him to join one of the campus singing groups. This particular group was noted for its conservative image. Several of the members came from wealthy families, and consequently, the group was invited to sing at exclusive country clubs and to entertain at private parties given by family friends of the group members. Mark did not feel he fit into this atmosphere, but he found it glamorous and often had fantasies that he would marry someone he met at one of the parties, and would thus permanently join this world. In sharp contrast, Mark had also made friends with several art school people, as a result of his studio art course. This was an entirely different group with entirely different values. They were overtly scornful of the "preppies" and criticized Mark for his singing group activities. They favored drug use and sexual experimentation in the interest of "creativity." Although Mark did not think he espoused these values, especially in relation to drugs, he observed that, when with this group, he felt relaxed in a way that he felt at no other time.

About the sixth therapy session Mark came to the conclusion that "I don't know who I am." He recognized for the first time that many of his decisions and much of his activity were the result of conforming to, or rebelling against what he saw as his parents' wishes. He recognized the burden that he felt the family placed on him as the "hope" of the family, since he had both intelligence and social skills. He began to see that his mother and father had rather different aspirations for him, and although they appeared to present a united front, the differences were communicated to him in subtle ways. He also talked some about his conflict with the family, especially his mother, around the issue of religion. He had been brought up as a strict Roman Catholic, but he had stopped going to church when he got to college. He had not admitted this to his parents and felt quite guilty about it and hypocritical because he continued to go to church when he was at home.

As therapy progressed Mark became more aware of his own wishes, and although many of his conflicts were not resolved immediately, he felt, after several months, that he had a much better ability to see the sources of his conflicts, and his symptoms were reduced. At one point he commented that "parts of myself do not fit together very well." He eventually made a decision to "take some time out" before making a career choice and was able to hold to this decision in the face of parental pressure. He realized that he had difficulty with commitment, and recognized that he would need to be clearer and more consistent in assessing his own feelings before he could make more far-reaching decisions. He also realized that he could experiment some, and that, if he made mistakes, it would not necessarily be disastrous, and such mistakes might even help him to make more satisfactory decisions in the long run.

DISCUSSION

Psychopathology and Diagnosis   Mark Nielsen came for treatment with a common complaint: he had just broken up with a girl friend and was feeling tense, having trouble sleeping, and was not functioning as well as he had been. However, in the course of the evaluation it became clear that there were other more serious problems, that all related to an uncertainty about his own sense of identity. He was unable to choose among various possible careers. He was not sure whether he was basically heterosexual or homosexual. He was torn between two groups of friends, each with different values and lifestyles. Associated with these conflicts was his inability to differentiate between what he really wanted and what he did in response to his parents' expectations of him.

Many adolescents and young adults have some conflict about issues related to identity, such as career choice, religious identification, and group loyalty. Usually these conflicts are merely a normal part of growing up, and even when causing severe distress, there is rarely any prolonged impairment in social or occupational functioning. However, when there is severe subjective distress about a variety of issues related to identity, as well as significant impairment in functioning, the diagnosis of *identity disorder* is made. In making this diagnosis, one needs to consider the possibility of a personality disorder such as borderline (see Case 12, "Angry Young Man"). In Mark's case the disturbance is not sufficiently enduring and there is no evidence of the wide variety of signs of instability, such as impulsivity, moodiness, and stormy interpersonal relationships, that are characteristic of borderline personality disorder.

Course Identity disorder usually begins in late adolescence, when individuals attempt to establish independent identities apart from their families, and is usually resolved in a few years, with or without treatment. If identity disorder becomes chronic, it may be impossible for the individual to maintain a stable work pattern, or to form lasting interpersonal relationships. In some cases identity disorder may develop into borderline personality disorder.

Treatment Mark's treatment has apparently helped him to feel better and to postpone his career choice until he is more certain about his own goals. It is not easy to predict the future course of his sexual orientation. Because he succeeded in having an enjoyable sexual relationship with a woman even after his homosexual experiences, it is apparent that he has both homosexual and heterosexual impulses. (On the Kinsey scale of heterosexual-homosexual balance, he would probably have gotten a rating of 4, indicating a lifetime pattern of slightly more arousal to homosexual stimuli than to heterosexual stimuli. A 0 on this scale indicates a history of arousal to exclusively heterosexual stimuli, and 6 is for exclusively homosexual arousal.) Hopefully he will be able to combine sexuality (homosexual or heterosexual) with intimacy. A less happy possibility is that he will develop a persistent homosexual arousal pattern, but be uncomfortable with it and yearn for the capacity to respond heterosexually with the possibility of a more traditional family life style. (This would be called ego-dystonic homosexuality. There is no corresponding category of ego-dystonic heterosexuality. The social pressures in our culture support heterosexuality, and therefore it is not surprising that no one has ever described a case of an individual with a heterosexual arousal pattern who wished to have it changed into a homosexual arousal pattern.)

CLOSE TO THE BONE

A 23-year-old woman from Arkansas wrote a letter to the head of a New York research group after seeing a television program in which he described his work with patients with unusual eating patterns. In the letter, which requested that she be accepted into his program, she described her problems as follows:

Several years ago, in college, I started using laxatives to lose weight. I started with a few and increased the number as they became ineffective. After two years I was taking 250–300 Ex-Lax pills at one time with a glass of water, 20 per gulp. I would lose as much as 10 pounds in a 24-hour period, mostly water and some food, dehydrated so that I couldn't stand, and could barely talk. I ended up in the university infirmary several times with diagnoses of food poisoning, severe gastro-intestinal flu, etc., with bland diets and medications. I was released within a day or two. A small duodenal ulcer appeared and disappeared on x-rays in 1975.

I would not eat for days, then would eat something, and overcome by guilt at eating, and HUNGER, would eat-eat-eat. A girl on my dorm floor told me that she occasionally forced herself to vomit so that she wouldn't gain weight. I did this every once in a while and discovered that I could consume large amounts of food, vomit, and still lose weight. This was spring of 1975. I lost nearly 50 pounds over a few months, to 90 pounds. My hair started coming out in handfuls and my teeth were loose.

I never felt lovelier or more confident about my appearance: physically liberated, streamlined, close-to-the-bone. I was flat everywhere except my stomach when I binged, when I would be full-blown and distended. When I bent over, each rib and back vertebra was outlined. After vomiting my stomach was once more flat, empty. The more weight I lost, the more I was afraid of getting fat. I was afraid to drink water for days at a time because it would add pounds on the scale and make me miserable. Yet I drank (or drink; perhaps I should be writing this all in the *present* tense) easily a half-gallon of milk and other liquids at once when binging. I didn't need the laxatives as much to get rid of food and eventually stopped using them altogether (although I am still chronically constipated, I become nauseous whenever I see them in the drugstore).

I exercised for hours each day to tone my figure from the weight fluctuations, and joined the university track team. I wore track shoes all the time and ran to classes and around town, stick-legs pumping. I went to track practice daily after being sick, until I was forced to quit; a single lap would make me dizzy, with cramps in my stomach and legs.

At some point during my last semester before dropping out I came across an article on anorexia nervosa. It frightened me; my own personal obsession with food and bodyweight was shared by other people. I had not menstruated in two years. So, I forced myself to eat and digest healthy food. Hated it. I studied nutrition and gradually forced myself to accept a new attitude toward food—vitalizing—something needed for life. I gained weight, fighting panic. In a rigid, controlled way I have maintained myself nutritionally ever since: 105–115 pounds at 5'6". I know what I need to survive and I eat it—a balanced diet with the fewest possible calories, mostly vegetables, fruits, fish, fowl, whole grain products, etc. In five years I have not eaten anything like pizza, pastas or pork, sweets, or anything fattening, fried, or rich without being very sick. Once I allowed myself an ice cream cone. But I am usually sick if I deviate as much as one bite.

It was difficult for me to face people at school, and I dropped courses each semester, collecting incompletes but finishing well in the few classes I stayed with. The absurdity of my reclusiveness was even evident to me during my last semester when I signed up for correspondence courses, while living only two blocks from the correspondence university building on campus. I felt I would only be able to face people when I lost "just a few more pounds."

Fat. I cannot stand it. This feeling is stronger and more desperate than any horror at what I am doing to myself. If I gain a few pounds I hate to leave the house and let people see me. Yet I am sad to see how I have pushed aside the friends, activities, and state of energized health that once rounded my life.

For all of this hiding, it will surprise you to know that I am by profession a model. Last year when I was more in control of my eating-vomiting I enjoyed working in front of a camera, and I was doing well. Lately I've been sick too much and feel out-of-shape and physically unselfconfident for the discipline involved. I keep myself supported during this time with part-time secretarial work, and whatever unsolicited photo bookings my past clients give me. For the most part I do the secretarial work. And I can't seem to stop being sick all of the time.

The more I threw-up when I was in college, the longer it took, and the harder it became. I needed to use different instruments to induce vomiting. Now I double two electrical cords and shove them several feet down into my throat. This is preceded by 6–10 doses of ipecac [an emetic]. My knees are calloused from the time spent kneeling sick. The eating-vomiting process takes usually 2–3 hours, sometimes as long as 8. I dread the gagging and pain and sometimes my throat is very sore and I procrastinate using the ipecac and cords. I sit on the floor, biting my nails, and pulling the skin off around my nails with tweezers. Usually I wear rubber gloves to prevent this somewhat.

After emptying my stomach completely I wash thoroughly. In a little while I will hydrate myself with a bottle of diet pop, and take a handful of lasix 40mg [a diuretic] (which I have numerous prescriptions for). Sometimes I am faint, very cold. I splash cool water on my face, smooth my hair, but my hands are shaking some. I will take aspirin if my hands hurt sharply . . . so I can sleep later. My lips, fingers are bluish and cold. I see in the mirror that blood vessels are broken. There are red spots over my eyes. They always fade in a day or two. There is a certain relief when it is over, that the food is gone, and I am not horribly fat from it. And I cry often . . . for some rest, some calm. It is foolish for me to cry for someone, someone to help me; when it is only me who is hiding and hurting myself.

Now there is this funny new split in my behavior, this honesty about my illness. Hopefully it will bring me more help than humiliation. Sometimes I feel a hypocrisy in my actions, and in the frightened, well-ordered attempts to seek out help. All the while I am still sick, night after night after night. And often days as well.

Two sets of logic seem to be operating against each other, each determined, each half-canceling the effects of the other. It is the part of me which forced me to eat that I'm talking about . . . which cools my throat with water after hours of heaving, which takes potassium supplements to counteract diuretics, and aspirin for torn hands. It is this part of me, which walks into a psychiatrist's office twice weekly and sees the liability of hurting myself seriously, which makes constant small efforts to repair the tearing-down.

It almost sounds as if I am being brutalized by some unrelenting force. Ridiculous to feel this way, or to stand and cry, because the hands that cool my throat and try to make small repairs only just punched lengths of cord into my stomach. No demons, only me.

For your consideration, I am

Gratefully yours,

Nancy Lee Duval

Ms. Duval was admitted to the research ward for study. Additional history revealed that her eating problems began gradually during her adolescence. At age 14 she weighed 128 pounds and had reached her adult height of 5'6" tall. She felt "terribly fat" and began to diet without great success. At age 17 she weighed 165 pounds and began to diet more seriously for fear that she would be ridiculed, and went down to 130 pounds over the next year. She recalled feeling very depressed, overwhelmed, and insignificant. She began to avoid difficult classes so she would never get less than straight A's and began to lie about her school and grade performance for fear of being humiliated. She had great social anxiety dealing with boys which culminated in her transferring to an all-girls school for the last year of high school.

When she left for college her difficulties increased. She had trouble deciding how to organize her time, whether to study, to date, or to see friends. She became more desperate to lose weight and began to use laxatives as she describes in her letter. At age 20, in her sophomore year of college, she reached her lowest weight of 88 pounds (70 percent of ideal body weight) and stopped menstruating.

As she describes in her letter, she recognized that there was a problem and eventually forced herself to gain weight. Nonetheless, the overeating and vomiting which she had begun the previous year worsened. As she was preoccupied with her weight and her eating, her school performance suffered, and she dropped out of school midway through college at age 21.

Ms. Duval is the second of four children and the only girl. The family is an upper-middle-class professional family. From the patient's description, it sounds as though the father has a history of alcoholism. There are clear indications of difficulties between the mother and the father, and between the boys and the parents, but no other family member had ever had psychiatric treatment.

When the letter was written she had had moderately severe symptoms for three to four years. She remained in the research ward for several weeks, during which time she participated in research studies and, under the structure of the hospital setting, was able to give up her abuse of laxatives and diuretics. After her return home she continued in treatment with a psychiatrist in psychoanalytically oriented psychotherapy two times a week which she had begun six months previously. That therapy continued for approximately another six months, when her family refused to support it. The patient also felt that while she had gained some insight into her difficulties, she had been unable to change her behavior.

Two years after leaving the hospital whe wrote that she was "doing much better." She had reenrolled in college and was completing her course work satisfactorily. She had seen a nutritionist and felt that form of treatment was useful to her in learning what a normal diet was and how to maintain a normal weight. She was also receiving counseling from the school guidance counselors, but she did not directly relate that to her eating difficulties. Her weight was normal and she was menstruating regularly. She continued to have intermittent difficulty with binge eating and vomiting, although the frequency and severity of these problems were much reduced. She no longer abused diuretics and laxatives.

DISCUSSION

Psychopathology and Diagnosis. Ms. Duval is suffering from a disorder that was first described nearly 300 years ago, and named *anorexia nervosa* in 1868. Although theories about the cause of the disorder have come and gone, the essential features have remained unchanged. Ms. Duval poignantly describes these features. She had an intense and irrational fear of becoming obese, even when she was emaciated. Her body image was disturbed in that she perceived herself as fat when her weight was average, and "never lovelier" when, to others, she must have appeared grotesquely thin. She lost about 30 percent of her body weight by relentless dieting and exercising, self-inducing vomiting, and use of cathartics and diuretics. Significantly, the dieting takes place despite persistent hunger; thus the anorexia, which means loss of appetite, is a misnomer. In fact, a common associated feature, present in this case, is bulimia—the rapid consumption of high-caloric foods, often followed by vomiting and remorse. When an emaciated patient with anorexia nervosa insists that she is fat, this suggests the presence of a somatic delusion, as might be seen in schizophrenia or depression. However, such a patient is generally not considered to have a delusion because she is describing how she experiences herself rather than disputing the facts of her weight.

Course   Anorexia nervosa usually begins in adolescence, and rarely after 30. Ninety-five percent of the cases occur in women, and are invariably associated with amenorrhea. Anorexia nervosa is a serious illness since, even with treatment, as many as 20 percent of patients die of starvation. The course is variable, including spontaneous recovery after one episode, repeated episodes, or a long, chronic course. Considerable weight loss may be seen in depression, and a variety of physical disorders, but the distorted body image and unusual eating behavior is not present.

Etiology   A variety of psychological theories have been proposed to explain this unusual disorder: rejection of a wish to be pregnant, guilt over aggression toward an ambivalently regarded mother, disturbances of family interactions, and an attempt to resolve a conflict over autonomy versus dependence. It has also been suggested that anorexia nervosa is a "phobic" avoidance of food reflecting a marked fear of obesity. Research in recent years has demonstrated that several neuroendocrine regulatory disturbances are present in patients with the disorder, but whether these disturbances cause the illness or are merely the result of the severe weight loss remains uncertain.

Treatment   Patients with anorexia nervosa usually do not acknowledge that they are ill, and may agree to medical care only when they are so emaciated and dehydrated that emergency treatment is necessary to prevent death. Such treatment involves restoring the chemical balance and normal nutritional state of the body, and must take place in a hospital. Although psychodynamically oriented psychotherapy, either inpatient or outpatient, has been the traditional treatment for this disorder, behaviorally oriented approaches have been found to be more effective in inducing weight gain and changing the abnormal eating behavior. In behavioral treatment the patient is rewarded for weight gain with increasing privileges, and little attention is paid to the underlying conflicts.

Prognosis   Even though Ms. Duval is doing better, the prognosis is still guarded. She is still preoccupied with eating, and like many patients with anorexia, she continues intermittent binge eating, although her weight is now stable.

TEASED

Richard Green, a $15^1/_2$-year-old boy of Jewish Italian extraction, was seen in consultation. He had been asymptomatic until the age of 13, about two weeks after his Bar Mitzvah, when he became depressed and suddenly developed many involuntary muscular movements. The symptoms began with eye blinking for one week, followed by neck and leg twitching, and then repetitive sniffing so severe that his nose bled. He developed echolalia, repeating the last few words of other people's remarks. For example, when his mother said "Dinner is ready," he repeated, "Is ready, is ready." In addition, he began to curse, especially when angry. He developed a spitting habit, and repetitively touched people. His symptoms increased with anger, changes in environment, and loud noises, even when a loud slapping noise was made by an examining doctor. Symptoms would decrease when he was quiet and unstimulated. During sleep these symptoms were absent. Prodromal symptoms were a strange feeling in his stomach, arms, or neck. Prior to this period, Richard's grades had varied between A and B; subsequently his grades deteriorated and he began to fail in school.

Richard had an outgoing, engaging personality. Although he tried to disguise the symptoms in "horseplay," he was soon jeered at by his schoolmates, imitated, and ridiculed. He responded to these provocations by withdrawing from his peers and becoming isolated and depressed. He channeled his energies into music, which became a refuge, but would not perform in front of others even though symptoms disappeared when performing. He began to question his sanity, recognizing that his behavior was extremely unusual.

Richard was the second son born to a Jewish father and an Italian mother. The children were raised as Jewish. His father was obese and hypertensive, as was Richard's older brother. His mother was an anxious, overprotective woman with a family history of mental illness, including two brothers who committed suicide. Richard was described as always being a difficult child and hard to please. He would demand that his mother be present when he awakened from a nap, and his mother in turn never left him with a babysitter. He had always been a fussy eater.

Richard was extensively evaluated at several major psychiatric and neurologic centers. Several neurologic examinations and electroencephalograms were normal. One neurologist diagnosed his symptoms as an "emotional reaction"; another diagnosed brain injury—"chronic brain syndrome with frontal lobe involvement." All laboratory tests were normal. An ophthalmologic examination, done because of Richard's extensive eye blinking, revealed no abnormalities, and the diagnosis was "psychogenic blinking."

The psychiatric diagnosis most frequently made was "passive-aggressive personality" (a condition in which there is resistance to demands for adequate performance in social and academic or occupational functioning; the resistance is expressed indirectly rather than directly in traits such as procrastination, dawdling, stubbornness, and "forgetfulness"). It was also noted that he had some obsessive-compulsive traits. He always kept his room immaculate, and was perfectionistic in his school work and chores at home. He had a tendency to repeat tunes, and preferred odd numbers, for example, always sitting in an odd-numbered seat in a theater. On the other hand, he was not overly concerned with cleanliness, and had no difficulty making decisions.

On psychological examination he obtained a verbal IQ of 111, a performance IQ of 68, and a full-scale IQ of 90 on the Wechsler Adult Intelligence Scale (WAIS). The interpretation of the Bender-Gestalt test (which requires copying a set of geometric patterns) resulted in two opinions: one psychologist interpreted the record as normal, the second as abnormal. The second regarded the marked discrepancy between verbal and performance on the WAIS and the abnormality on the Bender as sure signs of organicity.

Pharmacologic treatment resulted in the suppression of 99 percent of Richard's symptoms. Once diagnosed, his depression lifted. He no longer viewed himself as bizarre and resumed his former outgoing manner. When or if he was teased, he would respond by telling the person that he had a tic condition and could not help himself. At follow-up, ten years later, he was working successfully in hotel management.

DISCUSSION

Psychopathology and Diagnosis   Richard exhibits recurrent involuntary repetitive and rapid movements—tics. He also makes uncontrollable sounds—verbal tics. Frequently the verbal tics take the form of curses (coprolalia). This peculiar constellation of bizarre symptoms is a movement disorder called *Tourette's disorder,* after the neurologist Gilles de la Tourette, who in 1884 first described the condition.*

---

*Tourette first became interested in the syndrome when he translated an article by an American neurologist, George Beard, who in 1881 described fifty cases of a bizarre syndrome, "the jumping Frenchmen of Maine." This syndrome begins in childhood and is characterized by a bark and jump in response to a sudden noise or startling event. Echolalia and automatic responses to comments are also associated with the syndrome. In 1884 Tourette published an article in which he described nine patients with a variant of "jumping Frenchmen" that he called "tic convulsif." He outlined the symptoms which distinguished this syndrome as a new diagnostic entity. Although what is now referred to as Tourette's disorder differs slightly from this syndrome, Tourette's brilliant and insightful observations earned him the honor of having the syndrome named after him.

Although the verbal and motor tics are involuntary, with a great effort of will they can be temporarily suppressed. Characteristically, the tics are more frequent when the individual is anxious; they diminish during periods of relaxation, and are absent during sleep and orgasm.

Richard has other symptoms that are sometimes seen in patients with Tourette's disorder. He exhibits compulsions (sitting in odd-numbered seats) and various perfectionistic traits (keeping his room immaculate). Perhaps these represent an attempt on Richard's part to control his illness through magic, ritual, and orderliness. Apparently the compulsions and perfectionistic traits are not so severe that by themselves they interfere with his functioning. Therefore the additional diagnosis of obsessive compulsive disorder would not be made (see Case 4, "Keeping Things Straight").

Course Tourette's disorder is almost always apparent before puberty. It is usually lifelong, although there may be brief periods in which the symptoms are not present.

Etiology Because of the involuntary cursing, it is understandable why for many years it was thought that the disorder was an expression of unconscious conflicts about aggression. In the past, many patients with the disorder spent countless hours in unfruitful psychotherapy attempting to discover the psychological origins of their symptoms. The current view of experts in movement disorders is that Tourette's disorder is a neurologic illness, and that even coprolalia is basically an organic symptom that is known to occur in several recognized neurologic disorders, such as senility and general paresis (syphilis of the central nervous system).

Treatment The pharmacologic treatment given to Richard is the only treatment with demonstrated effectiveness in controlling the symptoms of the disorder. Obviously, individuals with such a disabling illness become self-conscious, withdraw from social contact because of embarrassment, and often become despondent about their future. Psychotherapy may be useful and even necessary to treat these secondary effects of the illness.

Prognosis Richard has done very well for the ten years during which he has been taking the drug. There is no reason to believe that this will not continue.

CASEY JONES

Donald, now aged 15 years, was first referred to the clinic at the request of his parents at age 3, because of overactivity and delayed speech development. He is the only child of his parents, who are British and reside in the United Kingdom. There were no problems associated with his birth, and his mother was sure he had been a normal, responsive baby until 9 months old, when he had severe diarrhea and had to be admitted to the hospital for treatment of dehydration. After this episode, Donald's mother felt that he became "odd and remote," though she could not describe his behavior clearly. Once over his illness, his physical development was normal, but he made no progress in speech, play, or sociability. At about age 2 he began to spend all his time aimlessly wandering around the house. While doing so he held a toy railway engine in one hand. He appeared not to look where he was going, but he never bumped into the furniture, or fell. He ignored his parents, other adults, and children, and seemed to avoid eye contact. His mother had to catch him and hold him in order to attend to him and feed him.

When first seen at the clinic at age 3 he was still wandering and did not understand or use speech or any other form of communication. Donald's mother disliked the idea of giving him drugs, which was suggested by the clinic, so she devised her own plan. Once each morning or afternoon she caught Donald, removed the toy engine from his grasp despite his screams, and held him on her lap for a short time before returning it. She slightly lengthened the time she held him each day, and gradually he ceased to attempt to escape and began to sit quietly, waiting until he could have his toy again. Once he had become used to sitting for 5 minutes, she began to show him a book with pictures of trains, which made him laugh with pleasure. Bit by bit, Donald's mother accustomed him to sitting down, first on her knee, then on a chair, while at the same time increasing the scope of his activities to include jigsaw puzzles, constructional toys, drawing, and listening to music. He also began to copy letters of the alphabet and his own name.

By $4\frac{1}{2}$ years old, Donald had ceased his restless wandering and was easier to manage. His eye contact had improved, but he still had a markedly abnormal behavior pattern. He had begun to speak, but echoed words and phrases heard in the past. He used such phrases to obtain what he needed and, in consequence, reversed pronouns. Thus he would say "it is time for your dinner" to indicate that he was hungry. He had some idiosyncratic uses of speech, for example, he used the term Sandy-dog to refer to any dog, because the family owned a labrador called Sandy.

When school age approached, he was assessed in order to decide on appropriate schooling. His score on non-language-dependent skills was above normal, although his language was around the 3-year-old level. It was decided to try him in a local special school for children of normal intelligence but poor physical health, because this had small classes and the staff were tolerant of unusual behavior.

At first Donald would not mix with the other children and spent playtimes absorbed in pictures and models of toy trains, which he had rapidly collected by searching every room in the school. During lessons he insisted that the books on the shelves should stand upright and spent most of the time jumping up from his chair to replace them in the required position, from which they promptly fell down again. Working with an agreed plan, the teachers gradually limited the time allowed for these repetitive activities until Donald accepted that books were tidied on arrival in the morning and trains were played with for 15 minutes once a day only.

Over the years Donald became more sociable, though still markedly naive and immature in relationships. Under the guidance of the teachers, his classmates tolerated his oddities, and teasing was kept to a minimum. However, he was always the last to be chosen for team games, because he was ill-coordinated, never understood the rules, and was given to such eccentricities as kicking the football into his own team's goal. By about 10 years of age, he had a good vocabulary and more or less normal grammar, though he was limited and pedantic in his use of language and could not hold a conversation on any subject other than trains. He did well in lessons that could be learned by rote, but was unable to cope with any that needed abstract thinking or creative imagination. He could read fluently, but his comprehension of written material was poor. Left to himself, he read only books about railways. He belonged to a train spotter's club.

Donald is now approaching school-leaving age, and his future is being considered by his family and the school staff. It is possible that, after a period of vocational training, he might find employment in, for example, simple clerical work, but this will depend upon local opportunities and the state of the labor market. The question of living arrangements also has to be examined. Donald would find it difficult to manage without the protection of his family. He will need careful training in the management of all the small details of everyday life, and even then, he might be disturbed by some unexpected crisis. An alternative plan would be to seek placement in a sheltered community for adults, perhaps one accepting all types of handicaps, or one that is especially for people with autistic behavior. The best solution can be found only by trial and error, and any placement will need to be reviewed from time to time to ensure that it remains appropriate for Donald's needs.

DISCUSSION

Psychopathology and Diagnosis Donald's mother noticed early in his life that he was not developing normally. Unlike a child who only has mental retardation, he was not merely slow in progressing through the expected developmental stages of sitting, standing, walking, talking, etc. Instead, he exhibited behaviors that are not normal at any stage of development. For example, he wandered aimlessly about the house, ignored other people, and used speech in a bizarre and uncommunicative manner. These distortions in the development of the multiple basic psychological functions that are involved in the evolution of social skills and language indicate a pervasive developmental disorder. The onset is usually within the first two-and-one-half years of life, as in this case, and early signs are often noticed from birth. Because of the age at onset (infancy) and the pervasive lack of responsiveness to other people (autism), this disorder is called *infantile autism.* Donald exhibited most of the classic features of this disorder, including the characteristic peculiar speech patterns such as *echolalia* and pronominal reversal (substitution of "you" for "I"), and peculiar interests or attachments to inanimate objects (trains). What is unusual in this case is the fact that Donald seemed to be normal prior to a physical illness that heralded the onset of autistic symptoms when he was 9 months old. In most cases of infantile autism, normal social responses never develop at all, and the child's behavior is recognized as abnormal within the first few months of life.

Course and Associated Features Although the disorder is chronic, approximately one-sixth of children with infantile autism eventually are able to work at a job, with only the residual symptoms of social awkwardness and ineptness. This good prognosis is usually associated with an IQ that is at least normal, and relatively intact language skills. It appears that Donald may be within this group. Unfortunately, about three-quarters of the children with this disorder score in the mentally retarded ranges on standardized intelligence tests. They remain severely handicapped and are unable to lead independent lives. In this group there is also often epilepsy or some other neurologic disorder.

Infantile autism, in its most typical form, is relatively rare and estimated to occur in two to four children out of 10,000. Overall, it is four times more common in boys than in girls, though the male predominance is higher than this among the less severely affected group, and lower among those who have it in more severe form.

Etiology Some child psychiatrists believe that infantile autism is a childhood form of schizophrenia, but in fact the course and family history are quite different, suggesting that infantile autism is unrelated to the adult psychoses. Infantile autism is a chronically disabling condition, though there may be variations in the degree of behavior disturbance over time due to biological or environmental factors. These fluctuations, superimposed on underlying impairments, are different from the episodic disorganization of the personality that is seen in schizophrenia. There is no increased prevalence of schizophrenia in the families of patients with infantile autism, as there is in the families of patients with schizophrenia.

The etiology of the disorder is unknown. It was once thought to result from a profound disturbance in the mother-infant relationship. Now the prevailing view is that a variety of biological disturbances, occurring before, during, or after birth, may disrupt crucial psychological development, resulting in this syndrome. The disturbed mother-child relationship is then viewed as a response to rather than a cause of the disorder. In Donald's case, the illness in his first year may have resulted in brain dysfunction. In approximately one-half of all autistic children there is historical or current evidence of some condition likely to be associated with neurological abnormality. Such organic factors are found more often in those who are severely mentally retarded as well as autistic.

Treatment   All children with infantile autism require appropriate environmental management and special education. Their handicaps and difficult behavior impose considerable burdens on the parents and siblings. The strain can sometimes lead to a breakdown of the parental marriage if no constructive help and emotional support is available from professional agencies, relatives, or friends. Donald was extremely fortunate that his mother and his teachers were sufficiently patient and creative to devise and carry out a program to reinforce his development of social and language skills. At the same time, his mother accepted his limitations and did not make undue demands on him. Her approach is now considered by experts in the area to be the most effective in treating children with this disorder. It was similar to the approach used by workers who have adapted the principles of learning theory in order to modify behavior problems and increase skills in autistic and retarded children. Their methods have been examined experimentally and shown to be helpful, whereas the approaches based on psychoanalytic theories have not been subjected to objective testing.

NOT STUPID

Mr. and Ms. Harold Brown took their 10-year-old son, Tom, to the school psychologist for testing at the request of the school counselor. It seemed that Tom had been failing in school, and his teachers felt that they couldn't get through to him. This was the final semester of the third grade for Tom and his most recent grades were as follows: Arithmetic—C; Spelling—D; Physical Education—A; Reading—F; Social Sciences—F. Tom's conduct was satisfactory, but his teachers often commented that they saw him staring off into space when he was supposed to be working.

Tom is a likable boy who seems to make friends quite easily. He plays well with other children and is active around the neighborhood. Tom also enjoys playing by himself. He has an elaborate set of building blocks called Legos and will spend hours building various houses and buildings. There are no discipline problems at home. Tom gets along with his sister who is five years younger than he, except for normal bickering that occurs when she gets into his toys. The only problem at home occurs when his parents try to get Tom to do his homework. They try to sit and read with him, but he gets fidgety and his parents usually give up after a short time. They have talked with his teachers about this. However, upon the recommendations of the teachers not to pressure Tom about homework, the parents discontinued this practice.

While talking to the psychologist, Tom's parents reported that he had a normal delivery and birth and that he walked and talked about the same time as other youngsters his age. He had a complete physical exam last year and was given a clean bill of health. His parents are puzzled by Tom's poor school performance. His father figures that Tom must not be applying himself at school and has attempted to lecture Tom about paying attention in class after every report card for the past two years. During the first grade Tom seemed to be doing and adjusting well in school. Second and third grades have been filled with academic problems. Tom's mother places the blame on the open classroom concept used at his elementary school. She feels that the open classroom is too disorganized an approach to allow Tom to do his work.

Both of Tom's parents have completed high school. His mother is an avid reader and will spend hours alone with a good book. Mr. Brown, on the other hand, is very activity-oriented. He did poorly in school himself and had to work very hard to achieve barely passing grades. He does not like to read and may have had a reading problem similar to Tom's when he was a child.

During the interview Tom was cooperative and talked freely with the psychologist. "I just don't like school" was his explanation for his poor school performance. "The teacher doesn't give us enough time to finish our work and picks on me about not getting my homework done" was another repeated comment. Tom feels that he has some good friends both in his neighborhood and at school. Some of his classmates do make fun of him because of his grades. "They call me 'stupid' sometimes when we are playing," he said in an angry voice. When asked, he said he did not think he was stupid, but was obviously wondering if that might be true. Tom was uneasy talking about school, but discussed in great length the buildings he had made with his Lego blocks.

After rapport was established with Tom, the psychologist began giving him both an intelligence test to assess his general ability level and an achievement test to assess his reading, spelling, and arithmetic skills. Tom approached the tests with apprehension, but was assured by the examiner that the tests would help him find out what the problems were and that he could not fail this kind of test. All he needed to do was try to do the best he could.

On the intelligence test Tom did remarkably well. He obtained a full-scale IQ score of 117, with a verbal subtest score of 116 and a performance subtest score of 115. All of these scores are in the bright normal range of intelligence. Thus, Tom demonstrated better than normal intelligence or general ability. The achievement tests were a different story. In arithmetic Tom scored at a beginning third-grade level. However, on both the reading and the spelling tests he was functioning at a mid-first-grade level. Tom became more restless and less attentive when he attempted the reading and spelling tests. He tended to read parts of sentences and make up or guess what the rest of the sentence said. Simple words, "the," "cat," and the like, posed no problem. However, his spelling of more complicated words was atrocious. "Board" was spelled "brod" and "people" came out as "popel."

Tom did not appear to have any discernible sound discrimination problems. His main problem seemed to be in translating speech sounds into appropriate verbal syllables and, conversely, breaking down written words that are in any way complex into syllables that are consistent and make sense while reading. This may involve some subtle sound discrimination problem. However, none was noted in the testing. There were indications that he had difficulty sequencing words properly. Tom would transpose words in a sentence as well as skip over words while reading. This certainly played a part in his tendency to make up or guess how the rest of a sentence read.

The results of this testing were discussed with the school counselor. Reading problems seemed to be at the root of Tom's academic difficulties. After first grade, reading became a more central element of the school curriculum and created problems over a wide range of school subjects. Tom's inattention in school is his way of avoiding the arduous task of making sense of the words and sentences he is reading. Since he has no way of knowing how or why other children find it so easy to read, he is not able to understand why he finds reading so difficult.

Subsequent to the testing, a special program of remedial reading was developed for Tom by the school counselor, and tutoring was provided to assist him in his other subjects. At first, Tom was very resistant to the idea of going to a "special" class for reading and wanted to remain with his friends in his regular class. It was obvious that he did not want to give the other children any more reason to make fun of him and to see himself as having a problem. He attended the remedial reading class reluctantly, but was cooperative in doing the work and began making friends in his new class. The remedial reading class had fewer children, so the teacher could give Tom more individualized attention. Tom seemed to enjoy the attention and began to be more responsible about doing his homework. The individualized attention of the tutor and the fact that he could work at his own pace with her also seemed to please him.

In the six weeks remaining in the school year Tom made significant progress in his reading. At the end of the semester he was reading at a beginning second-grade level, although his spelling remained at a first-grade level and showed only minimal improvement. He continued to have difficulty paying attention in his regular classes and was easily distracted by the other children. However, his work with the tutor enabled him to complete more of his class assignments and improve his grades. The school administration decided to promote him to the fourth grade with the understanding that the special programming would continue.

DISCUSSION

Psychopathology and Diagnosis   At first it seemed as if Tom had a general problem doing his school work. He was failing most of his subjects, and his teachers described him as inattentive. However, psychological testing clearly showed that the problem was neither with his general intelligence (which is above average) nor with his ability to focus his attention. The trouble was quite specific: as noted by the psychologist, "His main problem seems to be in translating speech sounds into appropriate verbal syllables and, conversely, breaking down written words that are in any way complex into syllables that are consistent and make sense while reading." This reading difficulty was apparently the basis for his inability to progress in other academic subjects which all depend heavily on reading skills. His "inattention" in class was apparently due to his frustration at not being able to do what his peers seem to do without any difficulty.

Often children like Tom develop a "failure" self-image and have problems relating to peers. They can become "class clowns" or appear immature to teachers and counselors. At times they will be referred for discipline or motivation problems, especially if they are given social promotions and the difficulties are not recognized until the later grades. In this case they can be misdiagnosed as simply emotionally disturbed, when the problems of immaturity and behavior are actually a consequence and not a cause of their specific developmental disorder. Tom's case represented a rather pure case of a reading disorder. Often a reading disorder is accompanied by hyperactivity, poor performance in other areas of functioning, and more prominent signs of frustration and distractibility than are evident in Tom's case.

Reading problems can be due to many factors: low intelligence, inadequate schooling, low motivation, or a more pervasive disturbance in attention or language. When, as in Tom's case, a specific reading disturbance appears to be the primary problem and cannot be explained by any of these factors, the diagnosis of *developmental reading disorder* is made. In the past, this disorder has been referred to as dyslexia. Research efforts are currently underway to determine the underlying deficiencies in this disorder. Although there are no definitive answers, deficiencies in visual perception and memory, integration of visual and auditory perceptions, recall problems, and verbal processing deficits have been hypothesized as the core problems for children with reading disorders.

The diagnosis of developmental reading disorder is only made when the clinician has been able to rule out environmental factors, such as poor schooling, or a chaotic family life that has resulted in poor motivation for learning. There is thus the general assumption that something must be wrong with the development of the central nervous system of children with this specific problem. Often some "soft neurological signs" (such as problems with coordination) are seen in these children. Therefore, it is classified as a mental disorder with other specific developmental disorders: developmental arithmetic disorder, developmental language disorder, and developmental articulation disorder. Because all of these conditions are generally diagnosed and treated within the educational system, rather than the mental health system, there is controversy as to whether or not they warrant classification as mental disorders.

Reading difficulty is often seen in the family members of children with developmental reading disorder. In fact, Tom's father apparently had similar difficulties, and even as an adult he does not like to read. In addition, developmental reading disorder occurs more frequently in males than in females.

Treatment and Prognosis Because of his difficulty, Tom has to work much harder to learn how to read than other children. He was fortunate to be placed in a special remedial reading program in which he will have both the extra time and the encouragement that he needs in order to compensate for his problem. It is likely that Tom will always have some difficulty with reading, but with the special program he will probably be able to handle these difficulties with greater ease and with a less detrimental effect on his self-esteem.

Although this type of problem is called a specific developmental reading disorder, the clinical picture is not always clear and specific. Children with this type of problem react in a variety of ways to the disorder, and a great deal depends on how the family and the educational system respond to the child. Depending on the child, the extent of the disorder, and the associated emotional and developmental problems, an interlocking network of problems is often generated by a learning disability. Strategies to remediate educational, discipline, and relationship problems should be designed on an individual basis for a child with any of the specific developmental disorders.

ORGANIC MENTAL DISORDERS

DIMINISHING ASSETS

Aside from a head injury of uncertain significance, sustained as a young man in the service, Mr. Abbot B. Carrington had no medical or psychiatric problems until the age of 56. At that time, employed as an officer of a bank, he began to be forgetful. For example, he would forget to bring his briefcase to work, or he might misplace his eyeglasses. His efficiency at work declined. He failed to follow through with assignments. Reports that he had to prepare were incomplete.

Although still friendly and sociable, Mr. Carrington began to lose interest in many of his usual activities. He ignored his coin collection. He no longer thoroughly perused *The Wall Street Journal* each day. When he discussed economics, it was without his previous grasp of the subject. After about a year of these difficulties, he was gradually eased out of his responsible position at the bank and eventually retired prematurely.

At home, he tended to withdraw into himself. He would arise early each morning and go for a long walk, occasionally losing his way if he reached an unfamiliar neighborhood. He needed to be reminded constantly of the time of day, of upcoming events, and of his son's progress in college. He tried to use electric appliances without first plugging them into the socket. He shaved with the wrong side of the razor. Mostly, he remained a quiet, pleasant, and tractable person, but sometimes, particularly at night, he became exceptionally confused, and at these times he might be somewhat irritable, loud, and difficult to control.

Approximately two years following the onset of these symptoms, he was seen by a neurologist, who conducted a detailed examination of his mental status. The examiner noted that Mr. Carrington was neatly dressed, polite, and cooperative. He sat passively in the office as his wife described his problems to the doctor. He himself offered very little information. In fact, at one point, apparently bored by the proceedings, he unceremoniously got up from his chair and left the room to wander in the corridor. He did not know the correct date or the name and location of the hospital in which he was being examined. Mr. Carrington was then told the date and place, but 10 minutes later he had forgotten this information. Although a presidential election campaign was then in progress, he did not know the names of the candidates. Despite his background in banking and economics, he could not give any relevant information concerning inflation, unemployment, or the prime lending rate. When questioned about the events of his own life, Mr. Carrington was also frequently in error. He confused recent and remote events. For example, he thought his father had recently died, but in fact this had occurred many years earlier. He could not provide a good description of his occupation.

The patient's speech was fluent and well articulated, but vague and imprecise. He used long, roundabout, cliché-filled phrases to express rather simple ideas. Sometimes he would use the wrong word, as when he substituted "prescribe" for "subscribe." Despite his past facility with figures, he was unable to do simple calculations. With a pencil and paper, he could not copy two-dimensional figures or a cube. When instructed to draw a house, he drew a succession of attached squares. Asked to give a single word that would define the similarity between an apple and an orange, he replied "round." He interpreted the proverb "People who live in glass houses shouldn't throw stones" to mean that "People don't want their windows broken." He seemed to have little insight into his problem. He appeared apathetic rather than anxious or depressed. There was no abnormality of muscle strength, reflexes, sensation, or gait.

A number of different laboratory tests were done. His blood was analyzed to look for various possible vitamin deficiencies (e.g., B-12) and/or endocrine disorders (e.g., hypothyroidism). A brain scan and an electroencephalogram were done in order to look for such lesions as a cerebrovascular accident (stroke), tumor, or subdural hematoma (a blood clot over the surface of the brain that may occur following an injury). All of these are potentially treatable diseases. Unfortunately, it was not possible to demonstrate a specific cause for Mr. Carrington's difficulties. The only laboratory finding of significance was that a computer-assisted tomography (CAT scan), a special x-ray procedure that allows one to see the outline of the brain, showed atrophy, or shrinking, of Mr. Carrington's brain.

DISCUSSION

Psychopathology and Diagnosis Although some of Mr. Carrington's symptoms, such as his apathy and quiet withdrawal, might be interpreted as signs of depression, it is apparent that his most important problem involves a progressive loss of intellectual abilities which is so severe that it has seriously interfered with his social and occupational functioning. Most prominent are his disorientation with respect to time and place, as well as a marked decline in his memory. The mental status examination confirmed this. Thus he did not know the correct date or place of examination (disorientation). Even when given this information, he could not learn it sufficiently well to remember it for more than a few minutes (short-term memory deficit). Nor could he remember personal and general events that happened in the past (long-term memory deficit). Other intellectual abilities were affected as well. Examination revealed an abnormal use of language, difficulty doing calculations, and troubles with a variety of different tasks that involved "constructional ability" (copying, drawing, etc.). Furthermore, it is apparent that Mr. Carrington has difficulty thinking abstractly, that is, finding the similarity between related words and interpreting proverbs. This syndrome of global cognitive impairment is called a dementia. A dementia is one type of organic mental disorder, a psychological or behavioral abnormality that is associated with transient or permanent brain dysfunction. It is to be emphasized that dementia refers to a severe degree of intellectual dysfunction. It is not synonymous with aging. The majority of elderly individuals do not suffer from dementia.

Etiology The cause of Mr. Carrington's dementia, however, is not immediately apparent. There was nothing in his past history to explain it. The head injury had occurred many years before and was followed by a full recovery, so it does not seem relevant to the present problem. He has not had a history of a stroke or any other neurological disease that could readily account for the mental deterioration, nor has he a history of chronic alcoholism.

The laboratory tests did not reveal any *specific* cause of the dementia. Such cases are called *primary degenerative dementia* (*primary* = first; *degenerative* = brain cell changes leading to loss of function.)

Course and Treatment Primary degenerative dementia may occur in elderly individuals, in which cases it has been referred to as senile dementia, or, more rarely, it may occur at an earlier age (presenile dementia), as in the case of Mr. Carrington. Both conditions are also sometimes known as Alzheimer's disease, named for the neuropathologist who first described the syndrome. At the present time there is no specific treatment or cure for this type of dementia. In the year since he was initially evaluated, Mr. Carrington has continued his slow, steady decline, and this is the typical course of this disorder. Because of the inexorable physical and intellectual deterioration, nursing will become increasingly necessary. It is not possible to predict how long Mr. Carrington will survive; this will depend on other factors, such as co-existing medical disease and how aggressively his physicians choose to treat infections. The average length of survival from the estimated onset of symptoms in patients with the presenile form of primary degenerative dementia is seven years.

A BAD DAY FOR
BANANAFISH

"Where's Dr. Kahn?" Ms. Landau demanded. "He's supposed to be the Chairman of the Department of Psychiatry, isn't he?"

"Yes, he is," I replied.

"Then where the hell is he? My brother said I was supposed to see him."

"He's in Russia for three weeks," I answered.

"Then let's get the hell out of here!" bellowed Ms. Landau as she turned toward her husband. I also glanced at Mr. Landau. We had both managed to cross our legs and fold our arms—almost simultaneously.

"I see," said Ms. Landau.

"Dr. Kahn asked that I assist him by taking a history and coordinating your medical work up."

"Coordinate my medical workup?" Ms. Landau mocked. "Work yourself up—if you're old enough. Come on, Hy, let's get out of here. Two-and-a-half years of psychoanalysis four days a week on that fake leather couch. A so-called training analyst whose dog supposedly humped the dog Freud gave Eric Erickson. Twenty-two thousand bucks, and this kid's going to do a *workup*. Hy, if you don't get me out of here this very minute . . ." "Here" happened to be the private psychiatric unit of the hospital. It is a locked ward.

"Relax," Mr. Landau urged. "Give Dr. . . . ." Mr. Landau squinted to read my name from the tag on my white coat.

Suddenly the door of the interviewing room burst open to reveal an explosive woman in her midforties.

"Dr. Sussman. When are you going to see me today?"

"In about 2 hours, Evelyn."

Not breaking stride or seeming to notice the Landaus, Evelyn barreled through the room toward me. She was wearing a billowy, fuchsia peignoir ornamented with five large gold and diamond brooches. Entangled among the brooches was an undiscernible number of thick gold chains of varying lengths. Both arms extended in exaggerated grace and were encircled with gold and silver bangle bracelets. However, attention was magnetically drawn to her face with its thick, white powder and generously applied orange lipstick.

"Dr. Sussman, darling, did I tell you my marvelous idea for redecorating the day room? We'll start with that ravishingly new William Morris paper from Scala-mandre . . ."

The soundproofed door opened again. Mr. Barnes, an athletic-looking aide, strode in.

"Excuse me, Dr. Sussman. Evelyn, let's go back to your room. The Doctor will see you in a little while." Discovering an opening amidst her jewelry, Mr. Barnes grasped Evelyn firmly by her upper arm.

"Ta-ta, Dr. S.! Barnes hasn't had any yet this morning. But don't you fret: there'll always be plenty left for you!"

The door closed. Mr. Landau and I turned back to his wife.

"Light me a bananafish, Hy. I don't believe I've come to this. This is a *certified* looney bin. I'm gonna be locked up for the rest of my life with manic depressives like Evelyn." Ms. Landau's hand was surprisingly steady as Hy lit her cigarette.

I had never heard anyone refer to cigarettes as "bananafish," and I couldn't remember what Seymour Glass used to kill himself with at the end of Salinger's story. It was my first year of practice as a psychiatrist. Every technical error that was possible to make, I had made. Short cuts through gratuitous familiarity were my specialty. But this time I managed to refrain from disclosing to Ms. Landau that I had read J. D. Salinger's short story, "A Perfect Day for Bananafish." She would have snapped closed on me like a bear trap. That she had correctly diagnosed Evelyn as having bipolar disorder was unsettling enough.

"You seem to be quite familiar with psychiatric terminology, Ms. Landau."

"My brother is writing a book on depression," she said.

Oh, Lord, I thought. Israel Landau, the well-known researcher in affective disorders, is her brother!

"You were expecting a passive hysteric, Dr. S?" Ms. Landau continued. "No such luck. I have a mossy-green depression. According to my brother, I meet all your so-called criteria for a major depressive episode. I wake up at 5:00 A.M., can't get back to sleep, and feel like a piece of crap. It's the worst part of the day, just like it's supposed to be. I have to wait 18 hours to go back to sleep. I come out of my sleep crying. No raveled sleeves of care get Scotchguarded for me." She looked annoyed at herself for her strained joke.

"How would you describe your mood, Ms. Landau?" I asked.

"You're really smooth, Doctor. My mood is lousy. Especially now that it's summer. It kills me to see people *appearing* to be happy. That's an expensive word, Doctor. 'Appearing' cost me 22,000 bucks. According to my analyst, all those jiggling and flexing summer phonies may be depressed sickolas just like me. My mood is crap, if you must know. I cry most of the day. Except in my analytic sessions, when I don't feel anything. I'm light years away from any feeling in therapy."

"Have you ever felt like harming yourself?"

"You mean killing myself, don't you Doctor Hedge? No. I don't *think* about it; I *dwell* on suicide. I *savor* the thought."

"Have you ever made an actual attempt?"

"Miriam says she can't kill herself because of the damage it would do to the children," Hy interjected.

"They're brilliant, Doctor," Ms. Landau continued. "My oldest boy is 14. He reads *Mourning and Melancholia* on the toilet instead of *Playboy*. He already explained to me that my suicide would be an aggressive act against the whole family, not just myself. But I'll fool that smart ass. I've hoarded thirty-five different types of Tampax. I'm going to kill myself with toxic shock."

"Not funny at all, Miriam," Hy interrupted.

"How is your energy, Ms. Landau?" I persisted.

"A few thousand megawatts less than Evelyn's. But I don't need energy, because I don't *feel* like doing anything. I don't *enjoy* doing *anything*." This with an emphatic glance toward Hy. "You forgot to ask me about somatic complaints, Dr. S. I have them all: headaches, backaches, stomachaches, premenstrual cramps, postmenstrual cramps, menstrual cramps. It hurts when I cough, it burns when I pee, and I can't swallow. My mouth is dry, and I have no blood pressure from that antidepressant drug that Dr. Rubin poisons me with. *He* says I have a 'low pain threshold.' *I* say I have pains everywhere but in my ass. That's what I go to psychiatrists for."

"How long have you been taking that drug?" I asked.

"Sixteen months. For the last twelve months I've taken over 350 milligrams a day of the stuff. But don't bother jabbing me for blood levels. They've already been taken: 150 nanograms per milliliter of serum. I believe that's within the therapeutic range. Now do you see why I need Dr. Kahn, Dr. S.?"

Everything *had* been done, and done right. For the life of me I couldn't remember the therapeutic serum level for that drug.

"I bet I can read your little mind, Dr. S.," Ms. Landau proceeded. "Simple mind, simple two-word thought: shock treatment."

"There's no shock involved, Ms. Landau," I responded mechanically. "That's why we call it electroconvulsive therapy. It's the seizure, not a shock, that treats the depression."

"A buzz by any other name . . . , that's why I'm here, Doctor. A whole covey of psychiatrists couldn't do a damn thing for me. Maybe New York Electric can."

"Let the Doctor decide what needs to be done," Hy advised.

"It'll come to shock treatment, Hy. You may as well get used to it. That's all they've got left." Ms. Landau was matter-of-fact.

That afternoon I was examining Ms. Landau prior to her electroconvulsive therapy. Dr. Kahn had called from Russia to instruct me to initiate treatments as soon as possible.

"What's wrong?" Ms. Landau demanded.

"Nothing's wrong," I lied.

"You keep listening at that spot. Who're you trying to kid?" I could not hear breath sounds in a segment of the lower lobe of Ms. Landau's left lung. Above that I kept hearing bubbling sounds as she breathed. Something in her lungs was very wrong. I tried to appear composed.

"Please inhale deeply, Ms. Landau," I instructed.

"I have cancer. I know it."

"Relax, Ms. Landau. Don't jump to conclusions. Would you please just breathe in deeply?"

"I won't take another breath until you tell me what you hear." She had grown on me. So quick and smart. It would be useless to conceal anything from her. That would only scare her more.

"I don't know yet. It sounds like rales," I replied, hoping her knowledge of medical terminology was limited to psychiatry.

"And what does that sound like?" she demanded.

"Like bananafish crying."

Follow-up Chest x-rays and bronchoscopy were ordered, which indicated the presence of a carcinoma in a bronchus of Ms. Landau's left lung. Other tests revealed that her carcinoma had metastasized to her liver and the left temporal cortex of her brain. It is interesting to note that following the diagnosis of her carcinoma and its treatment with surgery and chemotherapy she became less depressed. Her preoccupation with suicide ceased and her appetite improved, with subsequent weight gain. Her tearfulness and sleep difficulties also were ameliorated without any change of her antidepressant regimen.

Despite surgical, radiotherapeutic, and chemotherapeutic interventions, Ms. Landau died one year later from complications secondary to metastases of carcinoma of the lung.

DISCUSSION

Psychopathology and Diagnosis Ms. Landau was convinced that she had the classic symptoms of "depression": dysphoric mood ("I feel like a piece of crap"; "I cry most of the day"), lack of pleasure ("I don't *enjoy* doing *anything*"), suicidal preoccupation ("I don't *think* about it; I *dwell* on suicide"), apathy ("I don't *feel* like doing anything"), early morning awakening ("I wake up at 5:00 A.M., can't get back to sleep . . ."), and diurnal mood variation (mornings are " . . . the worst part of the day"). The many psychiatrists she had seen over the two-and-a-half years that she had had symptoms apparently shared her view and never seriously considered the possibility that her psychological symptoms were the manifestation of a physical illness.

Ms. Landau's "depression" was first treated with psychoanalysis, and when this had no effect on her mood, she received antidepressant medication. When she did not respond to drug therapy, even with evidence of therapeutically effective amounts of the drug circulating in her blood, she was referred for electroconvulsive therapy (ECT). ECT is often effective in the treatment of depression when other forms of therapy have failed (see Case 23, "Weeping Widow"). It was only during the pre-electroconvulsive therapy physical examination that signs of disease in her lung were detected. Further laboratory tests finally revealed the presence of carcinoma of the lung which had spread to other parts of her body. Her "depression" was now understood to be caused by the cancer, and treatment would have to be directed at the underlying physical disorder.

Physical illness, by affecting the central nervous system, may cause a wide range of psychological symptoms. In Ms. Landau's case, the symptoms were of a disturbance in mood—a pervasive and sustained emotion that colors the person's perception of the world—accompanied by other symptoms that tend to be present when the mood is depressed. Traditionally, serious disturbances of mood are called affective disorders (*affect* = a feeling, state, or emotion). When an affective disturbance is caused by a known physical illness, the diagnosis of the psychological symptoms is classified as an organic mental disorder and is called an *organic affective disorder.* The most common type involves depression, as in Ms. Landau's case, and may be caused by certain drugs and by many physical illnesses, particularly endocrine disorders, viral illnesses, and cancer. Less commonly, an organic affective disorder may present with elevated mood similar to a manic episode (see Case 22, "Cuckoo Clocks"), typically caused by an endocrine disturbance or by the taking of certain drugs, particularly central nervous system stimulants such as appetite suppressants.

There are other organic brain disorders (a collection of signs and symptoms without reference to the specific cause, due to central nervous system disturbance) that present with psychological and behavioral symptoms. The most common are delirium (see Case 51, "The Innkeeper"), dementia (see Case 47, "Diminishing Assets"), and organic delusional disorder (see Case 49, "Stoned").

The diagnosis of an organic brain disorder, such as Ms. Landau's organic affective disorder, requires evidence of a specific organic factor that is judged to be etiologically related to the psychological or behavioral disturbance. This evidence is obtained by means of a careful history, a physical examination, and appropriate laboratory tests.

Treatment   In many cases of organic affective disorder the underlying physical disorder is not recognized, and the patient is subjected to ineffective or even dangerous treatment. (ECT would have been dangerous to Ms. Landau, since her cancer had spread to her brain.)

Ms. Landau's cancer was surgically removed from her lung. It had, however, already spread to her brain and liver. Therefore, she received radiation therapy to shrink the tumors and chemotherapy to attempt to prevent their further spread. Although she had some relief from her depressive symptoms, it was transient, and she died due to further metastases.

This case shows the potential dangers of assuming a psychological etiology, and therefore failing to search for organic causes of depression. If a thorough physical examination had been done when Ms. Landau first sought help for depression, perhaps her cancer could have been surgically removed, her depression aborted, and her life saved.

STONED

Sharon Johnson, a 21-year-old woman, had a relatively uneventful childhood and early adolescence. There was no family history of mental illness. In school she was described as somewhat shy at first, but by high school she had a number of friends and occasionally dated. She was not a very assertive person in social situations, and she began to use marijuana as a result of peer influence when she was 16. Typically she would smoke four to six "joints" or marijuana cigarettes during a weekend. She occasionally felt slightly anxious when under the influence of marijuana, but did not experience any more serious symptoms. Following high school she attempted to find work but was initially unsuccessful. She had an interest in music and literature and decided to share an apartment with a group of young people who had similar interests. Soon after moving in, her marijuana use increased to two cigarettes every evening. About a week later she began to have unusual and frightening experiences that finally led to her being hospitalized. While recovering in the hospital and at her doctor's request, Sharon wrote the following description of her drug precipitated illness:

> One night while I was stoned on marijuana, as one guy talked I felt he was speaking about all the thoughts and feelings that were going through my mind. It was like being able to project all my innermost thoughts into the minds of others through some sort of hidden channel and having them reflected back in conversations or actions of the people around me. I was afraid, and my first thoughts were to run, because I felt my friends were into something I could not handle. I started to pay very close attention to what was happening around me and was on the alert for anything that might confirm my suppositions. I asked them what they were into and received a number of replies. "We're just like you are." "We want to help you." "There's not enough God in your life." "You don't know what life is all

about yet." I picked up my coat and ran for the door. Once I was outside, I thought the cold January wind would awaken me from a bad dream. But it didn't. Someone was coming after me. I could hear his footsteps behind me. I froze and started to pray loudly and uncontrollably. I had to get away. Maybe I was going to die or be raped. Something kept warning me to run. My imagination was running away with me. My thoughts were jumbled, and I thought my new friends had some supernatural power to read minds and perform other psychic acts. I felt as though the episode was some sort of conspiracy, that everyone knew what my next move would be, where I was going, and what I was thinking. A lot of things didn't dawn on me until this experience. There were hidden meanings in expressions, songs, and poetry that I shared with my friends. I investigated and looked for associations. When I heard conversations it seemed that I had thought of everything that was said before anyone said it.

The day after the experience began, I moved to my parents' apartment. I was feeling totally confused. I tried to decide who wanted to hurt me and why. I read book after book in a search for answers, and most of what I read seemed applicable to me. I was battling with my senses over this experience, and although part of me refused to accept the new reality I discovered, part of me still lived inside the separate reality in confusion.

I decided to have a consultation with a priest, who urged me to go on a weekend retreat. There I found myself in complete confusion. Everything appeared very mystical. The vestments on the altar contained the words "For Our Dead." I thought that I had died and was going through some initiation into adult humanity. Everyone seemed to be reacting in accordance with my thoughts. I was afraid as well as fascinated by my new discovery—communication without talking, testing the will of others, and watching them react. I experimented frequently by directing my thoughts to certain people, and they unconsciously picked up my thoughts and reacted to them. If I were talking to someone and thinking something unkind, the person's conversation would react accordingly. If I willed some action directly, it came to pass. My thoughts were running wild, and people's actions and conversations were in accordance with my will.

Sharon was hospitalized when her parents took her to a hospital emergency service approximately two weeks after her symptoms began. Her symptoms had persisted even though she had stopped smoking for several days. In the hospital she was initially treated with antipsychotic medication. After about a week her more florid symptoms diminished enough for her to engage in individual and group psychotherapy, which focused on her fears of leaving the parental home and establishing trusting relationships with others her age. Sharon remained in the hospital for approximately six weeks; at the time of her discharge she was free of symptoms. A follow-up interview three years later revealed that she had lived with several groups of friends in the interim and had worked steadily. There had been one additional brief hospitalization with similar symptoms which occurred about a year after her initial admission. She denied marijuana or other drug use at that time, but had recently terminated a close relationship with a man she had dated for six months. Her psychotic symptoms again remitted rapidly with antipsychotic medication.

DISCUSSION

Psychopathology and Diagnosis Sharon vividly describes a variety of psychotic symptoms. She felt that her thoughts were being communicated to others without her speaking. She believed that there was a conspiracy, that people were going to attack her, and that they could read her mind. Later she developed the belief that she had died and that her thoughts were controlling the actions of those around her. She attributed a special meaning to things that she saw, read, and heard (ideas of reference). Throughout the episode her thoughts were jumbled and confused, and she was fearful and hypervigilant.

The abrupt onset of these symptoms shortly after Sharon increased the amount of marijuana that she was smoking strongly implicates the drug as the cause of the psychotic episode. (It is now recognized that psychotic episodes induced by cannabis are more common than previously thought.) When a psychotic episode with delusions as the most prominent symptoms develops following the taking of a drug, this is called an organic delusional disorder, specifically *cannabis delusional disorder*. Other drugs that may cause a similar clinical picture are amphetamines ("speed"), phencyclidine (PCP), and LSD.

If we accept Sharon's claim that she had not used any drugs at the time of her second hospital admission, we have to question whether her first psychotic episode was wholly due to the marijuana. Perhaps Sharon would have become psychotic even without taking the marijuana, or, more likely, the marijuana and the immediate severe reaction to the marijuana precipitated a psychotic episode in a vulnerable individual. Given the available information, the most likely diagnosis for Sharon's second episode of illness is schizophreniform disorder, to indicate a psychosis with schizophreniclike symptoms lasting more than two weeks but less than six months. To what extent this diagnosis also applies, in retrospect, to her first hospitalization, instead of cannabis delusional disorder, is not known.

Predisposing Factors Because marijuana is so widely used, it would be very desirable to be able to identify individuals who are particularly prone to develop psychotic reactions following heavy drug use. It is known that individuals with severe preexisting psychopathology, such as schizophrenia, are especially likely to have such reactions. However, Sharon's case illustrates that there are individuals without apparent significant preexisting psychopathology who are nevertheless vulnerable to having a drug-induced or -precipitated psychotic episode.

Treatment Of course, if drug use is judged to have caused a psychotic episode, it is imperative to stop taking the drug. In some instances, the psychotic symptoms will disappear in hours, and no further treatment for the acute psychotic episode is necessary. In Sharon's case, even several days after she stopped taking the marijuana her symptoms persisted, and it was necessary to hospitalize her. Her psychotic symptoms were so pervasive that her judgment was seriously impaired, and without the structure of the hospital she might have acted in a way that would have been harmful to herself or others.

In the hospital Sharon received antipsychotic medication that is effective in the symptomatic treatment of a psychotic episode, whether the psychotic symptoms are due to a drug, such as marijuana, or due to a functional (nonorganic) psychotic disorder, such as schizophreniform disorder. As she improved, she received individual and group psychotherapy to help her better deal with the stresses in her current life.

Prognosis Ordinarily the prognosis of a single episode of organic delusional disorder is excellent, provided the individual does not continue to take the drug. In Sharon's case, she seems also to have another illness (schizophreniform disorder) that is quite separate from the difficulties caused by taking marijuana. Therefore, even if she remains drug-free, there is the possibility of another psychotic episode.

PSYCHOLOGICAL FACTORS AFFECTING PHYSICAL CONDITION

A STRUGGLE FOR SURVIVAL

Leonard Feldman wiped the perspiration from his brow and stuffed his rumpled handkerchief into his suit pocket as he left his internists's office. The frightening words that his internist had just spoken to him echoed over and over in his head: "ulcer . . . medications . . . psychiatrist . . . retirement . . . ." He could not believe it had really come to this.

Two months ago, shortly after his 62nd birthday, Mr. Feldman had appeared in the office of his internist complaining of a recurring sharp pain in the middle of his abdomen, just below his breastbone. His internist listened patiently as Mr. Feldman meticulously described the attacks that he had been having over the preceding several weeks. They appeared to come and go every several days, bothering him particularly when he was very busy at work or after eating an especially large, rich, or spicy meal. They did not seem related to physical exertion. His internist at first was not overly concerned. He had known Mr. Feldman for about twenty years, and during that period Mr. Feldman had frequently visited his office with one complaint or another. He had mild arthritis and gout, but had otherwise always been found in good health. Nonetheless, a series of medical tests was ordered, including an upper GI (gastrointestinal) series—an x-ray study to help visualize the esophagus, stomach, and duodenal portion of the small intestine—in order to locate the source of Mr. Feldman's discomfort.

It had taken Mr. Feldman nearly six weeks to arrange for several hours during which he could get away from his work as the president of a small company and have the test completed. His internist had just received the results from the radiologist several days before and had called Mr. Feldman in to discuss the findings. In fact, the x-rays showed a small duodenal ulcer that was no doubt causing Mr. Feldman's pain.

Mr. Feldman: Doctor, what can I do? I can't afford to be sick. There is no one else to do the business. I have worked too hard to let what I've built up go to pieces.

Doctor: Wait a minute. It's not serious yet, but it could be. Ulcers can bleed, and this can be a serious problem. It will heal if you take certain medications, but I must also tell you I feel you are under too much pressure at your work and you must find a way to take it a little easier. Sooner or later you'll probably want to retire, anyway.

Mr. Feldman: Doctor, you have known me for many years. You know that I'm not one to "take it easy." My business is all I have.

Doctor: I know it won't be easy and I've even thought that perhaps you should talk to someone who might be able to help you with the pressure.

It was at this point that the internist suggested referring Mr. Feldman for psychiatric consultation. He did know Mr. Feldman very well and realized that without considerable effort it was very unlikely that his patient would be able to change his deeply ingrained work habits and general outlook on life. Mr. Feldman told the doctor he would think about it, but as he left the office that day he was confused about what he should do. Four days later he spent a sleepless night, the first of its kind, due to the severe pain. The next day he called the internist and told him he was ready to see the psychiatrist.

During most of the initial consultation session with the psychiatrist, Mr. Feldman described his difficult life history. Both he and his wife had been confined for approximately two and a half years in German concentration camps during World War II. Like many Jewish families, each had lost innumerable friends and relatives, including their parents. Mr. Feldman's tale was vivid, both in the gruesome details of concentration camp atrocities and in the description of his attempts at coping and adaptation. "You did whatever you had to," he said, "in order to survive. Survival from one day to the next was your only thought. You did not think about next week or next month, only how to get from today until tomorrow." Mr. Feldman sometimes managed to obtain cigarettes for the soldiers who guarded the building in which he stayed. In return for this, he was treated somewhat more leniently by them. His release from the concentration camp after the war was a miracle he surely never expected. Shortly after his release, he met his wife in a refugee camp. They married and soon thereafter, having little to keep them in Europe, emigrated to the United States when Mr. Feldman was 28 years old.

On coming to the United States, they settled in New York City and lived in a flat on the Lower East Side of Manhattan. Mr. Feldman first worked in a local grocery store and later obtained a job in the shipping department of a clothing manufacturing firm. He studied the clothing manufacturing business very diligently, observing the manufacture of the products and the marketing to buyers. Because of his hard work and quick mind, he was promoted to bookkeeper where he learned the "business side" of the company. Finally, a supplier for the clothing company who was interested in expanding a small business that manufactured various types of fasteners that were used on clothing, such as snaps and hooks and eyes, invited Mr. Feldman to join him as a partner in return for a $5000 investment that the Feldmans had saved from his earnings. Five years later, the business had grown. The senior partner then died unexpectedly of a heart attack, and Mr. Feldman assumed total control and ownership of the business. Over the ensuing 25 years, the fastener business continued to grow. Originally employing only six people, Mr. Feldman now proudly stated that there were 45 individuals who worked for the company, and gross sales in 1978 had been five million dollars. Mr. and Ms. Feldman now live comfortably in a large stone house in a suburban New York community. Their two sons are both grown and married: one is a dentist practicing in Westchester County, the other a sportswriter for a New York newspaper.

The psychiatrist commented to Mr. Feldman that it seemed as if he had managed to achieve a relatively secure station in life. He suggested that many of Mr. Feldman's responsibilities, such as the education of his children, were complete, so that a slowing down might not only be feasible but also appropriate. Mr. Feldman was quick to object:

"No, no, no, no. You don't understand. This business, this business of mine does not last on its own. It depends on me. Every day I am involved in keeping it going. I know how to get the best price from the buyers. No one else does and believe me, if you don't fight back, the other guy will get you. This is what this business is all about. Someone wins and someone loses."

In describing the conduct of his business in a subsequent session, it appeared that Mr. Feldman viewed all interpersonal relations in a similar manner. Everyone, his employees included, was potentially in a position to take advantage of him and with everyone he felt he was defending himself.

Psychiatrist: But isn't there someone you can trust, feel comfortable with?
Feldman: Doctor, it's dog eat dog. The one who trusts loses. I have learned this the hard way in my business.

In fact, Mr. Feldman described his whole life as an "aggravation." He constantly ruminated about the details of his business and his interactions with his employees, his customers, and his wife. Because he felt he was frequently being taken advantage of or otherwise being threatened, he was unable ever to relax and was prone to fits of intense rage when interacting with others.

Mr. Feldman had grown up in a very poor family and his lifelong ambition was to become a comfortably well-off man. His childhood had been punctuated by frequent conflicts with his harsh, physically punitive, and devoutly religious father. When Mr. Feldman rebelled, such as by not following Orthodox Jewish rules for observing the Sabbath, his father would retaliate by strap beatings or guilt-provoking remarks such as lamenting "my business is not successful because God punishes me for your giving up the faith." Mr. Feldman ran away from home to live with an uncle at age 13. In a recurrent dream, Mr. Feldman pictures himself as a young apprentice working in a blacksmith shop who is constantly in fear of losing his job because his boss disapproves of him.

Mr. Feldman described his relationship with his wife as "not so peaceful coexistence." Apparently both his wife and his sons have learned to anticipate his rages and thus steer clear of issues that might provoke him. Mr. Feldman realized after the fact that his outbursts were out of proportion to the incidents that precipitated them, and he was often contrite. He had never struck anyone and described himself as "not an aggressive person."

Mr. Feldman's tenseness was visible to the psychiatrist. He sat rigidly on the edge of his chair with his brow furrowed and his jaws clenched. He described being upset and somewhat depressed at the internist's diagnosis of ulcer, the need for medicine, and the advice that he should "slow down." (Characteristically, Mr. Feldman over the years had always accepted his doctor's prescriptions for ailments such as his gout but, he admitted, only rarely did he fill them.) Mr. Feldman had taken minor tranquilizers like Librium and Valium on occasion over the years for his "aggravation."

The psychiatrist realized that were it not for the medical problem with the ulcer, Mr. Feldman would never have sought psychiatric help. While acknowledging the extremely competitive nature of his business, the psychiatrist believed that Mr. Feldman's perception of himself as always struggling for survival was no longer appropriate to his current circumstances. It was as if his early life experiences and particularly his experiences in the concentration camp had never ended. The psychiatrist hypothesized that his intense style of relating to his environment was a significant contributing factor to the development of his ulcer. The goal of treatment was thus to attempt to alter his usual behavioral style with the hope that this would not only be of benefit in itself psychologically, but would have a positive effect on the course of his duodenal ulcer.

Mr. Feldman was seen once a week; the initial approach was to determine his capacity for introspection and behavioral change based on self-understanding. He clearly was not accustomed to examining his motivations and fundamental assumptions about life. However, because he was very frightened by his medical condition, he was willing to accept the psychiatrist's suggestion that his work habits contributed to his being chronically upset and that this, in turn, was certainly not good for his ulcer. Therefore, after several months he reluctantly agreed on the wisdom of gradually relinquishing several of his responsibilities at the factory to younger employees and to begin to take two weeks off every six months (he had not had a vacation in ten years). Once having made this decision, he reported that he felt better, although he still had a lingering worry that he *might* be making a big mistake.

During the first six months of his psychotherapy his ulcer gradually healed and he no longer had any abdominal pain. Sessions were reduced in frequency to every other week and mainly dealt with supporting his efforts to take life a bit easier.

DISCUSSION

Psychopathology and Diagnosis Mr. Feldman consulted his physician because of his abdominal pain. After making the diagnosis of a duodenal ulcer, his physician referred him to a psychiatrist because he recognized that Mr. Feldman's longstanding way of dealing with his work and the rest of his life might well be a significant factor in the development of his ulcer and in preventing its healing, even with medication. The psychiatrist observed that Mr. Feldman had several maladaptive personality traits, such as his excessive devotion to work, his inability to relax, and his combativeness in interpersonal relationships. Because these traits were long-standing, maladaptive, and caused him considerable distress, the diagnosis of a personality disorder was warranted. Because the clinical features were not characteristic of any of the specific personality disorder types, except for some features of compulsive personality disorder, the actual diagnosis would be mixed personality disorder. It was these personality features that the psychiatrist believed were likely to affect his duodenal ulcer adversely.

Physicians have recognized for many years that certain physical disorders seem particularly aggravated by psychological stress. At one time a small group of these disorders, including duodenal ulcer, asthma, ulcerative colitis, rheumatoid arthritis, and migraine, were thought to be associated with specific psychological conflicts and personality styles and were called psychosomatic disorders. Later, evidence accumulated showing that a simple causal relationship between specific psychological conflicts or personality styles and the development of the physical disorder could not be demonstrated, and the concept of psychosomatic disorders was broadened into the concept of psychophysiological disorders. This concept encompassed a larger group of physical disorders in which it was believed that psychological factors played a role in the development of the physical disorders primarily through the overactivity of the autonomic nervous system. Psychophysiological disorders were subclassified according to the organ system that was involved. For example, duodenal ulcer was classified as a psychophysiological gastrointestinal disorder, and asthma as a psychophysiological respiratory disorder.

The diagnostic concept of psychophysiological disorders was unsatisfactory for many reasons. First of all, it perpetuated a mind-body dichotomy and the simplistic notion that psychological factors *caused* certain physical disorders, when in reality, psychological factors are better understood as playing a role in a multifactorial model of causation for all illnesses. It also artificially designated certain physical disorders that were presumably caused by psychological factors as "mental disorders," and the same disorders as "physical disorders," when no psychological factors could be demonstrated. The determination of the psychological role in such a disorder, for example, duodenal ulcer, was idiosyncratic and largely depended upon whether the diagnostician was a psychiatrist or an internist. Now, in cases where psychological factors are clinically judged to play a contributing role in the development, exacerbation, or maintenance of any physical disorder or condition, as in this case, the role of the psychological factors is noted as *psychological factors affecting physical condition*. The physical disorder, in this case duodenal ulcer, is separately noted.

Treatment In the past, psychological treatment of patients with "psychosomatic disorders" was directed at resolving certain specific underlying conflicts that were hypothesized to be specifically related to the physical disorder. This approach has by and large been abandoned, as it was recognized that such specific connections between psychological conflicts and physical disorders did not exist. More recently, however, specific behavioral techniques have been developed, often aimed more directly at the physical symptoms themselves. Examples include biofeedback in the treatment of hypertension and migraine headache, relaxation techniques for treating muscle tension, and social learning approaches to the control of eating behavior that results in obesity. However, for the majority of patients with physical disorders who receive psychological treatment to modify the effects of stress on the physical disorder, the psychological treatment is supportive and nonspecific.

Course and Prognosis   The physical illnesses for which psychological treatment is directed tend to be chronic. Although the newer behavioral approaches seem promising, it is too early to know to what extent they can substantially alter the long-term outcome of these disorders.

HISTORICAL CASES

Emil Kraepelin
(1856–1926)

Kraepelin, a Professor of Psychiatry in Germany, provided the basis for the modern classification of mental disorders. He used the natural history of the illness—its onset, course, and outcome—as well as its clinical picture as the basis for classification. Thus he differentiated maniacal-depressive insanity from dementia praecox (later renamed schizophrenia by Bleuler). He subdivided dementia praecox into three types: catatonic, hebephrenic, and paranoid.

His major textbook was first published in 1883, went into nine editions, and provided generations of clinicians with detailed illustrations of his diagnostic concepts. These two cases are taken verbatim from his *Lectures on Clinical Psychiatry*,* first published in 1904.

*E. Kraepelin, *Lectures on Clinical Psychiatry,* translated by Johnstone. Hafner Publishing Company, New York, 1968. "The Innkeeper," p. 97; "The Suffering Lady," p. 252.

THE INNKEEPER

Gentlemen,—The innkeeper, aged 34, whom I am bringing before you today, was admitted to the hospital only an hour ago. He understands the questions put to him, but cannot quite hear some of them, and gives a rather absentminded impression. He states his name and age correctly . . . Yet he does not know the doctors, calls them by the names of his acquaintances, and thinks he has been here for two or three days. It must be the Crown Hotel or, rather, the "mad hospital." He does not know the date exactly.

. . . He moves about in his chair, looks round him a great deal, starts slightly several times, and keeps on playing with his hands. Suddenly he gets up, and begs to be allowed to play on the piano for a little at once. He sits down again immediately, on persuasion, but then wants to go away "to tell them something else that he has forgotten." He gradually gets more and more excited, saying that his fate is sealed; he must leave the world now; they might telegraph to his wife that her husband is lying at the point of death. We learn, by questioning him, that he is going to be executed by electricity, and also that he will be shot. "The picture is not clearly painted," he says; "every moment someone stands now here, now there, waiting for me with a revolver. When I open my eyes, they vanish." He says that a stinking fluid has been injected into his head and both his toes, which causes the pictures one takes for reality; that is the work of an international society, which makes away with those "who fell into misfortune innocently through false steps." With this he looks eagerly at the window, where he sees houses and trees vanishing and reappearing. With slight pressure on his eyes, he sees first sparks, then a hare, a picture, a head, a washstand set, a half-moon, and a human head, first dully and then in colours. If you show him a speck on the floor, he tries to pick it up, saying that it is a piece of money. If you shut his hand and ask him what you have given him, he keeps his fingers carefully closed, and guesses that it is a lead pencil or a piece of india rubber. The patient's mood is half apprehensive and half amused. His head is much flushed, and his pulse is small, weak, and rather hurried. His face is bloated and his eyes are watery. His breath smells strongly of alcohol and acetone. His tongue is thickly furred, and trembles when he puts it out, and his outspread fingers show strong, jerky tremors. The knee reflexes are somewhat exaggerated.

. . . Our patient has drunk hard since he was 13 years old . . . At last, by his own account, he drank 6 or 7 liters of wine a day and five or six stomachic bitters, while he took hardly any food but soup. Some weeks ago he had occasional hallucinations of sight—mice, rats, beetles, and rabbits. He mistook people at times, and came into his inn in his shirt. His condition has grown worse during the last few days.

DISCUSSION

Psychopathology and Diagnosis The innkeeper is admitted to a hospital with a wide range of psychological and physiological symptoms indicative of impairment in multiple areas of nervous system functioning. He is not fully alert and appears unable to attend sufficiently to the questions to hear them correctly, although he seems to understand what is asked. This suggests a deficit in attention-focusing capacities and is known as clouding of consciousness. Also, the patient is noted to know his name and age, but to confuse the doctors with former acquaintances (referred to as disorientation to person). He believes that he is in a hotel rather than the hospital or, if in the hospital, he is not sure which one (known as disorientation to place). He is unaware of the current date and believes that he has been hospitalized for several days (called disorientation to time). He exhibits psychomotor agitation: he gets up and down from his chair and moves about, unable to stay seated and participate in the interview without frequent interruptions. He experiences many hallucinations and illusions, indicating disordered perception. He describes houses and trees vanishing and reappearing outside the window; he sees many pictures flashing before his eyes; he mistakes specks of dust for money.

The combination of clouding of consciousness and disorientation accompanied by psychomotor agitation and hallucinations strongly suggests an organic mental syndrome, known as a delirium. The innkeeper also has the delusion that he is being persecuted and may be killed in a plot of an unknown international society. Persecutory delusions are common in patients with delirium.

On physical examination he is noted to be flushed, with a rapid and weak pulse. He is bloated, his eyes are watery, and his breath smells strongly of alcohol. He has a furred tongue and an extension tremor of hands. His knee reflexes are hyperactive. This physical picture, in association with the long history of very heavy drinking, makes the cause of the delirium almost undoubtedly related to alcohol abuse. The case itself does not describe a recent reduction in alcohol use, which invariably precedes the development of this characteristic delirium, but the patient was forced in recent days to reduce his intake, because of physical complaints or limited supplies of alcohol, thus bringing on a withdrawal state. This case demonstrates that delirium caused by alcohol withdrawal, technically known as alcohol withdrawal delirium, has been recognized for many years. Kraepelin used the familiar term, *delirium tremens*, to diagnose this case.

Etiology   Individuals who consume substances that have the potential for physiological addiction invariably develop tolerance to the substance, that is, larger and larger amounts of the drug are necessary in order to produce an intoxicated state. This is true of alcohol and also of other types of drugs, such as barbiturates, opioids (e.g., heroin), and amphetamines. Once the individual has become physiologically dependent on a drug, abrupt reduction or cessation in use of the drug will precipitate a severe physiological and psychological withdrawal state. In some cases, drug withdrawal can be a life-threatening situation. Individuals who are withdrawing from alcohol, barbiturates, or similar sedative drugs may experience grand mal seizures, may go into coma, and may even die if medical intervention is not initiated. Ordinarily, it takes many years of daily consumption of a drug like alcohol in order to develop alcohol dependence, which the innkeeper also undoubtedly has. Certain other drugs, such as the barbiturates, may lead to dependence in a shorter time, since the body's metabolic processes are activated to break down the drug more rapidly, thus hastening the development of tolerance.

Treatment   There is no mention of treatment in Kraepelin's case. Today severe alcohol withdrawal is recognized as a medical emergency. A patient such as the innkeeper would be brought to a nearby emergency room where he would receive intravenous fluids if he appeared dehydrated or on the verge of shock (collapse of the circulatory system), and sedation to control psychomotor agitation and to guard against the possibility of seizures. Since it is not usually wise or feasible to sedate with the drug from which the patient is withdrawing, such as alcohol in this case, another sedative drug is commonly substituted. Hospitalization would last at least a week, during which time the patient would be gradually withdrawn from the alcohol by slowly reducing the total daily dose of sedative given. After about a week of gradual sedative withdrawal there is no longer a danger of a severe withdrawal syndrome. Chronic users of alcohol are often vitamin deficient and may show signs of this deficiency by an abnormal gait, incoordination, paralysis of the muscles controlling eye movements, and memory loss. To avoid this complication of excessive alcohol use, they are commonly given large doses of thiamine (vitamin B-1). Other drugs may be added to the regimen to help guard against the possibility of grand mal seizures.

Prognosis   With prompt and adequate medical treatment the prognosis for an episode of alcohol withdrawal delirium is good. However, since this is a complication of a chronic problem with alcohol, the long-term prognosis is not as positive. Many individuals who have had an episode of alcohol withdrawal delirium will go on to have future episodes. It is therefore imperative that treatment be instituted to combat the underlying problem, alcohol dependence. This treatment is usually begun while the patient is still hospitalized and being gradually withdrawn from alcohol. Commonly, arrangements will be made to have the individual approached by a representative of Alcoholics Anonymous, for example, and invited to participate in A.A. meetings while still in the hospital (see Case 17, "I Am Duncan. I Am an Alcoholic").

THE SUFFERING LADY

Gentlemen,—The young lady, aged 30, carefully dressed in black, who comes into the hall with short, shuffling steps, leaning on the nurse, and sinks into a chair as if exhausted, gives you the impression that she is ill. She is of slender build, her features are pale and rather painfully drawn, and her eyes are cast down. Her small, manicured fingers play nervously with a handkerchief. The patient answers the questions addressed to her in a low, tired voice, without looking up, and we find that she is quite clear about time, place, and her surroundings. After a few minutes, her eyes suddenly become convulsively shut, her head sinks forward, and she seems to have fallen into a deep sleep. Her arms have grown quite limp, and fall down as if palsied when you try to lift them. She has ceased to answer, and if you try to raise her eyelids, her eyes suddenly rotate upward. Needlepricks only produce a slight shudder. But sprinkling with cold water is followed by a deep sigh; the patient starts up, opens her eyes, looks round her with surprise, and gradually comes to herself. She says that she has just had one of her sleeping attacks, from which she has suffered for seven years. They come on quite irregularly, often many in one day, and last from a few minutes to half an hour.

Concerning the history of her life, the patient tells us that . . . she was educated in convent schools, and passed the examination for teachers. As a young girl, she inhaled a great deal of chloroform, which she was able to get secretly, for toothache. She also suffered from headaches, until they were relieved by the removal of growths from the nose. She very readily became delirious in feverish illnesses. Thirteen years ago she took a place as governess in Holland, but soon began to be ill, and has passed the last seven years in different hospitals, except for a short interval when she was in a situation in Moravia.

It would appear from the statements of her relations and doctors that the patient has suffered from the most varied ailments, and been through the most remarkable courses of treatment. For violent abdominal pains and disturbances of menstruation, ascribed to stenosis of the cervical canal and retroflection of the uterus, recourse was had five years ago to the excision of the wedge supposed to cause the obstruction, and the introduction of a pessary. At a later period loss of voice and a contraction of the right forearm and the left thigh set in, and were treated with massage, electricity, bandaging, and stretching under an anesthetic. Heart oppression and spasmodic breathing also appeared, with quickly passing disablements of various sets of muscles, disturbances of urination, diarrhea, and unpleasant sensations, now in one and now in another part of the body, but particularly headaches. Extraordinarily strong and sudden changes of mood were observed at the same time, with introspection and complaints of want of consideration in those about her and in her relations, although the latter had made the greatest sacrifices. Brine baths, Russian baths, pine-needle baths, electricity, country air, summer resorts, and, finally, residence on the Riviera—everything was tried, generally with only a brief improvement or with none at all.

The immediate cause of the patient being brought to the hospital was the increase in the "sleeping attacks" two years ago. They came on at last even when the patient was standing, and might continue for an hour. The patient did not fall down, but simply leaned against something. The attacks continued in the hospital, and spasmodic breathing was also observed, which could be influenced by suggestion.

After spending eight months here, the patient went away at first to her sister's. But after a few months she had to be taken to another asylum, where she stayed about a year, and then, after a short time spent with her family, came back to us.

During her present residence here, so-called "great attacks" have appeared, in addition to her previous troubles. We will try to produce such an attack by pressure on the very sensitive left ovarian region. After one or two minutes of moderately strong pressure, during which the patient shows sharp pain, her expression alters. She throws herself to and fro with her eyes shut, and screams to us loudly, generally in French, not to touch her. "You must not do anything to me, you hound, cochon, cochon!" She cries for help, pushes with her hands, and twists herself as if she were trying to escape from a sexual assault. Whenever she is touched, the excitement increases. Her whole body is strongly bent backward. Suddenly the picture changes, and the patient begs piteously not to be cursed, and laments and sobs aloud. This condition, too, is very soon put an end to by sprinkling with cold water. The patient shudders, wakes with a deep sigh, and looks fixedly round, only making a tired, senseless impression. She cannot explain what has happened.

The physical examination of the patient shows no particular disturbances at present, except the abnormalities already mentioned. There is only a well-marked weakness, in consequence of which she often keeps to her bed or lies about. All her movements are limp and feeble, but there is no actual disablement anywhere. She often sleeps very badly. At times she wanders about in the night, wakes the nurses, and sends for the doctor. Her appetite is very poor, but she has a habit of nibbling between her meals at all kinds of cakes, fruit, and jam, which are sent to her, at her urgent request, by her relations.

With her growing expertness in illness, the emotional sympathies of the patient are more and more confined to the selfish furthering of her own wishes. She tries ruthlessly to extort the most careful attention from those around her, obliges the doctor to occupy himself with her by day or by night on the slightest occasion, is extremely sensitive to any supposed neglect, is jealous if preference is shown to other patients, and tries to make the attendants give in to her by complaints, accusations, and outbursts of temper. The sacrifices made by others, more especially by her family, are regarded quite as a matter of course, and her occasional prodigality of thanks only serves to pave the way for new demands. To secure the sympathy of those around her, she has recourse to more and more forcible descriptions of her physical and mental torments, histrionic exaggeration of her attacks, and the effective elucidation of her personal character. She calls herself the abandoned, the outcast, and in mysterious hints makes confession of horrible, delightful experiences and failings, which she will only confide to the discreet bosom of her very best friend, the doctor.

DISCUSSION

Psychopathology and Diagnosis This woman presents with an unusual symptom, bizarre sleeping attacks that leave her unresponsive for several minutes many times a day, but which apparently have no physical cause. In taking a history, the clinician discovers that this woman has been plagued by physical problems since childhood. She has had toothaches, headaches, abdominal pains, menstrual disturbances, loss of voice, muscle contractions, heart problems, breathing problems, disturbances of urination, and diarrhea. For all of these symptoms she has received a myriad of the treatments of her day, including surgery, massage, electricity, bandaging, stretching, various kinds of baths, and country air. When a patient presents a long history of multiple, somatic complaints in many organ systems which are not traceable to a diagnosable physical disorder, this suggests the somatoform disorder, somatization disorder. This is one of the classic presentations of what used to be called hysteria. Kraepelin's diagnosis was *hysterical insanity*.

This clinical picture is often seen in association with certain personality attributes that have also been called hysteria in the past. Specifically, this patient engages in much dramatic, attention-seeking behavior during her examination: she screams, she gets very excited when being examined, and then later she begs forgiveness, sobs, and laments her unfortunate situation. She is also viewed as very selfish and manipulative in her interpersonal relationships in the hospital. She "ruthlessly extorts attention" from the hospital staff and demands extra time from the doctor, feeling neglected if she is not shown this preferential treatment. These personality characteristics, which are most certainly part of an enduring pattern of relating to others, indicate what would now be called histrionic personality disorder.

Course Somatization disorder commonly begins prior to the age of 30, and will often cause a patient to go from doctor to doctor and to submit to multiple medical tests, examinations, procedures, and treatments in order to reach a diagnosis and obtain symptomatic relief. Many physicians will extensively examine such patients, expecting perhaps that a subtle, undiagnosed physical illness may be accounting for the most recent complaints; but such a search is most commonly futile. After a time, unfortunately, some physicians will regard these patients as chronic complainers and may even overlook true organic illness. The danger to the patient of receiving unnecessary medical tests and surgical procedures, coupled with the expense of the repeated medical workups, make this illness a dangerous and costly one.

Treatment Since such patients are rarely aware of the psychological nature of their physical complaints, they are notoriously difficult to treat with psychological therapy. Many of them will not even be referred by their medical doctors to a mental health professional because, if such a course of action is suggested, they will adamantly refuse. If a referral is made, the mental health professional must avoid conveying to the patient the idea that the physical complaints, since they do not have an organic basis, are not actually being experienced. The therapist must find a way to demonstrate to the patient how physical complaints might be connected to psychological stress or conflict. This often can be approached by eliciting a very careful history from the patient of the psychosocial circumstances surrounding a particular complaint or preceding a period in which physical complaints were experienced. Connections may then be drawn by the therapist between the occurrence of a stressful life event and the onset of symptoms, and a suggestion may be gently made to the patient that perhaps this link has some causal significance. When the patient is, in addition, very demanding of others, as is the Suffering Lady, the slow process involved in most psychotherapies becomes a source of frustration, and maintaining a therapeutic relationship for the length of time necessary to bring about even a modest change is difficult.

Somatization disorder usually persists throughout adult life with periods of exacerbation and remission. Specific treatment approaches have not been designed to help the patient with multiple physical complaints not due to organic illness, such as have been developed to help the patient with chronic depression or a psychosexual dysfunction (see Case 24, "Learning to Cope" and Case 20, "Latin Lover"). The vast majority of patients with this disorder probably continue year after year in the practices of many internists, obstetricians, gynecologists, cardiologists, and other medical practitioners or, conversely, see dozens of different doctors and visit many hospitals over the course of their lives.

Josef Breuer
(1842–1925)

Breuer was a Viennese physician who collaborated with Freud in using hypnosis to treat patients with hysteria. The case of "Anna O" was abstracted from Breuer and Freud's *Studies in Hysteria*,* published in 1895. Anna O was treated and reported by Breuer. It was the case that suggested to Freud the possibility of a "talking cure"—later known as psychoanalysis.

---

*J. Breuer and S. Freud, *Studies in Hysteria*, translated by Brill. Beacon Press, Boston, 1937, p. 14.

ANNA O

Anna O was the only daughter of a wealthy Viennese Jewish family. She became ill when she was 21, in 1880.

> "Up to the onset of the disease, the patient showed no sign of nervousness, not even during pubescence. She had a keen, intuitive intellect, a craving for psychic fodder, which she did not, however, receive after she left school. She was endowed with a sensitiveness for poetry and fantasy, which was, however, controlled by a very strong and critical mind . . . Her will was energetic, impenetrable and persevering, sometimes mounting to selfishness; it relinquished its aim only out of kindness and for the sake of others . . . Her moods always showed a slight tendency to an excess of merriment or sadness, which made her more or less temperamental . . . With her puritanically minded family, this girl of overflowing mental vitality led a most monotonous existence."

She spent hours daydreaming, making up fanciful plots in what she called her "private theater." She was at times so engrossed in fantasy that she did not hear when people spoke to her.

In July, 1880, her father, whom she admired and "loved passionately," developed tuberculosis. From July through November Anna was his night nurse, sitting up with him every night observing his pain and deterioration, with the knowledge that he would not recover.

Her own health eventually began to decline:

> ". . . she became very weak, anemic, and evinced a disgust for nourishment, so that despite her marked reluctance, it was found necessary to take her away from

the sick man. The main reason for this step was a very intensive cough about which I [Breuer] was first consulted. I found that she had a typical nervous cough. Soon, there also developed a striking need for rest, distinctly noticeable in the afternoon hours, which merged in the evening into a sleeplike state, followed by strong excitement . . . From the eleventh of December until the first of April the patient remained bedridden.

"In rapid succession there seemingly developed a series of new and severe disturbances.

"Left-sided occipital pain; convergent strabismus (diplopia), which was markedly aggravated through excitement. She complained that the wall was falling over (obliquus affection). Profound analyzable visual disturbances, paresis of the anterior muscles of the throat, to the extent that the head could finally be moved only if the patient pressed it backward between her raised shoulders and then moved her whole back. Contractures and anesthesia of the right upper extremity, and somewhat later of the right lower extremity . . .

"It was in this condition that I took the patient under treatment, and I soon became convinced that we were confronted with a severe psychic alteration. There were two entirely separate states of consciousness, which alternated very frequently and spontaneously, moving further apart during the course of the disease. In one of them she knew her environment, was sad and anxious, but relatively normal; in the other, she hallucinated, was 'naughty'—i.e., she scolded, threw the pillows at people whenever and to what extent her contractures enabled her to, and tore with her movable fingers the buttons from the covers and underwear, etc. If anything had been changed in the room during this phase, if someone entered, or went out, she then complained that she was lacking in time, and observed the gap in the lapse of her conscious ideas . . . In very clear moments she complained of the deep darkness in her head, that she could not think, that she was going blind and deaf, and that she had two egos, her real and an evil one, which forced her to evil things, etc . . . there appeared a deep, functional disorganization of her speech. At first, it was noticed that she missed words; gradually, when this increased her language was devoid of all grammar, all syntax, to the extent that the whole conjugation of verbs was wrong . . . In the further course of this development she missed words almost continuously, and searched for them laboriously in four or five languages, so that one could hardly understand her . . . She spoke only English and understood nothing that was told her in German. The people about her were forced to speak English . . . There then followed two weeks of complete mutism. Continuous effort to speak elicited no sound.

"About ten days after her father died, a consultant was called in whom she ignored as completely as all strangers, while I demonstrated to him her peculiarities . . . It was a real 'negative hallucination,' which has so often been reproduced experimentally since then. He finally succeeded in attracting her attention by blowing smoke into her face. She then suddenly saw a stranger, rushed to the door, grabbed the key, but fell to the floor unconscious. This was followed by a short outburst of anger, and then by a severe attack of anxiety, which I could calm only with a great deal of effort."

The family was afraid she would jump from the window, so she was removed from her third-floor apartment to a country house where, for three days

". . . she remained sleepless, took no nourishment, and was full of suicidal ideas . . . She also broke windows, etc., and evinced hallucinations [of black snakes, death's heads, etc.] without absences [dissociated periods]."

Breuer treated her by asking her, under hypnosis, to talk about her symptoms, a technique which she referred to as "chimney sweeping." As the treatment proceeded, she had longer periods of lucidity and began to lose her symptoms. After eighteen months of treatment, as Anna prepared to spend the summer in her country home, Breuer pronounced her well and said he would no longer be seeing her. That evening he was called back to the house, where he found Anna thrashing around in her bed, going through an imaginary childbirth. She insisted that the baby was Breuer's. He managed to calm her by hypnotizing her. According to Ernest Jones, Breuer then "fled the house in a cold sweat" and never saw her again.

Anna remained ill intermittently over the next six years, spending considerable time in a sanatorium, where she apparently became addicted to morphine. She was often fairly well in the daytime, but still suffered from hallucinatory states toward evening.

By 30 she had apparently completely recovered, and moved to Frankfort with her mother. There she became a feminist leader and social worker. She established an institution for "wayward girls" and spoke out against the devaluation of women which she believed was inherent in Orthodox Judaism.

She never married, but was said to be an attractive and passionate woman who gathered admirers wherever she went. She had no recurrences of her illness and never spoke about it—in fact, she apparently asked her relatives not to speak of it to anyone. In her later years her attitude toward psychoanalysis was clearly negative, and she became quite angry at the suggestion that one of her "girls" be psychoanalyzed.

Anna died at 77, of abdominal cancer.

DISCUSSION

Psychopathology and Diagnosis The catalog of symptoms that Anna presented to Dr. Breuer at various points during her illness included almost the entire range of psychopathology. She was depressed and suicidal, without energy, anorexic, mute, and sleepless—all suggesting a depressive disorder. In addition, she had numerous symptoms that suggested a physical disorder, but for which no organic cause could be found. She had a persistent cough and headaches. Both legs and her right arm were paralyzed and the muscles rigid. Her neck muscles were also paralyzed. She had such severe visual disturbances (strabismus) that she could no longer read. When there is a loss or alteration of physical functioning that appears to be the expression of a psychological conflict or need, this is called a conversion symptom. Anna also had blackouts and long periods during which she seemed not to hear what was said to her. During these periods she was apparently experiencing rapidly changing states of consciousness, again without an adequate physical explanation (such as drug ingestion or disease affecting the brain). During these periods she had "temper tantrums"—she threw things and yelled at people. Altered states of consciousness, such as Anna experienced, in which an individual splits off an aspect of his identity, consciousness, or sense of self, are called dissociative states. Finally, Breuer reports that Anna had psychotic symptoms—hallucinations of snakes and skulls, and incoherent speech.

What are we to make of this complex and dramatic presentation? In 19th century Europe the illness was called *hysteria* and was a well-recognized affliction, occurring only in women (hence the name hysteria, derived from the Greek word for womb). A diagnostician of the 1980s would have a hard time accounting for such a myriad of symptoms with a single diagnosis. (Fortunately, there is not much call for such a diagnosis, since this clinical picture seems to be extinct, at least in the cities of Western Europe and America.) Using today's diagnostic concepts, the clinician would be forced to make several separate diagnoses to account for various aspects of the disorder.

Anna's depression is partially accounted for by the illness and death of her beloved father, but it seems to exceed the bounds of normal grief, and therefore cannot be considered uncomplicated bereavement, the technical term for a normal period of grief following the loss of a loved one. Instead, it appears that Anna had an episode of major depression.

Her physical symptoms without an organic basis lead us to consider a somatoform disorder. Since they are not part of a chronic pattern of multiple somatic complaints in many organ systems, as would be seen in somatization disorder (see Case 52, "The Suffering Lady"), the appropriate diagnosis is conversion disorder.

Since Anna's dissociated states do not conform to any of the specific types of dissociative disorders (psychogenic amnesia, psychogenic fugue, multiple personality), an additional diagnosis would be atypical dissociative disorder (see Case 9, "Possessed").

Finally, we are inclined to believe that Anna's psychotic symptoms are genuine and are not just being put on for dramatic effect. Since they do not appear to be associated with her major depression, yet another diagnosis must be made! Atypical psychosis, because it is a nonspecific diagnosis, is probably the best way to characterize her relatively brief and intermittent psychotic periods.

Admittedly, the sum of these diagnoses does not capture the essence of Anna O's difficulties. The attempt to diagnose her condition in modern terms demonstrates how diagnostic concepts have changed as the manifestations of psychopathology have changed over time.

Etiology The etiology of Anna's complex condition is a matter of speculation, as are the reasons for the disappearance of such a clinical entity. Freud believed that that "hysterical" symptoms were the result of sexual repression. Many modern clinicians see the origins of Anna's problems in the oppression of Victorian women. Both proposals are consistent with the rarity of the syndrome in societies in which there is greater equality of the sexes and less sexual repression.

Treatment When Breuer moved from the standard 19th-century treatment of hysteria, hypnosis, to the "talking cure" with Anna O (which she called "chimney sweeping"), he began the process that Freud developed into psychoanalysis, using the free associations of the patient as the major treatment technique. Although Anna was temporarily relieved of her symptoms, the treatment cannot be considered a success. She was ill for many years after her treatment with this method ended. If Anna were to consult a modern clinician, it is likely that she would be treated with some kind of "talk" therapy, perhaps together with drugs, and that particular attention would be paid to helping her use her considerable intellectual and creative talents for some purpose other than her "private theater."

Sigmund Freud
(1856–1939)

Sigmund Freud, the originator of psychoanalysis, attempted to explain the mechanisms by which unconscious conflicts resulted in the clinical manifestations of psychopathology. This case, first published in 1909, was abstracted from Volume III of Freud's *Collected Papers.*

*S. Freud, *Collected Papers,* vol. III, translated by Strachey. Hogarth Press, London, 1953. "Little Hans," p. 149.

LITTLE HANS

Little Hans's parents were friends and early followers of Freud who had agreed to bring up their first child with

> . . . no more coercion than might be absolutely necessary for maintaining good behavior. And, as the child developed into a cheerful, good-natured, and lively little boy, the experiment of letting him grow up and express himself without being intimidated went on satisfactorily.

Freud asked Hans's father to collect observations on the sexual life of his child, and received frequent letters reporting on Hans, beginning just before his third birthday. In this correspondence Freud found confirmation of many of his notions about infantile sexuality: Little Hans was preoccupied with his "widdler"* and believed that women, including his mother, also had them. Freud also learned that Little Hans's mother had threatened to cut off his penis if he continued to play with it, and that she often encouraged Hans to come into her bed and also allowed him to accompany her to the bathroom.

All went well until Hans was $4^3/_4$, at which time Freud received the following letter from his father:

> My dear Professor, I am sending you a little more about Hans—but this time, I am sorry to say, material for a case history. As you will see, during the last few days he has developed a nervous disorder, which has made my wife and me most uneasy, because we have not been able to find any means of dissipating it. . . . No

*Translator's term for the original German, "wiwimacher."

doubt the ground was prepared by sexual overexcitation due to his mother's tenderness; but I am not able to specify the actual exciting cause. He is afraid *that a horse will bite him in the street,* and this fear seems somehow to be connected with his having been frightened by a large penis. . . . I cannot see what to make of it. Has he seen an exhibitionist somewhere? Or is the whole thing simply connected with his mother? It is not very pleasant for us that he should begin setting up problems so early. Apart from his being afraid of going into the street and from his being depressed in the evening, he is in other respects the same Hans, as bright and cheerful as ever.

It was some months later that Hans remembered an incident which had, in fact, occurred just before his symptoms began. He had been walking with his mother and had been frightened when a large horse pulling a bus had fallen down and kicked its feet around violently.

The first evidence of the disturbance had then been noticed in the first few days of January (1908): "Hans woke up one morning in tears. Asked why he was crying, he said to his mother: 'When I was asleep I thought you were gone and I had no mummy to coax* with.' " Several days later, on January 7:

. . . he went to Stadtpark with his nursemaid as usual. In the street he began to cry and asked to be taken home, saying that he wanted to "coax" with his mummy. At home he was asked why he had refused to go any further and had cried, but he would not say. Till the evening he was cheerful, as usual. But in the evening he grew visibly frightened; he cried and could not be separated from his mother, and wanted to "coax" with her again. Then he grew cheerful again and slept well.

On January 8 my wife decided to go out with him herself, so as to see what was wrong with him. They went to Schönbrunn, where he always likes going. Again he began to cry, did not want to start, and was frightened. In the end he did go, but was visibly frightened in the street. On the way back from Schönbrunn he said to his mother, after much internal struggling: "I was afraid a horse would bite me." (He had, in fact, become uneasy at Schönbrunn when he saw a horse.) In the evening he seemed to have had another attack similar to that of the previous evening, and to have wanted to be "coaxed" with. He was calmed down. He said, crying: "I know I shall have to go for a walk again tomorrow." And later: "The horse'll come into the room."

Freud explained Hans's "morbid anxiety" as due to "repressed longing" for his mother, and fear of retaliation from his father. He counseled Hans's father as follows:

I arranged with Hans's father that he should tell the boy that all this business about horses was a piece of nonsense and nothing more. The truth was, his father was to say, that he was very fond of his mother and wanted to be taken into her bed. The reason he was afraid of horses now was that he had taken so much interest in

*Cuddle.

their widdlers. He himself had noticed that it was not right to be so very much preoccupied with widdlers, even with his own, and he was quite right in thinking this. I further suggested to his father that he should begin giving Hans some enlightenment in the matter of sex knowledge. The child's past behavior justified us in assuming that his libido was attached to a wish to see his mother's widdler; so I proposed to his father that he should take away this aim from Hans by informing him that his mother and all other female beings (as he could see from the maid) had no widdler at all. This last piece of enlightenment was to be given him on a suitable occasion when it had been led up to by some question or some chance remark on Hans's part.

There ensued a fairly quiet period during which Hans could be persuaded to walk in the park, but felt compelled to look at the horses: "I have to look at horses, and then I'm frightened."

After two weeks in bed with influenza, and then a tonsillectomy, his phobia became much worse. "He goes out on to the balcony, it is true, but not for a walk. As soon as he gets to the street door he hurriedly turns round."

In early March the family hired a new maid and later that month, with some persuasion, Hans consented to go to the zoo with his father. There he was afraid of the large animals but not the small ones, and would not even look at the elephant or the giraffe. "During the next few days it seemed as though his fears had again somewhat increased. He hardly ventured out of the front door, to which he was taken after luncheon."

It was during this period that there was much discussion between father and son about Hans's masturbation, about the nature of the female sexual apparatus, and about Hans's desire to get into bed and "coax" with his mother.

Freud had one session with Hans, during which he made a connection between the white horses that Hans was particularly afraid of and Hans's father, and explained to Hans that he was afraid of his father " . . . precisely because he was so fond of his mother."

In subsequent weeks Hans alluded to his fear that his mother and father would go away and leave him. Over a period of some months, Hans's symptoms disappeared, and he became closer to his father.

Freud saw Hans only once again, and wrote the following postscript to the case in 1922:

A few months ago—in the spring of 1922—a young man introduced himself to me and informed me that he was the "little Hans" whose infantile neurosis had been the subject of the paper which I published in 1909. I was very glad to see him again, for about two years after the end of his analysis I had lost sight of him and had heard nothing of him for more than ten years. The publication of this first analysis of a child had caused a great stir and even greater indignation, and a most evil future had been foretold for the poor little boy, because he had been "robbed of his innocence" at such a tender age and had been made the victim of a psycho-analysis.

But none of these apprehensions had come true. Little Hans was now a strapping youth of 19. He declared that he was perfectly well, and suffered from no troubles or inhibitions. Not only had he come through his puberty without any damage, but his emotional life had successfully undergone one of the severest of ordeals. His parents had been divorced, and each of them had married again. In consequence of this he lived by himself; but he was on good terms with both of his parents, and only regretted that as a result of the breaking up of the family he had been separated from the younger sister he was so fond of.

One piece of information given me by little Hans struck me as particularly remarkable; nor do I venture to give any explanation of it. When he read his case history, he told me, the whole of it came to him as something unknown; he did not recognize himself; he could remember nothing.

DISCUSSION

Psychopathology and Diagnosis   Freud's diagnosis of Little Hans was *phobia,* and the modern clinician would make the same diagnosis, because of Hans's irrational fear of and compelling desire to avoid horses. There are an almost unlimited number of objects or situations that may be the focus of irrational fear and avoidance behavior, but it is useful to divide phobias into three types. The most severe kind of phobia is agoraphobia and involves a restriction of activities due to a marked fear of being alone or being in places where sudden escape might be difficult or help not available in case of incapacitation (see Case 2, "Anxious Anne"). Social phobias are the rarest phobias and involve fear of situations in which the person fears that he or she may act in a way that will be humiliating or embarrassing. For example, the individual may be terrified of eating in restaurants, signing documents in front of witnesses, or speaking before groups of people. The most common, and generally the least disabling type of phobia, involves any other object or situation, and is called simple phobia. The most common examples of simple phobias are fears of animals (cats, dogs, snakes, insects), closed spaces (elevators), and heights. Thus in modern diagnostic terminology, Hans had simple phobia.

Hans had other fears as well. He expressed the fear that his parents might leave him, and had nightmares that they had. He was afraid to go to bed at night, and became visibly upset when he was separated from his mother. When a child experiences extreme anxiety on separation from major attachment figures beyond what would be expected given the child's developmental level, this is called separation anxiety disorder. Such children may worry unrealistically that something terrible will separate them from their parents, have many physical complaints on school days (justifying staying home with their parent), or refuse to go to school at all. Thus the modern clinician would probably also diagnose separation anxiety disorder, and might well judge that Hans's phobia was a symptom of the separation anxiety disorder.

Course   Most simple phobias develop in childhood and disappear by adult life even without treatment. Separation anxiety disorder is usually also limited to childhood, although in some cases it may persist into adult life.

Etiology   Freud focused on the fear of horses and attributed Hans's problem to his excessive love for his mother and resulting fear of his father. A modern clinician would want to explore other possible sources of Hans's anxiety, in particular his fear of losing his parents. The evaluation of Hans would undoubtedly involve sessions with his entire family. Freud notes in the postscript that the parents were eventually divorced, so it is a reasonable assumption that there were serious conflicts in the marriage and perhaps even threats, explicit or implicit, of separation. It is also now known that separation anxiety disorder is often precipitated by the loss of an important caretaker, other than the parents. Freud reports that a new maid was hired a few months after the phobia began. This raises the question of when Hans's previous nursemaid had left and what effect it had on Hans.

Treatment   Since most cases of simple phobia and separation anxiety disorder are likely to remit with time alone, we cannot say whether Freud's proxy treatment was instrumental in "curing" Hans. If Hans were seen in a clinic today, he might be treated with the same behavioral techniques that his parents used: they insisted that Hans accompany them on short trips into the street and park. This exposure to the phobic stimulus, often done in a slow and graded manner, is called systematic desensitization. The person with the phobia is regularly exposed to the phobic stimulus in order to desensitize them over time to the feared object or situation so that it becomes no longer fearsome. Undoubtedly, family therapy would attempt to work with Hans's parents so that they would recognize that some of their child-rearing practices (e.g., encouraging Hans to sleep with his mother and accompany her to the bathroom, threatening to cut off Hans's penis if he played with it) should be altered.

Prognosis   Freud's postscript provides us with confirmation of the generally good prognosis for separation anxiety disorder and simple phobia occurring during childhood. Hans's problem disappeared without leaving any permanent scars.

BIBLIOGRAPHY

INTRODUCTION

American Psychiatric Association: "Appendix F: DSM-III Field Trials: Interrater Reliability and List of Project Staff and Participants," in *Diagnostic and Statistical Manual of Mental Disorders,* 3d ed. American Psychiatric Association, Washington, D.C., 1980, pp. 467–481.

American Psychiatric Association: *Diagnostic and Statistical Manual of Mental Disorders,* 3d ed. American Psychiatric Association, Washington, D.C., 1980.

Greist, John H., James W. Jefferson, and Robert L. Spitzer (Editors): *Treatment of Mental Disorders.* Oxford University Press, New York, 1982.

Parloff, Morris B.: "Psychotherapy and Research: An Anaclitic Depression," *Psychiatry* **43,** November, 1980.

Rosenhan, D. L.: "On Being Sane in Insane Places," *Archives of General Psychiatry* **33,** 1976, pp. 459–470.

Spitzer, Robert L.: "On Pseudoscience in Science, Logic in Remission and Psychiatric Diagnosis: A Critique of Rosenhan's 'On Being Sane in Insane Places'," *Journal of Abnormal Psychology* **84,** 1975, pp. 442–452.

Spitzer, Robert L., Andrew E. Skodol, Miriam Gibbon, and Janet B. W. Williams: *DSM-III Case Book.* American Psychiatric Association, Washington, D.C., 1981.

Spitzer, Robert L., and Janet B. W. Williams: "Classification of Mental Disorders and DSM-III," in *Comprehensive Textbook of Psychiatry,* 3d ed. Williams & Wilkins, Baltimore, 1980, pp. 1035–1072.

Williams, Janet B. W.: "DSM-III: A Comprehensive Approach to Diagnosis," *Social Work* **26,** 1981, pp. 101–106.

ANXIETY DISORDERS

Agras, W. S. (Editor): *Behavior Modification: Principles and Clinical Applications,* 2d ed. Little, Brown and Company, Boston, 1978.

Burgess, A. W., and L. Holstrum: "The Rape Trauma Syndrome," *American Journal of Psychiatry* **131**, 1974, pp. 981–986.

Horowitz, M. J.: *Stress Response Syndromes*. Jason Aronson, New York, 1976.

Klein, Donald F., Rachel Gittelman, Frederick Quitkin, and Arthur Rifkin: "Treatment of Anxiety, Personality, Somatoform and Factitious Disorders," in *Diagnosis and Drug Treatment of Psychiatric Disorders: Adults and Children,* 2d ed. Williams & Wilkins, Baltimore, 1980, pp. 539–575.

Marks, I. M.: *Living with Fear*. McGraw-Hill, New York, 1978.

Marks, I. M., R. Stern, D. Mawson, J. Cobb, and R. McDonald: "Clomipramine and Exposure for Obsessive Compulsive Rituals," *British Journal of Psychiatry* **136**, 1980, pp. 1–25.

Mathews, A. M., M. G. Gelder, and D. W. Johnson: *Agoraphobia: Nature and Treatment*. Guilford Press, New York, 1981.

Mavissakalian, M., and D. H. Barlow: *Phobia: Psychological and Pharmacological Treatment*. Guilford Press, New York, 1981.

Rapoport, Judith L.: "Childhood Obsessive Compulsive Disorder," in *Diagnosis and Treatment in Pediatric Psychiatry*. Macmillan Free Press, New York, 1982.

SOMATOFORM DISORDERS

Chodoff, P.: "The Diagnosis of Hysteria: An Overview," *American Journal of Psychiatry* **131,** 1974, pp. 1073–1078.

Guze, Samuel B., R. D. Woodruff, and Paula J. Clayton: "A Study of Conversion Symptoms in Psychiatric Outpatients," *American Journal of Psychiatry* **128,** 1971, pp. 643–646.

Kenyon, S. E.: "The Hypochondriacal Patient," *The Practitioner* **220,** 1978, pp. 245–250.

Meister, R.: *Hypochondria: Toward a Better Understanding*. Taplinger, New York, 1980.

Woodruff, R. A., Paula J. Clayton, and Samuel B. Guze: "Hysteria. Studies in Diagnosis, Outcome, and Prevalence," *Journal of the American Medical Association* **215,** 1971, pp. 425–428.

DISSOCIATIVE DISORDERS

Leahy, M. R., and I. C. A. Martin: "Successful Hypnotic Abreaction After Twenty Years," *British Journal of Psychiatry* **113,** 1967, pp. 383–385.

Odencrants, G.: "Hypnosis and Dissociative States," in *Experimental Hypnosis*. Citadel, New York, 1965, pp. 416–420.

Prince, M.: *The Dissociation of a Personality*. Meridian, New York, 1957.

Schreiber, F. R.: *Sybil*. Warner Books, New York, 1974.

Taylor, W. S., and M. F. Martin: "Multiple Personality," *Journal of Abnormal Social Psychology* **39,** 1944, pp. 281–300.

PERSONALITY DISORDERS

Cleckly, H. M.: *The Mask of Sanity*, 5th ed. C. V. Mosby Company, St. Louis, 1976.

Hartocollis, P. (Editor): *Borderline Personality Disorders: The Concept, the Syndrome, the Patient*. International Universities Press, New York, 1977.

Kernberg, Otto: *Borderline Conditions and Pathological Narcissism*. Jason Aronson, New York, 1975.

Kohut, Heinz: "The Analysis of the Self: A Systematic Approach to the Psychoanalytic Treatment of Narcissistic Personality Disorders," in *The Monograph Series of the Psychoanalytic Study of the Child*. Monograph No. 4, International Universities Press, Inc., New York, 1971 (Second Printing 1974).

Lazarus, A. A.: *The Practice of Multimodal Therapy*. McGraw-Hill, New York, 1981.

Lion, John R. (Editor): *Personality Disorders: Diagnosis and Management*. Williams & Wilkins, Baltimore, 1981.

Mailer, Norman: *The Executioner's Song,* 1st ed. Little, Brown and Company, Boston, 1979.

Stone, M. H.: *The Borderline Syndromes: Constitution, Adaptation and Personality*. McGraw-Hill, New York, 1980.

SUBSTANCE-USE DISORDERS

Lowinson, J. H., and P. Ruiz (Editors): *Substance Abuse: Clinical Problems and Perspectives*. Williams & Wilkins, Baltimore, 1981.

Mendelson, J. H., and N. K. Mello: *Diagnosis and Treatment of Alcoholism*. McGraw-Hill, New York, 1979.

PSYCHOSEXUAL DISORDERS

Ellis, Albert, and Russel Grieger: *Handbook of Rational Emotive Therapy*. Springer, New York, 1977.

Green, R., and J. Money (Editors): *Transsexualism and Sex Reassignment*. Johns Hopkins Press, Baltimore, 1969.

Kaplan, Helen S.: *Disorders of Sexual Desire*. Brunner/Mazel, New York, 1979.

Masters, William, and Virginia Johnson: *Human Sexual Inadequacy*. Little, Brown and Company, Boston, 1970.

Meyer, Jon K., and D. J. Reter: "Sex Reassignment," *Archives of General Psychiatry* **36,** 1979, pp. 1010–1015.

Stoller, R. J.: *Perversion: The Erotic Form of Hatred*. Pantheon Books, New York, 1975.

Stoller, R. J.: *Sex and Gender,* vol. III. Hogarth Press, London, 1975.

AFFECTIVE DISORDERS

Akiskal, Hagop S., A. H. Bitar, V. R. Puzantian, T. L. Rosenthal, and P. W. Walker: "The Nosological Status of Neurotic Depression," *Archives of General Psychiatry* **35,** 1978, p. 756.

Akiskal, Hagop S., A. H. Djenderedjian, R. H. Rosenthal, and M. H. Khani: "Cyclothymic Disorder: Validating Criteria for Inclusion in the Bipolar Affective Group," *American Journal of Psychiatry* **134,** 1977, pp. 1227–1233.

Akiskal, Hagop S., and W. T. McKinney: "Depressive Disorders: Toward a Unified Hypothesis," *Science* **182,** 1973, p. 20.

American Psychiatric Association: *Task Force Report on Electroconvulsive Therapy*. American Psychiatric Association, Washington, D.C., 1978.

Beck, Aaron T., A. J. Rush, B. F. Shaw, and G. Emery: *Cognitive Therapy of Depression*. Guilford Press, New York, 1979.

Fieve, Ronald R.: *Mood Swing: The Third Revolution in Psychiatry*. William Morrow and Company, New York, 1975.

Freud, Sigmund: "Mourning and Melancholia," in *Standard Edition of the Complete Psychological Works of Sigmund Freud,* vol. 14. Hogarth Press, London, 1957, p. 243.

Friedberg, J.: *Shock Treatment Is Not Good for Your Brain.* Glide Publications, San Francisco, 1976.

Lakein, Alan: *How to Get Control of Your Time and Your Life.* McKay Publishing Company, New York, 1973.

Lewinsohn, Peter M., R. Munoz, M. A. Youngren, and A. Zeiss, *Control Your Depression.* Prentice-Hall, Englewood Cliffs, N.J., 1978.

Lewinsohn, Peter M., Linda Teri, and H. M. Hoberman: "Depression: A Perspective on Etiology, Treatment, and Developmental Issues," in *Perspectives on Behavior Therapy in the Eighties.* Springer, New York, 1982.

SCHIZOPHRENIC DISORDERS

Anderson, C. M., Gerard E. Hogarty, and D. J. Reiss: "Family Treatment of Adult Schizophrenic Patients: A Psycho-Educational Approach," *Schizophrenia Bulletin* **6,** no. 3, 1980.

Arieti, S.: *Interpretation of Schizophrenia,* 2d ed. Basic Books, New York, 1974.

Wing, John: *Schizophrenia: Towards a New Synthesis.* Academic Press, New York, 1978.

Wynne, Lyman C., R. L. Cromwell, and S. Matthysse: *The Nature of Schizophrenia: New Approaches to Research and Treatment.* John Wiley & Sons, New York, 1978.

PARANOID DISORDERS

Lewis, A.: "Paranoia and Paranoid: A Historical Perspective," *Psychological Medicine* **1,** no. 2, 1970.

Retterstol, N.: *Paranoid and Paranoiac Psychoses.* Charles C. Thomas, Springfield, Ill., 1966.

PSYCHOTIC DISORDERS NOT ELSEWHERE CLASSIFIED

McCabe, M. S.: "Reactive Psychoses and Schizophrenia with Good Prognosis," *Archives of General Psychiatry* **33,** 1976, p. 571.

Stephens, J. H.: "Long-term Prognosis and Follow-up in Schizophrenia," *Schizophrenia Bulletin* **4,** 1978, p. 25.

Vaillant, G. W.: "A Ten-Year Follow-up of Remitting Schizophrenics," *Schizophrenia Bulletin* **4,** 1978, p. 78.

FACTITIOUS DISORDERS

Sussman, Norman, and Steven E. Hyler: "Factitious Disorders," in *Comprehensive Textbook of Psychiatry,* 3d ed. Williams & Wilkins, Baltimore, 1980, pp. 2002–2014.

DISORDERS OF IMPULSE CONTROL NOT ELSEWHERE CLASSIFIED

Monroe, R. R.: *Episodic Behavioral Disorders.* Harvard University Press, Cambridge, 1970.

Monroe, R. R.: "The Problem of Impulsivity in Personality Disturbances," in *Personality Disorders: Diagnosis and Management.* Williams & Wilkins, Baltimore, 1981.

ADJUSTMENT DISORDER

Strupp, Hans H.: "Success and Failure in Time-Limited Psychotherapy: A Systematic Comparison of Two Cases, Comparison 2," *Archives of General Psychiatry* **37,** 1980, pp. 708–716.

Strupp, Hans H., and S. W. Hadley: "Specific Versus Nonspecific Factors in Psychotherapy: A Controlled Study of Outcome," *Archives of General Psychiatry* **36,** 1979, pp. 1125–1136.

Winer, J. A., and G. H. Pollock: "Adjustment and Impulse Control Disorders," in *Comprehensive Textbook of Psychiatry,* 3d ed. Williams & Wilkins, 1980, pp. 1812–1817.

V CODES FOR CONDITIONS NOT ATTRIBUTABLE TO A MENTAL DISORDER THAT ARE A FOCUS OF ATTENTION OR TREATMENT

Offer, D., and Melvin Sabshin: *Normality: Theoretical and Clinical Concepts of Mental Health,* 2d ed. Basic Books, New York, 1975.

DISORDERS USUALLY FIRST EVIDENT IN INFANCY, CHILDHOOD, OR ADOLESCENCE

Benton, A. L., and D. Pearl: *Dyslexia: An Appraisal of Current Knowledge.* Oxford University Press, New York, 1978.

Bruch, H.: *The Golden Cage. The Enigma of Anorexia Nervosa.* Harvard University Press, Cambridge, 1978.

Erikson, Erik H.: "The Problem of Ego Identity," *Journal of the American Psychoanalytic Association* **4,** 1956, pp. 56–122.

Erikson, Erik H.: "Identity Confusion in Life History and Case History," in *Identity, Youth and Crisis.* W. W. Norton, New York, 1968, pp. 142–208.

Halmi, Katherine A.: "Anorexia Nervosa," in *Comprehensive Textbook of Psychiatry,* 3d ed. Williams & Wilkins, Baltimore, 1980, pp. 1882–1891.

Howlin, P., R. Marchant, M. Rutter, M. Berger, L. Hersov, and W. Yule: "A Home-Based Approach to the Treatment of Autistic Children," *Journal of Autism & Childhood Schizophrenia* **4,** 1973, pp. 308–336.

Jenkins, R. L.: *Behavior Disorders of Childhood and Adolescence.* Charles C. Thomas, Springfield, Ill., 1973.

Kendall, P. C., and S. D. Hollon (Editors): *Cognitive-Behavioral Interventions: Theory, Research, and Procedures.* Academic Press, New York, 1979.

Koch, R., and J. C. Dobson (Editors): *The Mentally Retarded Child and His Family.* Brunner/Mazel, New York, 1970.

Levinson, H. N.: *A Solution to the Riddle: Dyslexia.* Springer, New York, 1980.

Rutter, M., and E. Schopler: *Autism: A Reappraisal of Concepts and Treatment.* Plenum Press, New York, 1978.

Shapiro, Arthur K., Elaine S. Shapiro, R. D. Bruun, and R. C. Sweet: *Gilles de la Tourette Syndrome.* Raven Press, New York, 1978.

Spivack, G., J. J. Platt, and M. B. Shure: *The Problem-Solving Approach to Adjustment.* Jossey-Bass, San Francisco, 1976.

Wender, Paul: *Minimal Brain Dysfunction in Children.* Wiley-Interscience, New York, 1971.

Wing, Lorna: *Early Childhood Autism,* 2nd ed. Pergamon, New York, 1976.

ORGANIC MENTAL DISORDERS

Chopra, G. S., and J. W. Smith: "Psychotic Reaction Following Cannabis Use in East Indians," *Archives of General Psychiatry* **30**, 1974, pp. 24–27.

Katzman, R., R. D. Terry, and K. L. Bick (Editors): *Alzheimer's Disease: Senile Dementia and Related Disorders*. Raven Press, New York, 1978.

Seltzer, Benjamin, and S. H. Frazier: "Organic Mental Disorders," in *The Harvard Guide to Modern Psychiatry*. Harvard University Press, Cambridge, 1977, pp. 285–297.

Spencer, D. J.: "Cannabis Induced Psychosis," *British Journal of Addictions* **65**, 1970, pp. 369–372.

Thacore, V. R., and S. R. P. Shukla: "Cannabis Psychosis and Paranoid Schizophrenia," *Archives of General Psychiatry* **33**, 1976, pp. 383–386.

PSYCHOLOGICAL FACTORS AFFECTING PHYSICAL CONDITIONS

Karasu, T. B.: "Psychotherapy of the Medically Ill," *American Journal of Psychiatry* **136**, 1979, pp. 1–11.

Schwartz, G. E.: "Psychosomatic Disorders and Biofeedback: A Psychobiological Model of Disregulation," in *Psychopathology: Experimental Models*, J. B. Maser and M. E. P. Seligman (Editors). Freeman Press, San Francisco, 1977.

HISTORICAL CASES

Freeman, Lucy: *The Story of Anna O*. Walker Publishing Company, New York, 1972.

Hyler, Steven E., and Robert L. Spitzer: "Hysteria Split Asunder," *American Journal of Psychiatry* **135**, 1978, pp. 1500–1504.

Sellers, E. M., and H. Kalant: "Alcohol Intoxication and Withdrawal," *New England Journal of Medicine* **294**, 1976, pp. 757–762.

Wolpe, Joseph, and Stanley Rachman: "Psychoanalytic 'Evidence': A Critique Based on Freud's Case of Little Hans," *Journal of Nervous and Mental Disease* **131**, 1960, pp. 135–147.

INDEX